CW01637780

BOEREJOOD

BOEREJOOD

One Man's Quest to Understand the Miracle of Democracy in South Africa

JULIAN ROUP

Paperback ISBN: 978-1-915490-23-0

A catalogue record for this book is available from the British Library.

EST. 2019

BLKDOG

www.blkdogpublishing.com

Other titles by Julian Roup for your consideration:

Life in a Time of Plague:
A Coronavirus Lockdown Diary

Into the Secret Heart of Ashdown Forest:
A Horseman's Country Diary

A Fisherman in the Saddle

First Catch Your Calamari: Travels with an Appetite

This Country I Call My Own

For Elise Roup

Jou bloed loop steeds deur die berge en kranse van ons land. Jou saad is die wêreld versprei. Jou liefde my erfporsie.

'Your blood still runs through the mountains and peaks of our land.
Your seed is spread across the world. Your love is my inheritance.'

Acknowledgments

The writing of a book like this is not the work of one person. I may have written the words but help came from many quarters.

So I must thank all those people mentioned in the book who gave so generously of their time and of themselves to help me better understand the miracle that occurred in South Africa and how they and it fare today. I am immensely grateful to all of them. I came as a stranger and I felt in many cases that I left as a friend. I hope as they read the book they will feel that too.

I thank Tracey Hawthorne for a fine editing job and for her continued encouragement.

Thanks also to my first three readers – Gerrit Boonstra, Yvonne Malan and my wife Janice Warman – who made invaluable suggestions and corrections, enriching the text and in some cases helping to spare my blushes. A special thanks to Susanne Bennell (Smit) who once more was there for me at a crucial time and with her corrections helped to improve the book considerably. Thanks must also go to Karin Cronjé and Fiona Archer, who helped me set up a number of the crucial interviews, which led to other interviews, which finally led to this book. 'n Baie groot dankie, nê. A very big thank you.

To my sister Jay, brother-in-law Guy and nephew Kirsten, who provided houseroom, board and lodging, emotional support, critical comment and encouragement to soldier on, making this book a reality, thank you so very much. To Maggie Davey, my publisher at Jacana, who is so much more than a publisher, and Chris Cocks at Jacana who pulled the book together at the end, a heartfelt thank you.

To my wife, journalist Janice Warman, who has edited this new edition with her customary precision, and who in the intervening years has herself published award-winning fiction and non-fiction based on the apartheid years in South Africa, *Class of 79* (Jacana, 2014) and *The World Beneath* (Walker Books, 2015) She has also reported on post-apartheid South Africa for British national newspapers and magazines, and thus brings her own knowledge to this new version of *Boerejood.*

And finally to my children, Dominic and Imogen, who gave me the time and space, encouragement and love to write this book. Thank you.

You have all helped this Boerejood to better understand himself, his country and both his peoples. Bless you all.

Julian Roup
East Sussex
August 2004-August 2024

They shall beat their swords into ploughshares and their spears into pruning hooks; nation shall not lift up sword against nation, neither shall they learn war anymore.
Isaiah II, 4

FOREWORD TO THE 2024 EDITION

In bringing out this new edition of *Boerejood* 20 years after it was first published in 2004, a decade after Mandela came to power at the head of the ANC after the 1994 election, I felt that it needed to be set in context. What has happened to South Africa since then? Many readers had reached out to me over the years to suggest a new book in which all those I interviewed for the first edition were asked for their opinion now, with 20-20 hindsight. This Foreword to the new edition tries to set the great excitement around the coming of democracy in the context of the last 20 years.

Recently, someone close to me said: "All I know is that the ANC has become the largest criminal organisation in South Africa." And this from a rock-steady citizen, not given to wild statements, and someone who has said for the past 44 years that he will stay to turn out the lights if necessary. He is going nowhere. He speaks for millions, I expect.

And who can blame them? When you read a phrase from *The Guardian*: 'State capture by the ANC Zuma Government, in cahoots with the Gupta family' (now in hiding in Dubai or Vanuatu or on trial in India for fraud and money-laundering) it is obvious that the country was treated as a private ATM by these people and their networks in the ANC. The miracle is that the country staggers on.

Thanks to Mandela, the feared 'night of the long knives' did not happen and the country was buoyant with optimism about the political reset. His great generosity of spirit set the tone and calmed the nerves of all who had lived in fear of black majority rule. It was a great time to be alive, to see the arrival of 'one man, one vote' finally manifested. One can only wonder how profoundly disappointed Nelson Mandela would have been at what the ANC has delivered as part of his legacy.

South Africa seemed finally to have outgrown and seen off its fears, Swartgevaar (black danger) and Rooigevaar (Red communist danger), and survived the Witgevaar (White danger) posed by the Afrikaners. Now all eyes were turned to the colours of Bishop Desmond Tutu's Rainbow Nation.

The ANC began well, says the BBC, 'with millions of small starter houses with electricity and toilets built for people who had lived in corrugated iron shanties for many years. The party says it has also delivered essential services to the poor, and more clinics and hospitals. The official estimate is that 1.4 million are still waiting for homes – although many believe that number is a considerable underestimate.'

But then the slide began with President Mbeki not tackling AIDS and Zuma turning the country into his own ATM. Hopeless, incompetent, corrupt governance has brought the country to its knees with unemployment rife and a new youth revolution one potential future outcome.

President Cyril Ramaphosa is not much better, as mired in ANC corruption and incompetence as his immediate predecessors. The country's infrastructure – power, water, education, have all crumbled. As has inward investment and the collapse of municipalities. There are few jobs and 40 per cent of the population is unemployed. The miracle is that the country is not in a revolutionary turmoil. It is the most unequal country in the world and among the most dangerous places to live. The economy is moribund, with virtually no growth in a decade and nearly half the adult population without work.

Basic public services are falling apart. In many parts of the country there is no clean water, while rolling power cuts have become a regular feature of daily life. One in five white South Africans have left and they are being followed by educated black middle-class professionals. The Rand is a basket case at R23 for £1, according to August 2024 foreign exchange markets. According to the World Bank, it has lost 97% of its value since 1980. There are 18,000 murders a year and 50 rapes a day are reported. Kidnapping children for ransom is on the rise.

Gruesome tortures and murders are a constant threat to the farming community. The police seem incapable of protecting citizens or solving crime. This in no way excuses the murderous times under apartheid that preceded it. The title of a book by Moeletsi Mbeki, Thabo's brother, *Architects of Poverty* (Pan Macmillan 2009), speaks for itself.

A leading South African writer journalist and editor, Max Du Preez, says in his book *A Rumour of Spring, South Africa after 20 years of Democracy*, (Penguin Random House, 2013) "My weather report says that winter will persist for a while, but there is a promise of an eventual spring. But it will be accompanied by a couple of thunderstorms."

Briers Van Rensburg, a mechanical engineer with extensive mining experience in South Africa, Africa and South America, who has been much involved in the country's mining infrastructure, says of South Africa's government: "Like a fish, it is rotting from the head down." He adds: "With the horrible example set by our political leaders, who are actively involved in kickbacks, payments and tender involvement to family and friends, it is not surprising that at every juncture where there is any money, the vultures settle to strip the carcass bare." He refers specifically to the Education Department, which has an enormous budget "and with that amount of money, there you will find the serious thieves. Rampant theft stops education in its tracks. Maintenance money is also stolen. The skills required to rebuild the country are not being acquired, due to the collapsing education system." His is a clear-sighted, well informed and very bleak view.

In the past year, a particularly dark development has taken place which sets the Israeli Netanyahu Govt and the ANC Govt on a course of confrontation over Gaza. The two countries that represent my DNA are now at each other's throats. South Africa has taken Israel to The Hague for its war in Gaza.

But now, with the 2024 general election results in and counted, the ANC has had a head-ringing slap from voters, down from 57 per cent of the vote to just 40 per cent. It finds itself in bed with 11 other smaller parties in a government of national unity and there is once more a moment of hope for the country.

Will it succeed or will it be squandered again? A growing black middle class wants grown up competent governance as much as the Indian, coloured and white minorities. The fact is that so much more could have been done had not so much money and energy been wasted by corruption and factional struggles inside the ruling party.

Addressing Parliament on Thursday, 18 July 2024, President Cyril Ramaphosa spoke of the country moving away from a Vulture Economy to a Country of Co-operation, like the Sociable Weavers and Red-billed Buffalo Weavers cooperating to build a communal nest together. Time will tell if we are going to be a nation of Weavers or Vultures; the Vultures have grown fat for 30 years, so a change is long overdue.

"We have an opportunity to make South Africa a better nation," said the President Nou ja, laat ons sien. (Ok, now let's see.)

It is not only in South Africa where the 'democracy train' has come off the rails. In Britain, we've just had 14 years of incompetent, corrupt, brutally uncaring Tory Government which has debased the country's reputation thanks to some of the worst politicians to besmirch the office of Prime Minister. And in France, it's been a close call with the far right of Marie le Pen's National Rally Party. And in the USA, the Trump-Republican MAGA show is still playing to packed houses as we await the outcome of the 2024 Presidential election. As I write this, Kamala Harris has just replaced Joe Biden as the Democratic candidate, to much joy among the faithful. But it seems she has a mountain to climb.

All of this has seriously undermined my faith in democracy. Long gone are the days when naively, I truly believed that one person, one vote would deliver peace, prosperity and a glorious future for South Africa.

It was Winston Churchill, the UK's wartime Prime Minister, who said in 1947: 'Indeed it has been said that democracy is the worst form of Government except for all those other forms that have been tried from time to time.'

And what of the racial issue, the thing that set us all at each other's throats for generations? Yvonne Malan, the Stellenbosch and Oxford-educated academic, says: 'When we met in 2004 at Stellenbosch to discuss *Boerejood*, we spoke about identity politics – at least in the South African context – and it seemed to be on the way out. Now we seem to be stuck in a new iteration of it. The ANC has long since abandoned any pretence of upholding the values of non-racialism. It died along with the Rivonia generation. However, amongst 'ordinary' South Africans, there is still hope. You see it in the Comrades Marathon, you see it when the Springboks play and you see it in everyday acts of kindness and solidarity. But it is not something we hear much about from our leaders.'

As the French are fond of saying: 'Plus ça change, plus c'est la même chose' - the more things change, the more they stay the same.

Amid the darkness that is South African politics, there are glimmers of hope. The 2024 general election, judged to be free and fair, gave the ruling ANC a shock. It seems, too, that there is a growing black constituency that is demanding good governance and an end to corruption. Both of these things are signs of hope.

On a personal note, my mother died before the publication of *Boerejood*, but my father was alive to read the book, which he enjoyed. He has since died and lies buried in the Jewish cemetery in Paarl, the place of his birth. My mother lies nearby in the Dutch Reformed Church graveyard. All that separates them is a mere 100 yards of earth and a sagging, single strand of rusty barbed wire. This was their choice, to be buried with their own people. They had found the courage to live together, but on death, each went back to their own.

Democracy's 'One man, one vote' has not brought solutions – equality, work, wealth and health. It has brought the opposite of those things and those hyenas in power still feast on the stripped carcass of this beautiful country. As Alan Paton, the author of the classic South African apartheid novel, *Cry the Beloved Country*, might say were he alive: 'The Beloved Country weeps yet.'

Julian Roup
East Sussex
August 2024

FOREWORD

Who am I? What am I? Why am I here?

These are questions that every human being wrestles with. In my case, having two conflicting heritages – Jewish and Christian – and having lived in a country beset with madness and cruelty, I wanted answers to those questions more than most. I had lived most of my life as a Jew. Now, at last, I wished to reclaim my other heritage – that of the Afrikaner, my mother's people, the only white tribe in Africa. I wished to find them and know them; I wished finally to enter their kraal, their laager, like the agteros, the last ox into the kraal, of my mother's idiom. *Boerejood* looks at the issues of growing up with a divided heritage, split loyalties, deadly opposites. It moves from a childhood swinging between two aspects of a personality, two inheritances, to a late adulthood in search of the Afrikaners. This book is a quest to find out how the Afrikaners are coping since Mandela walked free in 1990 and democracy arrived in South Africa, a decade ago, in 1994. It is also a journey of personal discovery to look more closely at the society that made me what I am.

I went in search of answers to questions that have puzzled me greatly. These included: Why did the Afrikaners go so quietly in the end? Why did they not opt to pull down the pillars of the temple like Samson, or commit themselves to a Masada-like suicide, if the thought of life under a black majority was so horrific? The Rhodesians, with a much smaller white minority, fought a rearguard action for 15 bitter years of bush war; the Afrikaners, it seemed, went with a whimper rather than a bang.

Why? I also wanted to know how the Afrikaners finessed their fear of swartgevaar, black danger, as they put it - for 50 years. How did they sell black majority rule to the volk? How do the Afrikaners live with this new reality - the one they feared the most? Have they changed, and if so, how? What do they tell their children? What are their hopes for the future? Do they wish to live as a protected minority in a rainbow nation, or do they still yearn for a place of their own? What stories do they tell themselves from the past, the present, and what will be their future story? What have they become? And what have I become?

In researching this book, I revisited many of my old haunts in the Cape, meeting as many Afrikaners as I could. This makes it a partial view, perhaps, but as this book is also one of my own history and my life in South Africa, it must be focused on the Cape. If the result is seen as my impression only, I am content, as that has been my aim.

Ten years after democracy arrived in South Africa - 342 years after the Cape was discovered and settled by the Dutch - I was going in search of the soul of this white African tribe, wishing to discover how they fared. Did they feel themselves safely in the kraal of their own community and culture or did they feel it was a holding-pen for future slaughter? And was the emasculated bull, the ox, an image that had new meaning for the Afrikaner? This beast that had once pulled the settlers' wagons across a continent, tough, strong, patient: did it now have a new symbolic value? The ox was the chosen sacrificial animal for centuries - were the Afrikaners to be some kind of sacrificial animal, compensating Africa for the hurt it had suffered at their hands?

I would follow the image of the last ox and see where it led me.

IN SEARCH OF THE AFRIKANERS

I find it strange that I wish to write about the Afrikaners, having spent a lifetime away from Africa, a total of 24 years in England. I would not have thought that the Afrikaner was a subject I'd ever want to write about. I, and many others with far greater reason than I, loathed them, these hypocritical racists, these church-going lovers of black and coloured women, this second, self-proclaimed Chosen People. These were the people who would, given the chance, happily have backed Hitler, glad to see the back of that other Chosen People – the Jews, my father's people.

This Afrikaans tribe was the people whose greed and fear and intellectual dishonesty condemned millions of fellow South Africans to a life on the fringes, to unrealised potential, poverty, disease and death. This was the people who had cost me my country. Hating what they were doing in my name as a white South African, I felt the need to make the one protest I was capable of – leaving. So I left for England in January 1980.

No, I had no love for the Afrikaners, this bull-necked tribe of biltong and boerewors eaters, worshippers of rugby players. My God, we had nothing in common – except for my mother, Elise Louw. She gave the lie to everything I felt for her people. It was her courage and love that had faced down her family, even as they cursed her on her wedding day when she married a Jew. She it was, who, putting her own convictions to one side, raised three children in the Jewish faith. Her own faith till the day she died was Dutch Reformed Christianity. As embodied in her, the faith was a constant example to me of forgiveness, that central tenet of the philosophy of Jesus. Truly, she embodied all that was best in Christianity – and this despite the condemnation of a Dutch Reformed dominee she went to, seeking advice and help about the central conflict in her life, a Christian raising Jews. 'You will burn in hell,' he told her with relish. She managed once more to do what she always bid us do: turn the other cheek.

Growing up as a Jew, it was not surprising that my feelings were for the underdog, the oppressed, the persecuted. And the underdog was ever before my eyes. I fished and swam and rode on the beaches of Blouberg, enjoying my privileged freedom less and less as I became more and more politically aware; I had the image of Robben Island and all it stood for right in front of me, just eight kilometres away.

No, indeed, I had no love for the Afrikaner.

But my mother and other individual Afrikaners gave me pause, made it difficult for me to condemn them all out of hand. I fought this inclination to condemn, a quality that they exhibited so horribly, an ability to condemn whole peoples because of the colour of their skin, their faith, their beliefs. I could not help but notice the kindness and generosity of neighbours to this strange, mixed-up family of mine. Even as prime ministers and presidents walked past our home at Blouberg, all dressed in their Sunday black, off for a stroll down the whites-only beach, I had other examples to balance the great evil I saw all around me.

There were the stories my mother told me, stories of courage and endurance against overwhelming odds, stories of her people, a small nation, ''n handjievol' – 'a small handful' as she described them – against the teeming black millions of Africa. This was a volk who, seeking their own freedom, ventured deep into the heart of this inhospitable continent, over mountains with straining ox teams, in the face of drought, hostility and war.

I was forced to admit that they had a vitality, these people, a robust attitude to life. They lived with gusto, and they loved the land. This was something that spoke powerfully to me. They felt themselves to be Africans, of Africa. They were not going anywhere. They had the power and intended to keep it. This, for better or worse, was their place and here they would live or die. It was an attractive quality, often lacking in English-speaking South Africans, who looked to England, America, Canada, New Zealand and Australia.

The embattled Afrikaner, it was said, had the respect of the blacks. They understood the blunt Afrikaner's approach and mistrusted the two-faced double-dealing of the English-speaking community, which paid lip service to liberal values and, when push came to shove, voted en masse for the Nationalists. You knew where you were with the Afrikaner. It might not always have been pretty, but there it was.

These people were shaped by Africa; its harsh realities were in their blood. They were a frontier race, pioneers, with all the rough and ready qualities needed for that task, the subjugation of land and people. Despite my every instinct, there was deep in me a bitter respect for the Afrikaners.

My Jewish grandfather Herman Roup was passionate in his defence of the Afrikaner, whom he said had been prepared to trade with him when he was a penniless immigrant, a nobody. He had traded with Afrikaans farmers all his life and had achieved prosperity as a result. And my own father not only chose to marry an Afrikaans girl, but would also say, 'The Afrikaners made me. They employed me and promoted me in their businesses, they backed me financially when no one else would, and later they became partners in my business. I owe the Afrikaner a blood debt. Our family's good fortune has been built with the help of the Afrikaner.'

Being what I am, a Boerejood, I cannot write about the Afrikaners without looking too, however briefly, at the Jews. I'm proud of their achievements and sometimes less than pleased by their actions. They are, after all, family.

A newly published book, *Community and Conscience – the Jews in Apartheid South Africa* by Gideon Shimoni reaches conclusions I can't argue with. Shimoni writes: 'There is nothing in this record [of Jews in South Africa] deserving of moral pride, neither does it warrant utter self-reproach. From a coldly objective historical perspective this was characteristic minority-group behaviour – a phenomenon of self-preservation performed at the cost of moral righteousness.' That strikes me as about right.

I think of Rabbi David Sherman, the Reform rabbi who was a fixture of my youth and my intellectual and spiritual development. His sermons, coolly dissecting the iniquities of apartheid, formed an important part of my thinking on race and injustice. I was proud to stand by his side as I read from the Torah on the day of my bar mitzvah at the Reform Synagogue in Sea Point in 1963.

I'm less proud of the role played by Percy Yutar, the Jewish State Advocate in the Rivonia trial of Nelson Mandela and his colleagues. But I think too of Helen Suzman and the many Jews who stood up and vocally opposed apartheid.

As always, wherever you look, at whichever end of the political spectrum, there are Jews in the mix. There are good and there are bad. As in all groups, there is an equal proportion of heroes and villains.

But it was the Afrikaners whom I now wished to meet and understand. I wanted to sit with them in their homes, on their farms, in their wealth and in their poverty, in their churches, their businesses, their innermost sanctums, if they would let me in, into their universities and into their minds. I wanted to meet their leaders, their priests, their poets and writers, their farmers and workers, their young and their old. I wanted to hear the stories they told themselves and their children. I wanted to know their hopes and fears for their future, and how they spoke of the past.

I would be going in search of the soul of a people, my mother's people, a people I had never really known. It would be a quest entered into with as much of an open heart as I could muster.

I would be going in search of many things; but one in particular, the answer to a question I had wondered about for years. Why did the Afrikaners relinquish power so quietly?

How had Afrikaners come to do this unthinkable thing? Did the story of Piet Retief not keep them awake at night, guns in hand, waiting for Africa to reclaim its own? Would the Afrikaners, like the once-dominant Moors in Spain, be relegated to a footnote in history as the tale of Africa unfolded? The Moors were beaten in battle and sent packing, the Afrikaners voted for a change that would diminish their role to that of a cipher. How was this possible?

I had many questions. I wanted to know how it was possible for me to have misjudged Afrikaners so. I had made the biggest decision of my life – to leave South Africa – based on a belief that they would never willingly submit to black rule, and that the ensuing bloodbath would involve me as a member of the South African Defence Force, as I had done my national service and was liable for call-up in the event of a national emergency. I wanted no part in that. So I left, and was astonished and amazed 14 years later to be proved wrong when they and other whites opted for reason rather than the bigoted stupidity I had expected, and went quietly, relinquishing power voluntarily in an orderly manner. On the scale of mistakes I've made, you could say this was a big one. This was a judgement call that I had got completely wrong. Perhaps this trip, this voyage of discovery, would show me a truer picture of the Afrikaners.

I began by contacting Afrikaans friends and family, people I hadn't spoken to for 30 years, unsure of my reception. I need not have worried; they offered help generously. Beginning with these people, I asked them to suggest others I might speak to, people who could speak for the Afrikaners as they had been and as they were now. They didn't disappoint me; they found me an extraordinary group of human beings to speak to, and I began a journey that would teach me many things.

I left England for South Africa in June 2003, almost a decade after Nelson Mandela had walked free, and a century since the Bittereinders (those Afrikaners who had fought the British to the bitter end) had left the country for South America after the Anglo-Boer War (1899-1902). I was intent on reading this latest chapter in the life of the Afrikaners.

Hybrid Vigour

As a horseman, I knew that my fairly unusual gene pool was, genetically, a great advantage – hybrid vigour is not something to be sneezed at. I can never be accused of in-breeding. All those jokes about second cousins blithely pass me by. I am an outcross if ever there were one.

This mix made for an unusual household in a truly bizarre country, and although I loved the country, I left it at the age of 30. So it's not surprising that my life has been a search for an independent identity, a land of my own, a country of my own and a language of my own. On the surface, it would seem that England provided the solution to all these issues – but this is both right and wrong. The search to find my place in the world, physically and spiritually, is a journey that I'm still on.

I never learnt to speak or write Hebrew, despite Hebrew lessons twice a week and synagogue on Friday nights and Saturday mornings until I was about 14 and began to assert myself. And my Afrikaans was poor, a sort of kitchen language that allowed me to communicate with our servants, but not much use outside the house.

My parents went through an understandably lengthy courtship, thanks to the mutual antagonism of their two communities. My mother's family wasn't exactly thrilled by the match and my father's family was equally aghast. But after 15 years of on-off romance, they finally married, in 1948, the year the National Party came to power.

My mother's people, the Afrikaners, have a strange attitude to the Jew. Many are, very generally speaking, subject to all the usual anti-Semitic feelings. This attitude is confused by the fact that they also identify with the Jews as a Chosen People. And thus we got the weird relationship between the apartheid Nationalist government and that of Israel – a mix of anti-Semitism and military respect that didn't stand in the way of diplomatic and economic links and considerable trade in armaments.

This benighted couple, my parents, decided that if they had children they would raise them in the Jewish faith. How this decision came about, I'm not sure. Perhaps my father felt that in this way he would not be completely opting out of Judaism; and for my mother, knowing her, it would have been an act of love, the final proof that she had not a scrap of her people's anti-Semitism.

The irony inherent in this decision is that according to ancient Jewish law one cannot be Jewish if one's mother is not Jewish. And though my mother wasn't particularly interested in her religion when young, she never converted to Judaism. (Had she converted, we, her children, would be seen as 'proper' Jews.) In her later years, she began to be greatly bothered by what she had done. She began attending church regularly on Sundays at Wynberg and Blouberg, depending on where we were at the time. Towards the end of her life, she also attended prayer meetings at friends' homes as well as at our house.

She was much helped in her religious dilemma – the ever-more-committed Christian raising so-called Jewish children – by a wonderful priest, Doctor Johan van der Merwe, whom she met at the Dutch Reformed Church in Blouberg. His encouraging words reassured her that of all the teachings of Christ, the greatest was that of love – to love thy God, and thy neighbour as thyself – and that this placed her and her decision to raise Jewish children beyond the reach of hellfire. She was greatly relieved by this judgement from someone who was a Doctor of Divinity and who headed the seminary for training Dutch Reformed priests in the Cape.

My mother warmed to Dominee van der Merwe even more when he briefly joined my brother Herman on a hitch-hiking tour of Israel in the 1960s, after Herman had spent three months on a kibbutz, sexing turkeys and trying it on with Dutch and Scandinavian girls who had been attracted to the kibbutz ethos. Herman was in search of his true identity and the experience of Israel and contact with Israelis gave him a greater sense of being Jewish, though he, like my sister Janine and I, married out of the Faith.

How my father managed to convince the rabbis of the Reform Synagogue in Cape Town, admittedly liberal though they were, to accept his brood of three as the genuine kosher article, I will never know. But he was a great salesman in his youth and has a huge, some would say overwhelming, personality, and he got his way.

And he didn't leave it at that. My father became a force within the Reform movement and helped significantly to see a temple built at Wynberg. He sat on committees and was a general thorn in the flesh of many of his fellow worshippers. 'The bloody Jews are driving me crazy,' he'd say. It was an expression we got used to at an early age. (What the Jewish God made of all this I look forward to finding out one day.)

So, to my mother's horror I, and five years later my brother, were circumcised, a few days after our respective births. She was comforted by Esther, her mother-in-law, who, while she did not approve of her daughter-in-law, was not going to be deprived of her grandchildren. After all, they had come down on her side of the religious divide and so she could be magnanimous. Esther's words of comfort were, 'Nonsense! It's nothing! It's the only pain a man ever feels in this life!' I also had a bar mitzvah at 13, as did my brother, and my sister a bat mitzvah. On the way to the synagogue, accompanied by my mother among others, Granny Esther, dear old thing that she was, said to me, 'I want you to promise me that you'll marry a nice Jewish girl when you grow up.' Too stunned by this gross act of insensitivity to say much, I mumbled, to my everlasting shame, what must have passed for assent. But, like my siblings, I too married out of the Faith.

This religious duality had its lighter and its bittersweet moments. When my mother's dominee came round each year to collect funds for the church, my father would take great delight in providing a seriously large cheque – with this proviso: 'Make sure that you tell everyone how much the bastard Jew gave and then they won't be able to give less!'

My mother's prayer group once discussed the apartheid issue. Most of the group opted, not surprisingly, for the view that God had intended apples to be apples and pears to be pears, and that never the twain should meet. My mother offered the thought – borne out by our family – that fruit salad had merits worth considering. It stopped the conversation dead for a while, I'm told.

And talking of food, the food on our table suffered an identity crisis; it was neither one thing nor the other. Of this you could be sure, though: it was not kosher. We ate milk with meat, and bacon and eggs were a breakfast staple. But lunch or supper could be chopped herring or chopped liver, beef with carrots and prunes, pickled herrings, red herrings or corned beef. There might be those Afrikaans staples, tamatiebredie (tomato and lamb stew), waterblommetjiebredie (stew of lamb with water hawthorn flowers) or gesmoorde snoek (a dish of fish and rice like kedgeree). Desserts might include melktert (milk & cinnamon tart), koeksisters (crisp plaited mini doughnuts in syrup), waatlemoenkonfyt (watermelon jam) or the more conventional items of the English kitchen.

Most people think their mothers are special; mine really was. She was funny, irreverent and brave, though she never saw that; she was also kind and loving, and could not tolerate bullshit, bragging or pretension. She was a remarkable woman whose principles I try to live my life by – not always successfully, it must be said.

My parents met at the roller-skating rink in Paarl in the 1930s and my father taught my mother to 'cross' going round corners – that is, putting the outside foot over the inner one to ease one's way smoothly round. It was a good start, for they would need to find a way of smoothing their path round the corners of life rather more than most. Theirs was an illicit love affair in this small, gossipy place. My father's family had come from nothing and were now well known and respected within both the Jewish and Afrikaans communities locally; my mother's family, born to wealth and privilege, had been reduced to abject poverty.

They had also to put up with taunts from their peers. My

mother recalls being asked time after time by Jewish girls in the town, 'Why don't you leave the Jewish boys alone?' – as if she were working her way through them single-handed.

When she matriculated from La Rochelle Girls' School, my mother wished to study to be a physical education teacher. The school said she certainly had the grades for university, but her family could not afford it. So, instead, she joined her sister Mabel in the small, chic dress shop she had established in the town. It was a good place to hear the latest and be in at the start of dresses designed for special occasions, dances and balls, which would later be discussed – both the impact of the ball gown and the ball. My mother loved it.

One day an elderly woman came into the shop and browsed through the clothes on display. When my mother offered her assistance she said, 'I'm just looking.' And that, in fact, is exactly what she was doing because when she left, Mabel said to my mother, 'Elise, do you know who that was? It was Leon's mother, coming to inspect!' That was the only contact my mother had with her future mother-in-law until years later, when she and my father had been married for some years, living and working in Johannesburg, and my mother flew down to Paarl to be with her mother, who was dying. 'My kind, wat jy nie sal waag nie!' ('My child, it's amazing what you are capable of doing!') her mother said to her, speaking of the plane journey and perhaps so many other things, including a Jewish husband.

I have said my mother was brave, and I will give you an example. Before she left Paarl to return to Jo'burg, she decided to take her courage in her hands and call on her parents-in-law. She described to me many times how she stood outside their door – a door that had been barred to her for all the 17 years of her courtship with my father and subsequent three years of marriage – and knocked tentatively. Grandpa Herman answered the knock. My mother said that all she could manage to say was, 'Mr Roup, I am Leon's wife.'

Herman threw the door open and said, 'Come in, come in, my child. You know, I myself nearly married an Afrikaans girl.' They never looked back and a real love grew between them.

My Jewish grandmother took longer to come round, but

Herman Roup was nothing if not master in his own home, so the citadel had been stormed. My father was very proud of my mother for this achievement.

My paternal grandmother, Esther Rosenthal, an English Jewess, arrived in South Africa at the age of three months with her family in the 1880s, setting up home at Riversdale in the Cape. Her husband-to-be, my Jewish grandfather, Herman Roup, based in Paarl after his epic journey out of Lithuania, was busy criss-crossing the Cape doing business with farmers, buying up their produce and selling it on.

Family legend records that one day, in Laingsburg, a Mrs Tromp, an Afrikaans farmer's wife, asked him why a good-looking chap like him was not married. He told her that those he liked would not have him. She said she had just the wife for him and described the daughter of a Jewish ostrich-feather buyer based in Riversdale. Herman decided to investigate, found the house and knocked on the door. Esther, who had been working hard, had her hair up in strips of cloth and was not looking her best. Nonetheless, three months later he met her in Cape Town, where she arrived to stay with an aunt, bringing ostrich feathers with her to sell, to provide spending money. Six months later they were married. He had found the woman for him, someone who shared his work ethic.

In the years that followed, Esther Roup's work ethic led to her enjoying (if that is the right word) an almost legendary reputation in Paarl. In fact, she was notorious. She would think nothing of walking into the home of a newlywed Jewish couple to berate the young wife for not being up and at it, cleaning, dusting and cooking at the crack of dawn. She and her husband made a formidable pair.

There is a story about my grandfather that I love for its theatricality and bloody-mindedness. He had heard that a fellow Jew in Paarl, an attorney, was spreading word that he, Herman, was less than honest. Herman bided his time and, on Yom Kippur, the Day of Atonement, the most holy day in the Jewish calendar, he stood up in the synagogue, pounding his pew to get the rabbi and the congregation's attention. Six foot four inches tall, blond and blue-eyed, with a very determined chin, he was a commanding presence. He said word had reached him of the slanders of this man. He invited the by-now trembling gossiper to come forward and repeat his allegations before the altar, the Torah, the word of God and the gathered congregation. The man rose from his seat, slunk out of the synagogue and was not heard from again on this subject. Years later, on Herman's death, this man came to condole, and my father shut the door in his face. The acorn does not fall far from the oak.

This couple, Herman and Esther, had four sons, Nathan, Henry, Abraham and Leon, the youngest being my father. He was a sickly child and dyslexic, having inherited his father's word blindness. His three elder brothers were academically outstanding and good sportsmen to boot. Nathan, the eldest, was the real star, the apple of his parents' eye. When he died at 27 from enteric fever it broke something in them that never healed. There was silence around their home as the young man fought for life. Straw was spread on the road outside to deaden the sound of passing carts, and when he died, Paarl came to a halt.

I believe my father, Leon, has spent his life trying to close the gap between himself and Nathan in his parents' eyes, and at 91, after decades of huge personal and financial success, still feels he has a way to go. That is life, and that's families for you.

In the years of their courting, my parents broke up for some time to give each other the opportunity to find someone more suitable from their respective backgrounds. My mother dated a number of Afrikaners and Dad some Jewish girls, but nothing clicked and so they finally married.

My arrival on the scene, after the loss of a first child, made things considerably easier with their families in Paarl. They would drive out from their home in Cape Town on a Sunday afternoon and at four o'clock, as they turned into the street where my Jewish grandparents lived, all the neighbours would be out on their stoeps, supposedly taking the air. Herman would come storming out to the car, gather me up and say at the top of his voice, 'Hulle is net nuuskierig om te sien hoe 'n baster-joodjie lyk!' ("They're all just curious to see what a little half-caste Jew looks like.")

My parents' early difficulties and their upbringing in

Paarl, close to the soil, gave both of them a robust, almost peasant, respect for thrift, hard work and solid, down-to-earth values; they mistrusted anything too intellectual or arty. Herman Roup was a regular visitor to their home in the Cape Town suburb of Newlands. On arrival, he'd inspect the contents of the kitchen cupboards and the fridge. Then, shaking his head, he would take my mother by the hand and order his driver to take them to Claremont. There, he would go from butcher to fishmonger to greengrocer, stocking up and warning each merchant that while his daughter-in-law might easily be fooled, he was not, and he wanted the best, and in future she too should only get the best.

I watched my mother once, many years later, applying this approach in London, with mixed results – whizzing through the hanging shelves of Harrod's, accompanied by the squeaks of distraught salesladies, and in Oxford Street, fingering the fruit on costermongers' barrows, to their fury.

She described herself as materialistic and loved beautiful clothes. She was always immaculately turned out. To help her achieve this, she bought two wigs on a trip to Italy. She would wear one while the other was at the hairdressers – both done in the bouffant style of the '60s.

Once, on a trip to Israel, my sister Jay heard a muffled cry from the Tel Aviv airport booth where my mother was being searched by some no-nonsense female Israeli soldiers. 'O, my Here, hulle het my pruik af! Hulle soek 'n geweer onder my pruik! Janine, kom help!' ('They've taken my wig off and are looking for a gun! Come help me, Janine!') Life with my mother was never boring.

She had no problem laughing at herself or walking in my father's shadow, winking as she did so when his favourite stories emerged for the millionth time. A favourite maxim when my father was on the warpath and she was, as usual, taking the brunt, would be to point out that her approach was based on Christ's teaching, to turn the cheek seventy times seven. When we threatened to tackle him, she would urge, 'Ag, my kind, wees maar die minste, wees maar die minste.' (Oh, child, rather be the lesser one, be the lesser one.')

She got her own back when rabbis came to call, inevitably

staying for a meal. Invariably there would be some un-kosher element in the food – bacon, or cream and meat, or something just not on. This would tickle her no end as she watched them tucking in with gusto. Afterwards she would hoot, 'Hulle het nie geëet nie, hulle het gevreet!' (They did not just eat, they gobbled it up!')

A litany of fearful, funny and coarse family sayings accompanies me through life. Afrikaans, English and Yiddish expressions, there is one for each and every occasion. But my mother's great favourite was the Italian expression 'Que sera sera'. It summed up her fatalistic take on life. And her most stinging rebuke was that someone was an 'asgat', whatever that meant. I think it referred to anyone wishy-washy, weak-willed or hopeless.

Her own mother's nickname was 'Baby', well earned because of her tendency to cry at the drop of a hat, something my whole family has inherited. This lachrymose fearfulness showed itself in another of my mother's regular statements: 'As jy kinders het, het jy altyd groen koring op jou land' – meaning that one's children are, unlike a farm crop, never harvested and safely stored in the barn under cover, but are always out there, subject to hail, rain-damage or depredation by pests, a never-ending source of worry. Now that I am a father myself, I am less irritated by that sentiment than I was in my youth, and understand the love and fear inherent in the expression.

When she thought something or some statement utterly ridiculous, my mother would mutter under her breath, 'Ag, gaan skeit op die ys,' a double entendre meaning either 'go and skate on the ice' or (what she really meant) 'go and shit on the ice'. She was also deeply canny in the ways of the world and not above teasing us, pretending ignorance. Picking up on our teenage slang, she was quite capable of saying, 'Oh, keep a cool tool!'

My father had just as many, if not more, favourite maxims. From his much-quoted father he would repeat 'one door closes and another opens' after any setback we had, or 'in business, you need to stand with a gun in one hand and a knife in the other'. He also had a selection of Afrikaans sayings: 'As lekker te lekker is, is lekker nie meer lekker nie' (Too much of a good thing) and 'Stank vir dank' (Just a bad smell by way of thanks). And if he said it once he said it a thousand times: 'The road to hell is paved with good intentions!' He was fond of describing people without manners as 'grobbejongs' (coarse or crude boys) and he spoke of 'cholloming', or dreaming, as in 'Let's chollom that he behaves like a mensch.' A mensch, of course, was the highest form of praise. It betokened someone who was a true human being, the real McCoy, a person of real worth.

It was a strange childhood, in that it left me feeling neither one thing nor the other. I did not feel Afrikaans and I did not feel Jewish. I did not know what I felt, but I knew I was different. Sometimes I wondered which part of me was the Jewish and which the Afrikaans bit. In adulthood, I would joke that had I been able to arrange things with God I would have had the top half, above the waist, Jewish, giving me the best shot at brains; and the half below the belt Afrikaans, with the sexual stamina and rugby-playing legs that came with it.

I remember walking along the beach at Bloubergstrand, where I most came into contact with the Afrikaans community. Stopping to chat to adult friends and neighbours of my parents, I always got the impression that they struggled to get 'vatplek', to get to grips, with who and what I was. I could not blame them. In a way this led me to sympathise with the black and coloured peoples around me, who were quite often even greater mysteries to whites. In my case, the confusion came not because I was completely foreign, but because people speaking to me were looking out for the foreignness in among the Afrikaans breeding, like one of those lava lamps where two colours move about in a body of oil but never mingle. In me they mingled, but neither I nor anyone else could see the join.

My genetic inheritance also ignited a land hunger, a desire for soil of my own that comes as much from my maternal Afrikaans farming family as from my landless, wandering Jewish family. The saying 'Without land a man is only half a man' is one I could subscribe to. Over the years, I visited many places in many countries, with the thought that they might provide the solution – a permanent homeland that wet and culturally cool England could never be.

France, Portugal, Spain, Greece, the USA, Italy – all were contenders at one time or another. My footsteps, and the hoofbeats of my horses, have crossed continents in search of this mythic homeland, half-wandering Jew, half-landless Afrikaans farmer. Maybe the old Irish saying 'He wandered the world in search of the answer and he returned home to find it' may yet prove true.

Bootstraps

For those of us who have known Afrikaners mainly in their time of power and wealth when they ran the country, it is often difficult to remember that one of the greatest problems faced by them was poverty. The poor white Afrikaner was the rule rather than the exception in the first half of the twentieth century. Afrikaners had fought and lost two wars which cost them a third of their population by some counts and had impoverished them, and this was then followed by the Great Depression. They were generally not wealthy farmers; rather, they made up the rural poor who had to pull themselves up by their bootstraps and for whom the arrival of an Afrikaner government in 1948 was a godsend.

My mother told me many stories as I grew up about her people and her life in Paarl. A number of them illustrate the reality of rural poverty very well. Her father, Andries Abraham Louw of Kuiperskraal, had grown up with great wealth on his parents' farm in Paarl, but when he inherited the farm, he had not been a success. My mother would say, 'Hy het agteruit geboer,' (he farmed backwards) and after many struggles, including one with the bottle, he found himself with a wife and eight children and no income. The community took pity on him and found him a sinecure job driving the post cart round Paarl.

The family, like so many others on the economic edge of disaster, kept a pig in the backyard of their modest home in Paarl to help them survive the winter. As late autumn approached, the time came for the slaughtering of the pig. On the day the knives were sharpened and the kitchen prepared for this annual event, my mother would take refuge under her bed to avoid the terrible screaming of the pig as it was stuck and then butchered. She told how her mother and the family's maid would use every last bit of that pig, making sausages of various kinds, then pickling some of the meat and smoking other parts. It was vital to their seeing the winter through.

Theirs was not a soft life; and it was also a life without shoes for many, she said, and told me the following story about a neighbour's son. The Paarl valley lay quiet beneath the heat of the summer sun, stilled with Sunday. Rows of vivid green vines swooped down the hills to red dust roads, marking it out as a wine-producing area. To one side of the valley rose the huge round dome of rock that gave the place its name – 'de Pêrel' (the pearl), in the language of the Dutchmen who had first set European eyes on it. It was an apt name, for when the rains came the domed rock gleamed wetly, like the fruit of some gigantic oyster.

On the far side of the valley bulged the grey-blue mass of the Hottentots Holland mountains, the first boundary between the Cape and the great open spaces of Africa proper to the north. Caught between these two rock masses, the place was an oven in summer.

The valley was dotted with farms, focused on the highest man-made object in 30 kilometres, the steeple of the Dutch Reformed Church, topped by a brass cockerel flashing semaphore messages in reflected sunshine to the god of these African Dutch. Suddenly church bells, reminding of duty to God, disturbed the Sunday quiet. In many homes of the Afrikaans community excitement mounted, as this was no ordinary Sunday. Today many young people would be confirmed into the brotherhood of Christ.

Ludovic, the eldest son of the village butcher, whose large family lived next door to my mother's family, was up early to see the sunrise on this important day. His bare feet kicked up little bursts of red dust as he ran. At 16 he had never worn shoes. His father worked from four in the morning until eight at night, cutting meat and serving customers, and his income did not run to providing shoes for all his many children.

Too excited to sleep, Ludovic ran up the hill to see the sun rise from the slopes below the rock. He wanted to be the first person in the valley to see the sun come over the mountains on this great day – the day he would wear shoes for the first time.

It was something he had been waiting years for. To him, it meant leaving behind childish things and becoming a man. He would shortly be joining his father in the butchery business, and there was a girl too, whom he was going to marry once he had saved up enough.

His bare feet had concerned him greatly. It wasn't that he minded for himself – years of walking on bare soles had toughened his feet to the point where he couldn't feel the sharp gravel or the full heat of the roads in the summer. But some of his friends had been wearing shoes for a long time now and he worried that his girl would think him of little worth because he still went without shoes like a young lad.

Now, as he heard the bells ring out, he ran for home till his lungs burned. About half a mile from his house, he stopped. It wouldn't do to arrive home heaving and sweating like the horse that pulled his father's cart. Today he would carry himself with as much dignity and pride as the dominee himself.

His mother and father were already dressed for church and the maid had almost finished dressing his youngest sister. Usually, his mother would have scolded him for being late, but on this morning she just smiled and said, 'Maak gou!' ('Hurry up').

Breathing shallow and fast, Ludovic walked into the bedroom he shared with three of his brothers. There, next to his bed, the shoes stood, gleaming black, the leather stiff and uncreased. The shoes were the exact pair he had pointed out to her in the shoe-shop window in Lady Grey Street. The laces were not yet crossed through the eight brass-ringed eyes; it was another example of his mother's intuitive understanding of her son. Bending down quickly, he picked them up, one in each hand, and held them to his cheeks, the smell of new leather making him dizzy with joy.

Hurriedly he sponged himself clean, then dressed: starched white shirt, blue-black tie, black socks and his confirmation blue suit. Sitting down, he quickly laced up the shoes and then slipped in his left foot. Toes and heel wiggled in, then stopped. The shoe was too small!

He tried again but he could simply not get his foot past a certain point. Worried, he tried the other shoe. It, too, was too small. Nonplussed, he sat looking at his feet half inside the shiny leather shoes. He felt his world crumbling. Then, suddenly, he had an idea.

A few minutes later, gasping, he pulled the shoes on, and this time they fitted snugly. Smiling with triumph, he laced them up tightly and went to join the rest of the family, blushing as he did so. His mother kissed him and his father shook his hand. It was a proud moment.

At the church, Ludovic collapsed. He had gone forward with the other boys in their dark blue suits and the girls in their white dresses, but at the altar, he crumpled. A whisper ran through the congregation: 'It's Ludovic, the butcher's son.'

The dominee and two church elders rushed to help him and noticed blood on the royal-blue carpet. The boy lay unconscious and they struggled to loosen his clothing. Then they saw that the blood came from his shoes. Quickly they unlaced them and pulled them off. Transfixed, they watched as the blood oozed from the boy's axe-severed toes.

Another story my mother told me was of an earlier time, just after the turn of the century. A young lad had gone up with some companions to play on and around Paarl Rock. This was something local children did, as my mother did in her time, sliding down the smooth face of the rock on logs and getting soundly spanked when they returned home for ruining their clothes in the process.

On this earlier occasion, the boys played up there in that eyrie overlooking Paarl until one of the lads fell with a shout into a deep crevice in the rock. He was badly hurt, and after struggling to no avail to reach him, his companions sent for help. The boy's father and other men arrived with ropes. They struggled for hours to find a way of releasing the boy, who was in agony and desperate. As the hours wore on, the father and friends battled to release the lad, so near and yet so far, all of them beside themselves with anguish, driving themselves to try, try desperately to find a way to free the boy and end his pain, to return him to his father. The boy waited in hope and fear, trusting that a way would be found, but slowly realised that he was hopelessly caught. His and his father's pain cannot be grasped. Finally, unable to stand his agony any longer, he begged his father to put him out of his misery and shoot him.

My mother couldn't say how long the father wrestled with this hell on earth, but eventually the cries of the boy proved too much and the man shot his son. The story has come down the years, a parent's worst nightmare and a symbol of a brutal time.

These were no fairy tales; the boys, the rock, the toes, the shoes, all existed, part of my mother and father's childhood in Paarl.

Meanwhile, my Jewish grandfather was also busy pulling himself up by his bootstraps, building a business in Paarl. Throughout his life, he lived in intimate contact with the Afrikaans farmers with whom he traded animal hides, seed, sacks, horses, donkeys and mules. His reputation for straight dealing was legendary in a trade notorious for tricky practices, and one of his biggest coups was an order from the British army for 10,000 horses for their forces in India. This he fulfilled by importing animals from the Argentine.

Herman was not an easy man; he had a volcanic temper, and a huge determination to do things his way. This determination was what had helped him survive his personal odyssey out of Lithuania. He had arrived in the Cape penniless, starting from scratch in a strange new continent, handicapped by a lifelong inability to read or write, a curse that has come down the generations in my family to haunt us. His love and respect for books, however, was great. On his deathbed, he made a request that to me has a particular significance. Jews never destroy their old prayer books and bibles and Torahs; they bury them in the same way that a person would be buried in the graveyard, in consecrated ground. As my grandfather lay dying, this illiterate man said, 'Bury me by the books.' And that indeed is where he lies today, hard by the old religious texts of Paarl's Jewish community.

Part of Herman's story was about having to deal with the emerging political restlessness of the Afrikaner in the 1930s. The fascist Greyshirts were active in South Africa, their words falling on fertile soil, as an impoverished people living under the colonial yoke sniffed an opportunity to free themselves at last in the looming world conflict. Herman heard that there was to be a Greyshirt rally at the Paarl Town Hall and went to see the mayor. He told the man that if the rally went ahead he would burn the place down. Knowing Herman Roup was not a man to make idle threats, the meeting at the Town Hall was cancelled and held somewhere else, somewhere rather more discreet.

These were the stories I grew up with, the true coin of my inheritance, the tales that would place me equally in two communities and in neither.

Cadillac Prayers

I remember the smell of the leather car seats, large and electronically controlled. They'd glide forward or back, go up or down, and tilt. The car was a Cadillac, one of a series my father had in the 1950s and '60s, huge, black, ostentatious boats on wheels, which squealed as you turned the slightest corner.

I would accompany him in one of these monsters now and then to his bakery, a massive industrial complex in Lansdowne, a suburb of Cape Town. The factory employed 600 people producing bread, biscuits and cake, in shifts round the clock, day and night, seven days a week.

The immense weight of the car doors closing created a tomb-like feeling inside, an oppressive atmosphere not helped by having to listen to my father saying his prayers – his habit since I was old enough to understand that he was not actually speaking to me.

'Shema Ysroel, Adonai Elohainu, Adonai Echad. Hear O Israel, the Lord thy God, the Lord is One.' He would begin and end with this prayer. It's the cornerstone prayer of the Jewish faith and it means 'Listen'. It continues in its second line and onward to admonish the faithful to 'Love the Lord God with all your heart, and with all your soul and with all your might.' It felt terribly wrong to me, forced to be present at a dialogue between my father and his God. There seemed something unnatural at this forced intimacy in which he prayed for himself and his family and me. It was strong stuff for a 6-year-old at 8 a.m.

In later years, when I came to read up about this faith I

had found myself born into, I discovered in Deuteronomy that God had an ambivalent attitude towards his Chosen People. Besides the story of the Ten Commandments, the unfortunate incident of the Golden Calf and the 40 years wandering in the desert, Deuteronomy makes plain that God did not choose Israel to enter Canaan because of the Hebrews' righteousness. Rather, it was because He wished to punish the wickedness of the nations already inhabiting the land. The God of Abraham intones, 'Know therefore that the Lord your God is not giving you this good land to possess because of your righteousness, for you are a stubborn people!'

I sympathised. If my father was anything to go by, God did indeed have his hands full.

As if by magic, my father managed to make my mother's religion disappear into anonymity. It was years before I understood that I was half Christian.

The words of the psalm: 'By the rivers of Babylon, there we sat down and wept when we remembered Zion' were very real to me.

But as I grew up, my Afrikaans heritage, like a strong weed, broke through the cracks of my consciousness and took hold of my mind at some deep unconscious level. My mother would tell me, 'Onkruid vergaan nie.' (You can't get rid of weeds). And the truth of that was borne out for me by the strength with which my Afrikaans heritage gradually climbed up my trunk and invaded my soul.

There are Afrikaners who were a part of my youth and my journey into manhood. They were people who stood out: Kobus Meiring, MP for Paarl and former Administrator of the Cape, and one-time partner in my father's business as MD of Sasko, our milling partners; André Brink the writer, behind whom I had queued at Paula's Bakery in Grahamstown while studying journalism at Rhodes University; Dr Johan van der Merwe, the Zionistic Afrikaans dominee who had been such a help to my mother; writer Rian Malan, with his 'traitor's heart'; Frederik van Zyl Slabbert, whom I heard lecture at Rhodes University once or twice. There were many others too.

And there was my immediate Afrikaans family. The men were mostly dead, but their wives and families lived on. I remember Uncle Pierrie, known as 'Kake' Louw (his jaw having been dislocated in a rugby game) and his wife Aunt Susanne and their children André and Elna. Oom Pierrie worked as a motorcar mechanic in Paarl. His brother Toetie and wife Linda also lived in Paarl, coughing out their last cigarette-stained breaths, childless, but with miniature white fluffy dogs for company in their small house; and just up the road, in a much nicer part of Paarl, my Jewish Uncle Abie and wife Hannah, who amid the dark wood panelling and Persian carpets were also shortly to be victims of cigarettes and cancer. I met their children Nathan and Sandra at rare family gatherings, and Atta Matthee, the stout cook who raised them when their mother died.

Atta joined our household years later when the kids had grown up. She felt a true bond with them and kept their pictures by her bedside till she too died. She was buried, unforgettably, on a rain-lashed midwinter day in Paarl. The coffin floated in the flooded grave, refusing to settle, as the mourners screamed and cried hysterically around the raw mud-stained mouth of her last resting place.

In Franschhoek, there was the lovely old Cape farm of the great Springbok rugby player, Boy Louw, my mother's cousin. I recall the cool dappled light of the farmyard, shaded by massive oaks and edged with creamy whitewashed walls that flaked softly at the touch, the sweet smell of silage and of lucerne bales stored in cavernous barns, spot-lit with sunrays and dancing dust motes. I think we visited twice. In Stellenbosch, down the road, my mother's youngest sister Ena lived with her husband Bertie and my cousins Albie, Jacques and Bertie junior. I recall the morning and afternoon teas she served us, scones and grated cheese, and apricot jam and delicious iced cakes; and my sense of being a foreigner in a foreign place.

Just outside Paarl there was Aunt Hester, the highly strung wife of my mother's dead brother, the brickmaker and farmer, Andries Louw, whom my mother described as working all his life 'soos 'n werkesel.' ('like a work mule')

There was Aunt Lena, a formidable former schoolteacher who had been married to another of my mother's brothers. We occasionally saw their younger son Ben and their daughter Rika. Ben, a brilliant boy who described himself as 'Louw by name and low by nature,' arrived once at our Newlands home in a green MG sports car, a glamorous figure studying at the University of Cape Town.

These were some of the people who slipped in and out of my childhood. Visiting South Africa now, I wished to connect with this half-foreign culture and note once more the tastes and smells of Afrikaans cooking, re-read Herman Charles Bosman, and walk, and ride, and drive through the land again. I wished to feel the ache in my shoulders induced by Blouberg's icy waters, and watch the sun set over Table Mountain. I wanted to be part of the light that bleaches the skies and thickens the shadows beneath the trees, see the birdlife and the particular flora of this place. I wanted to speak to those who had been there during this latest chapter in the country's history.

The Afrikaans Landscape

The Afrikaners have never had time to sit and contemplate the land in peace, unthreatened by outside forces. Their history is one of struggle, and this is what has formed them. Looking for national characteristics is always a dicey business, but it strikes me that there are qualities and behaviours that can be described as 'Afrikaans'.

The Afrikaners are great family people, and the women are a powerful presence in the community – perhaps one of the qualities that entitles them to call themselves 'Africans'. It's also a very physical society – there's a great deal of kissing and handshaking and hands on shoulders and knees. It's all terribly un-English. There's very little small-talk; there's no 'conversation-lite'. It's all straight to the beef, the big stuff – life, love, politics, religion, family, sex, money. And there's a powerful feeling of being a discriminated-against minority. It's all so reminiscent of the Jews.

Living in England is the very opposite of these two cultures. Here we keep it light, distant and private, as much as possible. But every time I go to France and enter a shop, I'm struck afresh by just how different things are to Britain. On the French side of the Channel the relationship between people is much more reminiscent of the Jewish and Afrikaans communities I grew up in. There's a lack of a generation gap, the relationships between young and old are generally good; there are few tearaways. There's also an emphasis on manners.

I like the cheery 'Bonjour, monsieur' called out as you enter a bakery, a call that you're required to respond to with a 'Bonjour, madame'.

The glue holding the community together is evident everywhere. It's a formal society in which the presence of the ancien régime is still in evidence. England seems like a free-for-all after France, and quite attractive for being so. But France still has a culture and civilisation based on mutually recognised and accepted manners. In many ways it reminds me of parts of Afrikaans-speaking South Africa in its mix of warmth and formality.

When speaking of the Afrikaners it is necessary to ask, as with any people – who are the Afrikaners? Are we speaking of the Cape Afrikaners, or those of the Free State, or of the old Transvaal? Are we speaking of the farming Afrikaners or the integrated city dwellers? Are we speaking about Afrikaans speakers – but then what of the Cape coloureds? Are they part of the Afrikaners? Are we speaking of the intellectual elite or the poor white Afrikaners? Do they all qualify as Afrikaners; are they more or less Afrikaans? Or are they 'Afrikansers' as some refer to themselves? What do the Afrikaners say about the divisions among them? Are they superficial, or are they deep and divisive?

Afrikaners seem to share many traits. There's a robust, no-bullshit quality about them, a practicality, a deep, unblinkered knowledge and wisdom about the land they live in. The place doesn't come to them filtered through another culture, as it comes to the English South Africans. For the Afrikaners, South Africa is their only yardstick, so there are no liberal blinkers, no political correctness, and as a result there are few surprises. They know the indigenous population in a way that most white English-speaking South Africans simply do not (with obvious, honourable, exceptions). In a strange way, the English speaker has been most effectively corralled by apartheid and his or her loyalty to another culture, a non-African culture.

The Afrikaners stand apart from this group, because they are also abused survivors. There's no question that the Boer wars against the British left a bitter legacy. These were unjust wars, recognised as such in Britain at the time by ever-larger groups of people. I've mentioned the strength of Afrikaans women, who are largely unsung heroines in the story of the Afrikaners. It's interesting to note that it was only when the British placed these formidable women – who had kept the home fires burning during the wars – behind barbed-wire fences in the first known concentration camps, that the war began to turn in the favour of the British.

These were wars that cast a long shadow over South Africa. The suffering of the Afrikaners of the time is alive and raw in the minds of their descendants. And like many an abused child, the Afrikaner became in turn a bully and an abuser. His experience of unfair persecution by a more powerful culture taught him nothing, and his brutality when he got his chance to abuse his black and brown compatriots was as evil as that done to him fifty years earlier.

We learn nothing and seem condemned to repeat our savagery as a species, time after time, century after century. No one's hands are clean. We need to remember that 'he who does not learn from history is condemned to repeat it'. University of Cape Town academic André du Toit argues in a compelling paper that if there had been a Truth and Reconciliation Commission after the second Anglo-Boer War, things might have been rather different in 1948. We will never know.

There is a coarseness to Afrikaners, an unsqueamish calling of a spade a spade. Their curses and their swearing have an earthy robustness that's a joy to use – 'Kakstories, twak en stront!' (bullshit stories, nonsense and rubbish) Yes, they are familiar with bullshit and have little time for it.

I used to argue futilely with my mother that things were never as simple as right and wrong, black and white, that truth was often grey. She would have none of it. There was a wish to have things straight, cut and dried, no compromises. And she would say, 'My country, right or wrong!' In this, I think, she was saying, perhaps unconsciously, 'They may be bastards, but they're my bastards.'

I cannot know for sure – but I can guess, or venture a guess, because I grew up so very privileged myself – that the Afrikaners felt as princes in this land, surrounded as they were by poverty, superstition, the deeply rural culture of subject races, with foreshortened views of geography and history, and no written language. They must have felt men apart, and the best among them must have felt something of a moral obligation, and the worst, the terrible thrill of dominance. But, good or bad, both impulses sprang from the same place: cultural superiority. Education and a European history of book learning set them apart, lords in this barbaric place.

And, like princes, they would also have known their vulnerability, known that their very difference, their relative wealth, their land, their livestock, their culture, might so easily give offence, eliciting hatred, greed, scorn, misunderstanding. The Afrikaners might well have felt as princes in this Africa of theirs, but they would never have felt secure; surely too much was at stake and the arithmetic of its peoples never very promising. Did this give rise to fear, and is it this fear that made them such hard, unforgiving taskmasters, such slave drivers?

Or is this wholly wrong? Did the Afrikaners merely feel they were survivors, brutalised by Africa for centuries, living rough, making do, trekking ever further from their civilised roots, the Bible and the gun their last vestiges of a European culture that had spawned them, but which now in this brutish place had been all but burned out of them? Were they in their own minds so different from the savage tribes that peopled this place? Not princes at all, but white paupers, acculturated lost individuals alone in a society of individualists? Is it this that formed their intolerance?

What effect did the land have on its owners? We tend to romanticise land, believing ownership to confer status, to ennoble its possessor, a god of acres in love with his farm, lord of hills and valleys and woods and vineyards and fields, a place of far horizons. A place where he could 'lift up his eyes unto the hills whence cometh his help,' as it said in his Bible.

This is not the only truth about land. A farm can grind you down. The European peasantry certainly doesn't hold with any notion of the land ennobling them. Rather, they see it as a bitter taskmaster, a place that holds them captive, a cross on which drought, flood and pestilence try their very souls. 'The city' is the place of wealth and ease and luxury, not the land. Which view did the Afrikaner hold, in the past and now?

Afrikaans painters and poets give us a hint as they express a love of the land that is quite unequivocal. 'Gee my 'n roer in my regterhand, gee my 'n bok wat vlug oor die rand' (give me a gun in my right hand and a deer that flees over the land) speaks of a love of the chase in this landscape. In paint, Pierneef, David Botha, Gabriel and Tinus de Jongh, and a host of others' mountain scenes, vast arid landscapes, or Cape Dutch homesteads speak eloquently of a love for the land.

This is a country in which one can observe people approaching from a great distance: its spaces bathe visitors in light, lending them a mythic quality. It is a land that belittles them too – puny figures in a landscape fit for giants. It would be strange if these vast spaces did not haunt the Afrikaans soul and lend a strange perspective to his worldview. In the same way that a sculpture placed in a landscape transforms that place and is itself transformed, so too, the Afrikaners placed in Africa transformed it and were in turn transformed by it.

There are, it seems, forces attracting and repelling the Afrikaners between the city and the farm. I think at best it's an uneasy balance that always swings back towards the land, the agrarian world being his natural habitat. The city is a place of almost Biblical perversions – a Sodom and Gomorrah – while the land is a place of greater significance than mere grass and stones and trees; this is the world in which the souls of the Afrikaners are restored. Yet the church was always situated in the town or city and the Afrikaners are nothing if not sociable – hence the tension between the town and the countryside.

The city was home to foreign influences, Jews, Portuguese, Greeks and the bloody English in particular. So there is within the Afrikaners an uneasy balance between the two realities of their world, the cities and the plain. Their image of themselves as men of the land, a man of distant places and far horizons, sits uneasily in a city coffee shop, restaurant or theatre. The Dutch Reformed Church with its own elemental view of the world is the one urban institution that sits comfortably across this divide. But one cannot ignore the fact that Afrikaners produced some very pleasant towns – Paarl, where my mother lies buried, Stellenbosch, Franschhoek, Tulbagh, Ceres, Swellendam, Caledon, Malmesbury and

Bredasdorp – urban spaces, but open to the countryside.

Yet this rural tranquillity was a mirage. South Africa always struck me as a whirlpool. The internal currents of the place were so immense they forced your view inwards and down, till you felt you were drowning in its politics. The view outwards, abroad, to other realities, other options, was not just obscured; it was obliterated by the power of that whirlpool, unleashed by the currents in the stream of consciousness that was South Africa.

These are, as I understand it, some of the forces, some of the issues, some of the cultural imperatives that formed the Afrikaners. While grasping some of the issues, I suspect that one has to be born an Afrikaner and live as one, to possess the key to truly understanding them. I could see a lot from the outside but was also on occasion confused by the view.

I remember leaving my parents' holiday home in Blouberg in the 1960s to spend a weekend on a friend's farm in Durbanville. So close to Cape Town and my urban reality, it was a world apart, in time and space. Here existed, it seemed to me, the remnants of a medieval, feudal world. There was a quietness on the farm that was accentuated by the silence of the servants and the sound of the wind over vast wheat fields, dipping and swaying as if to an unheard orchestra. Before the large rambling farmhouse lay huge dogs, boerbuls (mastiffs). Almost unable to move for their size, they reclined like stone lions before a Roman villa. We went horse riding and it irritated and amazed me that every few hundred metres one of us had to dismount to open a gate. I'd thought I was headed for unfettered countryside and kilometres of open riding, unhindered by fences or roads. But in fact this was a land under duress, hard at work growing things. The horses were thickset animals of Friesian blood with straight shoulders and a high action that made for a jarring, thunderous ride, so unlike the loping comfort of thoroughbreds.

After church on Sunday, we sat down to an enormous meal, spread on a vast round table with a lazy Susan revolving in the middle, carrying a bewildering array of wonderful things. At the end of the meal I stood up with the rest, some 20 people at least. I took a few steps towards the door and then stopped to allow others to go through first, but there was no one. I looked back in confused embarrassment. All the family and guests, bar me, were kneeling by their chairs while the paterfamilias prepared to pray. The servants had come in from the kitchen for this after-dinner prayer ritual too, and were kneeling by the kitchen door. I sprang to my chair and fell to my knees and, covered in blushes, did my best to be calm.

Afterwards I went with the sons of the house to their father's study. Here lay the great iron-bound family Bible from which he read a passage and spoke a while about its significance. We left then to rest in the quiet gloom of my friend's room, shuttered against the heat outside. I felt far, far away from my own world that was in fact just 30 kilometres away. I felt as if I had gone back to another time, another place.

History is Trouble

History is trouble. When there is no trouble, there is no history, and my background teems with history. Because of this aspect of my life, my family, both alive and dead, take on a dimension in my mind that is unusual, I suspect, by normal standards. I have heard their stories so often they colour my life completely.

When I face choices, I often wonder how these forebears might have acted in my place. In the beginning, as a lonely boy, it was a way of peopling my universe. In matters of money, politics, religion and love, I have a chorus of mentors, all singing out advice and direction with equal and confusing conviction.

The story of how my maternal grandmother met my maternal grandfather was the first I remember being told by my mother. I loved the tale and always thought of this grandmother, Magdalena, whom I never met, as the girl by the window.

Magdalena Aletta Kirsten stood expectantly at her bedroom window. Her slim fifteen-year-old figure looked gawky in the short dress of childhood that she still wore. She was coltish but there were definite signs of budding womanhood in the pout of her lips, the hollow of her back and soft curve of her jaw beneath her delicate ears. The chin, however, had a decided firmness, and though the face was lovely, the eyes came as a shock. They were so dark they looked black beneath black eyebrows and a swing of straight blue-black hair. Her gaze was direct and had the power to arrest one in mid-stride.

Unselfconsciously, she rubbed one firm-calved leg against the other in a stroking movement that held all the pent-up excitement of a cat's quivering tail as it sights a bird. She was tense with waiting. Gazing with rapt attention from her window, she waited for the guests to arrive - and for one guest in particular.

Down her line of vision, sentinel oaks marked the generous width of the carriage drive to the great white gateposts of the Kirsten farm. Beneath the trees in the cool green shadows of evening the squirrels and turtledoves scampered and fluttered.

The Kirstens were giving their annual harvest ball, and the farm looked its best. Everything about the estate had that freshly washed look that comes from hard work and loving care. For almost a week Magdalena's mother, Jacomina Hendrina Kirsten (formerly Jacomina Basson), had been directing the preparations for the dance. Nothing had been forgotten, from the chalk for the dance floor in the voorkamer to the freshly cut hydrangeas filling huge copper bowls. There was chilled sparkling wine as well as peach brandy and red wine from their own farm. To the side of the farmhouse was a flickering fire beneath a slowly turning ox on a spit, the roasting meat sending delicious smells across the farm. The fire threw fantastic shadows onto the curved gables of the whitewashed home of this old Cape family.

Promptly at six o'clock the carriages and carts bearing guests began to arrive. Some of the younger male guests came on horseback. Each time Magdalena heard the sound of a single ridden horse, she dug her nails into the palm of her hand, the tiny scimitars she made turning first white and then red.

Magdalena would not be attending the ball. She was far too young, only a child, her mother had scolded her gently. 'Do you want to be leaving us already? You, our youngest?' No, she had to be content with watching for his arrival from her bedroom window.

At 6.30 p.m., with the hubbub in the house and gardens making hearing difficult, she still caught the sound of a single horseman, so closely was she listening. By now it was dusk proper and the horse and rider were quite near to the house before she could see them clearly. It was him!

Magdalena made a decidedly unladylike moan in her

throat as she caught sight of the high-stepping grey and the lithe young man sitting so erect in the saddle. No animal deserved to be so beautiful, she thought. The stallion's tremendous presence spoke of an almost human awareness of its own good looks. The rider collected the horse under him and it danced into the lamplight.

As Andries Abraham Louw dismounted, Magdalena knew, come hell or high water, she was going to make him notice her somehow. She crossed the room to one of the dark stinkwood kists and opened the lid. The smell of lavender and camphor rose from the folded fabric within. She chose a dress she wore to church because it was longer than most. Working carefully, despite her wildly beating heart, she began to unpick the hem. If she were clever, it would almost be long enough to pass for an evening dress and no one would notice the rapidly unpicked hem in the candlelight.

Suddenly a thought struck her: she had no high-heeled shoes. Like a wraith, she slipped silently next door to her sister's room and found a pair of leather pumps that fitted well enough.

She gasped with fright when she returned to her room. Waiting for her was her nursemaid Dinah, with an affronted look about her. Magdalena sat on the bed next to her oldest confidante and told her everything.

Shaking her head but with a conspiratorial smile, Dinah began to cut through the hemming stitches. Next, she fetched coals and an iron and pressed the dress. Magdalena slipped into it and looked at herself in the mirror. It was just fractionally too short. Dinah solved the problem with a lace petticoat. She helped put the girl's hair up, leaving it full in the nape of the neck. A single white camellia finished the coiffure to perfection.

Dinah stood back, amazed – the child was transformed. Fear of her master and madam was forgotten in her love for this young beauty.

It would be different, Dinah told herself, if she was helping the kleinnooi (little mistress) to snare a scoundrel. But wasn't Andries Louw one of the biggest catches in the whole Paarl valley? Didn't his family own more land than any other three put together? No, this was a good thing!

To be fair, there was also a little self-interest in Dinah's reasoning. She knew that she would accompany Magdalena in marriage as surely as the silver hairbrushes the girl had inherited from her grandmother. 'O meisie, vanaand gaan jy harte breek.' (Oh, my girl, tonight you are going to break hearts). Years later, thinking back on this night, Dinah would wonder if she had done the right thing.

Magdalena tottered towards the door, unsteady on the unaccustomed heels. Dinah said, 'Nee, kleinnooi, jy moet soe stap!' (No little mistress, this is how you must walk). Heavily, and with all the dignity of her weight, Dinah mimed her imitation of a lady's correct carriage. Back straight and chin up, with slow, measured steps, she crossed the room. The performance elicited hysterical giggles from Magdalena, but she knew the maid was right. The whole effect would be spoiled if she acted her age tonight.

Dinah let her out of the room. 'Gaan steel sy hart,' (Go, steal his heart), she whispered. Magdalena was nervous and admitted as much to herself. She bit her lips, bringing bright red colour into them. But as she thought of the prize, her black eyes flashed and her chin rose resolutely. Her confidence was boosted by the fact that neither of her family's two oldest retainers recognised her as she drifted past them into the voorkamer.

Here, fate took a hand in the matter. Coming towards her, carrying two drinks, was Andries himself. In the way he stopped she could see the effect her unexpected appearance had on him. But it was the eyes that gave the clue to how she looked. From the moment they detected her they never stirred from her face, even as a silence grew around them.

'Goeienaand. It is Magdalena, isn't it?' he asked and looked quizzically at her.

All she could manage was the faintest nod. He had the social grace to recognise her difficulty and the daring to solve it. Putting the drinks down on a table beside him, he took her by the hand and led her onto the dance floor. They were waltzing before she knew how it had happened and all the time their eyes spoke silently.

Six months later, on her 16th birthday, they were married at a glittering wedding in Paarl. Their honeymoon gift from

Andries' family was a beautiful farm. The couple was happy and, despite her youth, Magdalena soon won for herself the reputation of an accomplished hostess. The farm became her second love, so much so that her coloured servants nicknamed her 'Maakskoon' (Clean-up). Guests would hardly be out of the house when she would have her servants polishing their boot marks out of the gleaming yellowwood floors.

The couple was favoured with eight children that lived. The children were their wealth, for fortune did not smile on Andries as a farmer. Life became hard, and Magdalena learned to live with tears.

But for me, Magdalena, my mother's mother, is always the girl by the window, waiting for love.

Chameleon

There is a small, brown soapstone carving of a chameleon, bought in a Simon's Town antique shop last Christmas, that stands on the windowsill by my bed in Sussex. It is a constant reminder of many things in my Cape Town childhood, but the link with its living, breathing cousins in the Hebrew School garden is the strongest.

I suppose I must identify with the chameleon, to some extent. It would be surprising, given my background, if I did not relate to this strange beast in some way. Perhaps my mix of influences - Lithuanian, French, Norwegian, Dutch, English, Jewish, Christian - makes me more pliable, more accepting of other influences, more prepared to blend into a multi-layered background. South Africa would, decades later, come to be described as a Rainbow Nation, a setting that would suit the particular attributes of a chameleon, a beast capable of changing colour at will. What an asset that would have been in the apartheid years.

And yet there is a hesitation to identify too closely with this animal; it made my flesh creep with its weird revolving eyes, sucker- pad feet and long, glue-like tongue that could flash out four times its body length and whip flies and other insects into its maw.

But at the age of 10, as I played in the garden of my Hebrew School, my Chaida, in Wynberg, I was not aware of these sophisticated, complex issues; I was simply fascinated by chameleons. I attended Chaida twice a week to learn to read Hebrew, an essential precondition for my bar mitzvah, my rite of passage into the adult Jewish world. It was here, in the garden of this part-time school, that I discovered the chameleons, living in the guava trees of the overgrown garden at the back of the spooky Victorian four-storey house.

Chameleons are reclusive creatures, hiding themselves among the leaves and branches, shy, yet scheming, flicking out that tongue and hauling in sustenance, just like a writer. The chameleon (there was always just one at a time) seemed a solitary character, gently swaying and vibrating like a tuning fork to the most sensitive sounds and hidden rhythms. I liked the chameleon's mystery and the fact that once carefully removed from its perch and placed on a stick – I would not have wanted it on my hand, I was far too squeamish – it made a wonderful weapon with which to terrify girl pupils. It goes without saying that I made scant progress at my Hebrew studies – just sufficient to perform my bar mitzvah.

The years of learning Hebrew did nothing to induce a cultural pride in me; rather, I felt, it set me apart from my fellow pupils at SACS (South African College School), something I hardly needed more of. Hebrew was just something else I had to learn that I did not wish to learn. It also set me apart from my own mother, who would, at my father's insistence, accompany us to synagogue on the high and holy days of the Jewish calendar. She would not attend the usual Friday night and Saturday morning services but would be there for Yom Tov and Yom Kippur when we would fast for 24 hours, no food or drink passing our lips, hoping that God would write our name in the 'Book of Life' for one more year.

Inevitably, there would be a wait for my mother to join us in the car for the journey to shul on these most holy of days. Finally, with my father's temper stirring, she would hastily get into the car. Having taken particular trouble with her appearance, her sense of herself was bound up minutely with how she looked. She had been a stunning girl, tall and dark, and was still a beautiful woman in her forties and fifties.

Walking into the packed Wynberg Reform Synagogue, I was always sensitive to the glances that came our way, this brood of so-called Jews with their shiksa mother in her expensive clothes. Those were the times I would happily have exchanged my fate for that of the chameleon, quietly at peace in his leafy fruit tree, changing colour to suit the shade of green, or light, or time of day.

But Jews and Christians had long been part of my inheritance, a mix that preceded my mother's arrival on the scene. I recall a story my father told me about Herman, his own formidable father, who had built up an agricultural merchants' business in Paarl. During the Depression, his bankers said that there were overdraft problems. There was some discussion between his sons and his partner about calling in the debts of farmers who were two years in arrears. Herman picked up the notices that were due to be sent out, tore them in half and dumped them in the bin. 'Do you think I'm going to let you chase these people for money?' he asked. The matter ended there. The Jews and the Afrikaners intertwine in my family history, in and out of each other like a plate of spaghetti.

At Christmas we gave a nod to our mother's heritage. We didn't have a Christmas tree, but the family exchanged Christmas cards with friends and neighbours and we children had pillowcases packed with presents (from Father Christmas) pinned to the end of our beds on Christmas morning. There was no church going, but there was a big traditional Christmas lunch with turkey and flaming pudding and the rest of it, all served up at Bloubergstrand where we would be based for the summer months of the year.

Here we were, fish out of water, the Blouberg community being almost exclusively Afrikaans farming families enjoying their beach homes once the harvest was in. I recall as though it were yesterday walking down the beach, splashing through the last gasp of waves, bracing myself for an encounter with neighbours. Good manners meant they would greet me, and I would have to reply, in Afrikaans. It was a training for later years when I was occasionally required to stand up and make impromptu speeches. I found then, as I had at Blouberg, that a bit of practice in advance was no bad thing; that selecting a topic or two, and then trying out some phrases, all paid handsome dividends. But, as a shy boy, inarticulate in Afrikaans, it was an ordeal, and the awkwardness engendered in me by this experience pushed me away from my Afrikaans heritage rather than towards it. Those Afrikaans families meant well, but they entrenched my shyness. Had they simply ignored me, doubtless I would have resented it as much. It wasn't easy for them or for me.

Christmas would bring with it my great annual ordeal – taking gifts to half the homes in Blouberg. It was my parents' way of thanking our neighbours for the avalanche of fresh fruit, vegetables, meat and preserves they sent us from their farms over the summer holidays. Our driver Pieter Brill and I would load the car with fancy iced Christmas cakes and large four-pound tins of biscuits from our factory, Enterprise Bakeries. And then my trial by Afrikaans would begin. I could not simply knock on a door, say thanks for past gifts, present our own and go; that would have been easy. Whoever answered the door had to be told who the gift was from, and then, invariably, I was gently hauled in, despite my protestations, to meet the family and the inevitable hordes of friends who were staying. 'Mense, dit is Leon en Elise Roup se oudste klong, Julian!' (People! This is Leon and Elise Roup's oldest son, Julian). Thus I would be introduced to everyone, told to sit, given a drink and asked in some detail about myself and my parents. And all of this in Afrikaans. I would struggle to reply; my Afrikaans, dreadful at the best of times, would emerge in a mix of kitchen patois and English. It must have been horrible to listen to. Patiently, Pieter Brill would wait in the car outside.

One mustn't forget that for these people, including my mother, the second Anglo-Boer War (1899 -1902) was barely over. It was as fresh in their memories in the 1950s as though it had happened yesterday. It was their Holocaust, their interned women and children dying from disease and starvation by the thousand. They believed firmly, and some still today, that the British had fed their prisoners ground glass to do away with them. There was a lasting legacy of hate.

There was, too, subsequently, the iniquity of an education based on English in which even speaking Afrikaans was not tolerated. And here I was, mangling their language and demeaning it with the Cape coloured argot spoken by our servants. These visits were not my finest hour, and I was always grateful to escape. I would get back into the car like a diver coming up desperate for air. And then it would be on to the next house and the next, the whole process repeated each time.

By the end of the morning I would be a wreck. But even then I realised with what kindness I was met, with what discretion I was treated, and though in my teens I took violently against their politics, I could not condemn Afrikaners completely. My mother had made sure of that.

She had brought me up to understand that South Africa had been settled by her people, the Afrikaners. She made plain the suffering and the bravery required. As a horseman myself, with a great love of open country, I had some grasp of the problems of traversing landscape on horseback, which made the feats of mad courage required to take ox wagons across mountain ranges into unknown, uncharted territory very real to me.

I grew up with the story of the Boer leader, Piet Retief, and the duplicity of Dingane, the Zulu chief who invited the Retief party to a parley and then brutally murdered them, including Retief's young son, with the words 'Kill the wizards!' The history of the Great Trek away from the English-dominated Cape, a saga of hardship, of laagered wagons, the rattle of musketry, the harsh realities of Africa, the savagery and distinction of the fight the Boers put up for four years against the might of the British Empire – all of this was told to me by my mother, a mother I loved passionately, a mother who told me that one could not trust a 'kaffir', that they were 'wreed', cruel, barbaric and uncivilised. These were my bedtime stories. It went deep, and much of it has stayed.

As I grew up, my liberal inclinations set me on a different path, but I would not claim to be free of racism. I would be lying if I did, I argued with my mother. She was a believer in her Bible as the word of God, verbatim; and she believed that white was white and black was black and there was no place in the middle for some grey compromise with truth, my position on so many things.

She would say when we argued politics, 'Ons Afrikaners is 'n handjievol teen die swart miljoene.' (We Afrikaners are a small handful against millions of blacks).

So there were two movies running in my head

simultaneously – the Jewish heritage of suffering and intellectual energy and the Afrikaans story of frontier heroism against overwhelming odds. No wonder I was a confused young man. It struck me then that the way of the chameleon was not a choice open to me – I could not change my colours easily. I had to make a hard choice, and my human and cultural 'colouring' would play a major part in that choice.

Anthony Appiah, Professor of American Studies and Philosophy of Harvard and Princeton universities, who writes on diversity and multi-culturalism, says, 'We make ourselves up from a toolkit of options made available by our culture and society. We do make choices, but we do not determine the options among which we choose.'

In the final analysis, that is humbling. We are what we are because of what we find lying around us. And in that sense, I was lucky. I found more lying around me than most.

BLURRED IMAGES

There is a strange, atmospheric occurrence visible from the beaches of Bloubergstrand that takes place during the very hottest days of summer. When conditions are right, Robben Island, a low, flat presence on the horizon with a lighthouse at its centre, transforms itself through the agency of heat, light and mirage into a city in the sky. The place transmogrifies into what looks like a square-ended cargo carrier loaded with blocks of flats.

To me as a child, it was a magical thing, and perplexing too. How could the nature of a place change so dramatically? I wondered how it was possible to be two such different things, even as I recognised in myself a duality that was unsettling. A movement in the plates of my double heritage, as they slipped past each other, caused earthquakes of insecurity. The one an ancient reality, the other more modern, both were fixated with God, wilderness and promised lands.

What was I? Was I an island, unique unto myself, alone, in a sea of incomprehension? If no man is an island, was I then just a cargo-load of feelings with each half of the ship headed in different directions? The latter seemed closer to the truth.

And adding confusion and interest was the issue of my black blood. I would enjoy teasing my mother, pointing out press articles quoting academic research that had established beyond doubt that the Afrikaner had a considerable amount of black blood, hardly surprising after three and a half centuries on this continent. It seems that the average Afrikaner had 19 per cent.

Now I was to be a literary pilgrim on a quest in search of

the Afrikaners. Where would I find them, and in particular those Afrikaners that I can relate to, who would settle my internal ambiguities for me, bring me to a peace with the Afrikaner within? Would I ever find such people? Would I find a quality in them that I would recognise in myself? Surely I would.

If I had been distanced from myself by this confusing dual heritage, both of which had the power to embarrass me in some ways, there was another isolating presence in my life as I grew up – wealth. When I was 15, we moved to Bishopscourt, home of Cape Town's most privileged residents, from Newlands, a far more unpretentious place by comparison. I soon found that sitting on the hill of privilege had an isolating effect, as much as the Cadillac and driver that took me to school and the ponies and horses I rode on my own. To a boy insecure about his own worth, wealth was just another reason to suspect the motives of those wishing to be close to him.

There can be no question that the move to Bishopscourt changed us as a family in some profound way. If one were superstitious, there were early signs that this would not be an auspicious move. But in 1965 my parents decided to buy a plot in Bishopscourt. The argument went that the move would provide much more afternoon sunlight, a fair comment on damp Newlands afternoons but less than honest. Although my mother had named our Newlands home 'Mon Rêve' she had been driving the byways of Bishopscourt for some years in her small black and white Karmen Ghia, admiring the homes and the gardens and the ambience of wealth so graciously displayed.

My father's business had done well and he decided that the time had come to show his formidable, widowed mother, his wife and the world that he was ready for Bishopscourt and all it entailed. He found a steeply sloping two-acre site near the crest of the hill in Primrose Avenue, covered in pine trees, which had recently come back onto the market as the result of a divorce.

This inauspicious start for our new home didn't seem to bother anyone overmuch. There were also previous unnamed tenants on that steep hillside; holes dug deep in among the pine-tree cover bore witness to the presence of 'bergies'. These subterranean tunnels were the homes of these San-like people, who lived on the very fringe of society, seemingly able to subsist on bread and the blue bottles of methylated spirits that were a sure-fire shortcut to an early death.

The plot was close to the massive old almond hedge that had once formed the first of the Cape Colony's borders back in the seventeenth century. It was, I suspect, on the borders of what my father could afford financially as well.

Bulldozers moved in and unceremoniously re-landscaped this last piece of native ecosystem, planing the hillside into three terraces through which a steep driveway sliced. Stone retaining walls kept the terraces from slipping down the hill during the worst of the lashing winter storms, and lawns and shrubs did the rest. A swimming pool was installed on the lowest terrace and two dogs, an Alsatian and a Weimaraner, the first of many, took up residence in the dog kennel on the deck that ran round the outside of the house. The deck, which facilitated discreet exits from bedrooms to the garden, was a great boon for teenage children.

The driveway was edged with oleander trees, the poisonous but colourful Mediterranean plant that provided a mix of pink and apricot flowers throughout the summer. Another deadly plant took up residence just below my bedroom window – the castor-oil plant, whose leopardskin-patterned seeds attracted interest from every passing child. A palm was planted hard by the circular pond at the front of the house into which a fountain splashed. Over the years this palm grew huge, and its swishing branches kept up a soft susurration throughout the summer, while in winter it seemed to lash itself into a frenzy.

There were fig trees, loquat trees, bulrushes, bottlebrush, silver trees in which long-tailed Cape sugarbirds fluttered, bougainvillea of various hues, a rose garden that was pruned and sprayed and which provided flowers for the family graves in Paarl. There was also a vegetable patch discreetly to one side of the garden, which provided tomatoes, beans, squash and lettuce. A massive poinsettia hedge that abutted Primrose Avenue provided a screen of privacy.

Looking after this domain was Ben Winslow, a short, slow-moving man with a keen intelligence and a philosophical mindset, not particularly keen on gardening. His dream, in fact, was to farm pigs in Springbok, the remote Namaqualand town from which he came. He was of an indeterminate age, I suppose in his fifties, and he looked forward to this agricultural idyll with more doggedness than hope. My father and Ben kept up a kind of running war for years over the garden, the issue being that one thought everything in the garden was perfect, while the other thought it a far cry from perfection. The amazing thing was that Ben remained with my father for years and years. To understand the relationship, one had to have grown up in South Africa.

It was a tense household, thanks largely to my father's business-induced stress, inherited temper and dictatorial ways. The staff coped as best they could, tucking chins in and giving a show of dumb obedience, a technique for coping with life in the Roup household that I had to admire.

My sister Janine, aged 13, and brother Herman, aged 10, came and went, living their own more rational lives, Janine doing well at school and already having a boyfriend, Herman playing rugby and starting to make a success of athletics. Their lives, I now know, were as fraught as mine, but at 15 one doesn't see very far, certainly not into the lives of others, or I certainly did not.

So there I sat, surveying the mountain and the vast plain of the Cape Flats, barely seeing it, more involved with adolescence, internal turmoil, an emotional volcano. It's hardly surprising that I chose to date girls from the English-speaking community. They had a coolness, an underplayed emotion so different from the Jewish and Afrikaans girls I knew.

I left Bishopscourt to go to school, to go riding and occasionally to visit friends down the road. After the fiasco that was school, I left home to do the obligatory nine months of army national service in Oudtshoorn. I came out in a bewildered state of mind. I was finished with the army but did not yet feel that I was a civilian. Something of the army experience would not wash off.

This was in the late '60s, a time when the world was changing, being grasped by the young, a new beginning. This was to be our time. I felt very little of that. I had no real idea who I was or what I wanted. I was filled with a thousand inchoate feelings, longings, desires, but most of all I wanted to meet a girl, someone who would love me as I loved her.

I went to parties with friends and I danced with girls. It was summer and I was 19, anything was possible, but very little happened. I remember getting drunk for the first time. It wasn't a happy experience.

We went to the beach a lot, Clifton mainly, and this was both exciting and depressing. The place was awash with beautiful girls, girls way out of my league, and hundreds of boys and young men who seemed to me to be that much more assured and confident. They knew how to speak to girls in just the right way, a light bantering tone that halted these beautiful, beguiling creatures and drew them into the male circles while I lay to one side pretending to read.

And then one night a friend suggested I join him and a few others at a party in Newlands. There I met a girl with green eyes and long blonde hair and my life changed forever. I can't recall speaking a single word, just dancing with my face buried in the lovely meadow scents of her hair. It was to be three years before I emerged from behind that blonde silk tepee. She was slight and I carried her easily, but it was she who took my weight and hammered out the last of boyhood on the anvil of her body, turning me into the man I would become. She loved me and I loved her, and life was good, the sweetest that I could remember.

Later, after dropping her at home, I would drive back to my own place, a flat in Wynberg, the windows open and a small breeze blowing through the car. I'd be thirsty with kisses, my lips sore, and before me the image of her eyes. I knew then what it was to be a man. It was a feeling of fulfilment that came with responsibilities. But I was not ready for that and so felt less of a man. The boy in me wanted the gift but was not prepared to pay the price.

I went away and became someone else. Once or twice I tried to see her before it was too late, but she was proud and sent me on my way. In the end she married someone else, and then remarried and is, I believe, happy at last. The years rolled on and I too married. But I never forgot her, and she rides behind me yet in the dunelands of my mind, beneath the sun, the wind ruffling her hair, murmuring down the years of our togetherness. My sister sees her occasionally. They live in the same city. Some time ago she said that she would like to speak to me, just once more, for the sake of closure. I do not wish that. I do not seek closure. I wish, perhaps selfishly, to keep her by me, at least my image of her that is forever young, riding as a couple through our golden time, young forever.

I was a mixed-up kid who became a fairly mixed-up man. I went into the family business and sold biscuits for seven years, stacking supermarket shelves, in and out of the cool storerooms and busy stores trying to catch managers' eyes, selling them biscuits while their customers clamoured for attention.

Looking back, there were times of calm when my island world lay quiet and then there were times when it changed into something else and I struggled with my life as it rocked and swerved and changed shape. In the pain of growth, my reality was like that island off the coast of my childhood, a clear image on the horizon, then later different, a strangely changed place, a mirage. It was a childhood and adolescence of blurred images and identities.

Things Change

It is possible to be many things in one life. Is that also true of a people, a nation? Can a people evolve, wishing for change and acting on it? Whether the desire for change can be collectively and actively willed I don't know, but time brings with it imperatives that do change people, and possibly nations, or so we believe. But is it true?

Today, Germany, for example, has a close, almost intimate relationship with Israel, but is anti-Semitism truly dead in the hearts and minds of the Germans? I would like to think so, and the Germans would have us believe it. In South Africa, we have the example of the New National Party, for so long the embodiment of the Afrikaners' political will, now in bed with the African National Congress.

As I set off on the journey south, I asked myself, how was this possible? Was such dramatic change credible, feasible? We have read of the conversion on the road to Damascus; was this what had happened here – a conversion on the road to Perdition? What had been the Afrikaners' response to black majority rule? Besides the NNP's extraordinary decision to join the ANC politically, there had been other manifestations of change brought about by this cataclysmic event called democracy. There were the many horrific instances of fathers murdering their whole families and then themselves – perhaps opting for death rather than dishonour and powerlessness? Some argue that this tribal trait of 'taking out' whole families go back a long way and is not, in fact, something new, nor unique to Afrikaners.

Was there a new sexual openness between the races?

What did the escalating emigration figures say about the state of mind of Afrikaners? Had there been a religious renewal or confusion? What of a cultural flowering or withering? Was there bewilderment or a new resolve, a new certainty? What was happening among South Africa's social workers, doctors, psychiatrists and mental institutions? Were they busier, fuller or emptier than usual? Did Afrikaners still feel themselves to be of Africa and would they remain in Africa, or would they head north to rejoin De Flaamse Blok, the Flemish Block, in Belgium, harvest the prairies of North America (as some already had, taking seasonal work), study abroad in Holland, Germany, England and the USA, and then think again?

I have wondered if change within an individual can be an indication of the possibility of change within a whole people. I do not know, but I do know from my own life that, while change is possible, the deep wellsprings of character and personality do not really change. We learn to put a better face on things, we disguise our shyness and insecurity – we seem changed, but in reality, we are not.

The major motivations of my life have been a wish for peace, quiet, contemplation and a desire to be artistically creative. Yet, once clear of the demands of school, I have been a part-time soldier, a biscuit salesman, a journalist, a public-relations consultant and now a writer. So it seems that my earliest ambitions have, throughout a changing life on three continents – Africa, America and Europe – lain dormant, festered, hurt, and finally come to the surface in a great torrent of words.

One's history is sometimes described as having weight. How can that be? History, after all, is what has shaped us and it is part of our flesh, and we do not feel it as weight, until perhaps we are much older and its weight hurts our knee joints and our soul. In my case, my personal history was so ever-present, so overwhelming in its density, as the grandson of an almost mythic figure who had crossed continents and wrestled with demons and come through brilliantly, leaving a glowing reputation; and as the son of a powerful and successful father, employer of hundreds, that my immediate history weighed me down somewhat, carrying with it expectations I felt myself totally incapable of achieving. And there he was, my mother's father, beckoning in the shadows, a failure by the standards of the world, a drunken ghost, saying, 'Well, follow me then, I am why you are as you are. In the end we are all the same – dust!'

These people haunted me and do so still. They set measures and yardsticks that I felt I would never match or that I feared I would match all too well.

My Jewish grandfather had a saying: 'Go out into the world and be a man!' I lived in terror of the world, the world of mercantile success, the hustle and bustle of business and the pressures to earn a living, and from a very early age my desire for peace and quiet led me to think with longing of a monastic, ascetic life, the life of a monk withdrawn from the world in a silent whitewashed cube, communing with God.

I knew that my circumstances put me light years beyond such dreams. There was a business awaiting me, a father's expectations, family commitments, and a cultural stance that put such thoughts into the realm of insanity. There had, in fact, been just such a decision, taken by the daughter of one of my father's partners. Her early Catholic religiosity had led to her giving up the things of this world and then a lifelong incarceration in the keep and care of nuns. There would be no tolerance for such nonsense in me.

So, after I had finished with army training, my troubled father, concerned about me and my future, sat down with his accountant and together they decided that a business course at Cape Town Technical College would be a perfect fit for me. It was a disaster, and I spent more time goofing off on Clifton Beach than I did in class.

One day our incongruously named economics lecturer, Mr Luck, asked me to come forward and explain the basis of the law of supply and demand. He wished to embarrass me for my absences and he succeeded all too well. I walked forward as if to the scaffold and then relied on my old school habit of taking the mickey out of myself before anyone else could. It was funny and they laughed and the law of supply and demand will not have been put in quite that way before. But as in the way of another family saying – 'Good straw, bad straw and the last straw' – it was the last straw, and I walked out of Tech for good after just six months.

A week later, I reported for work at Enterprise Bakeries, aged 20, with a catastrophic academic record and a sense of insecurity that must have been evident to anyone with half a mind. I was to be a biscuit salesman in my father's business. I felt a complete fool.

I must have had some good teachers there, because with a lot of help, my gift of the gab and a sense of massive desperation, I made a go of it. I was by no means a brilliant salesman, but I managed. I remember the sense of dislocation I felt as I watched myself play this role from a position somewhere above my head, an ever-present observer of myself, this ridiculous puppet.

As I walked through the factory – something I tried to do as little as possible – I felt the eyes swivel to watch the boss's son. God knows what they made of me. I couldn't gauge anything; all I felt was an overwhelming sense of shame and worthlessness. I knew that but for my father I would not even have had a job interview. It was corrosive stuff and it's a miracle to me that I survived seven years of it.

But there came a night when I was 27 and I held a gun in my hand and the temptation to end the madness was almost overwhelming. I don't know to this day what stopped me. I think what I felt was that I was dead anyway and that turning myself into a corpse would solve nothing. I felt, too, that having nothing to lose anymore, I would live each day thereafter with more courage. This 'almost-death' released the real me, empowered me. I had been thinking about a new life for a long time, desperate, uncertain and afraid, but at last I acted.

I told my father that I would be leaving the factory to study journalism at Rhodes University as a first step to leaving the country. He took it in a calm and subdued way. I don't know what he made of this decision, or whether he saw that he spoke to one who responded as a corpse. But for once he kept his temper under control and the die was cast. Shortly after that he sold the business and I became a journalist.

I tell this story to illustrate the fact that the individual can change, can act to save himself. Is this true too of a people? Had Afrikaners gone through a similar dark night of the soul, I wondered?

Afrikaners always reminded me of the ostrich, head determinedly in the sand, not seeing the coming storm, not wishing to see the coming storm. I always thought ostriches rather ridiculous birds. I watched them when I did my national service in Oudtshoorn. On the day I left, it rained for what seemed like the first time in months, and I saw a sight that has stayed with me to this day: it was magical. The ostriches, hundreds of them in the flat stony fields that run up to the Outeniqua mountains, were dancing in the rain. These huge, stately birds had their wings outstretched and it looked as if they were doing a quadrille. They were no longer ungainly, but beautiful. I pulled the car over onto the hard shoulder and watched in amazement.

I wondered now whether the ostrich's power to surprise me would be displayed in equal measure by a people who for a long time I had seen as the breed's human counterpart. Were Afrikaners dancing in the rain? I hoped so.

ARABIER

To be a Jew is to be a pariah in the eyes of many people. There's something profoundly suspect about this gypsy race that lives among decent, Christian, God-fearing nations as interlopers within the gates of honest people. Here are a people, I have heard it said, with no loyalty but to themselves, and to money, before everything else. And, my God, they are 'slim, skelm en uitgeslaap'(clever, crooked, devious.) In fact, there is not much good to say about them.

I have heard this said so many times, in so many ways, and recently once again here in England. This, after all, was the first nation to expel the Jews, in 1290 on the orders of Edward I shipping them out of London and leaving many on a tidal island in the Thames estuary to wash away to perdition as the waters rose.

There's no place except Israel where the Jew is truly welcome. South Africa is no exception – I have heard bad things said about Jews by English, Afrikaans and black South Africans, and once even by a Chinese shopkeeper in Cape Town on whom I called in my capacity as a biscuit salesman.

I had been calling on him for years, unavailingly; he simply would not buy our biscuits. One day I thought I would try a new approach. I'd forget the special offers, the sales pitch, the fact that in his area our biscuits sold well with a good profit margin. (See? Good Jewish thinking!) I asked him why he was so adamant that he would not buy our biscuits. Irritated beyond measure by my weekly presence and my refusal to take no for an answer, he levelled with me. 'I hate Jews, you see, and I know that Enterprise is owned by Jews. So I will never buy their biscuits.'

It was obvious in the way he told me this that he had no idea of my personal family connection with the firm. This was my chance, and something devilish in me (some will doubtless say the Jew in me) came out with the following argument. I asked him to imagine what it must be like working for Jews and having each week to explain why one solitary customer would not buy your biscuits. I told him his refusal to buy was leading to my persecution by the bloody Jewish owners and that my job was probably on the line. I looked at him with as much suffering as I could evoke. To my absolute astonishment he took pity on me and placed the first of many orders. When I left, I had to hold hard onto myself until I was some distance off, driving away in my car before I laughed, but it was a bitter and twisted kind of laughter, believe me.

Friend, wherever you are today, let me tell you this: you are not alone, and I also understand a little of what you were going through. Here in England, we have Chinese South African friends who tell us that their reason for emigrating was that in South Africa they were first too black and then they were too white. All of us have our problems; the Jews are not unique.

I found similar problems in the army. A staff sergeant lost his cool with an infantryman who simply could not tell his right leg from his left and consequently made a mess of marching. 'Van der Merwe, jy is so kak sleg soos 'n fokking Jood!' ('Van der Merwe, you are as bloody shit as a fucking Jew'), he shouted at poor van der Merwe. There was a small silence, a hush, as 5,000 years of history rushed over us.

One must offer the staff sergeant some modicum of respect for the fact that his shouted comment gave him pause. 'Is daar Jode hier tussen julle?' ('Are there any Jews here among you?') he asked in a strangled tone.

'Ja, Sergeant,' I yelled. 'Ek is.' ('Yes, sergeant, I am.')

His reply was instant and he smiled as he said it. 'Ag kak Roup, jy's net 'n fokken Arabier.' ('Ah bullshit Roup, you are just a fucking Arab.)

There was laughter and for some time after I was known as 'Arabier'.

In the years following the army, I had some interesting comments from the fathers of girls I dated. One girlfriend's father, with an English-speaking and Christian background, was not best pleased by my arrival. He said, among other things, 'Why don't you take the six million chips off your shoulder?' and 'You've got to remember your people are inclined to run to fat.' These are just two of the gems I recall. I tried to shrug this stuff off, but it wasn't always easy.

These things left me feeling unsure about my cultural identity, the two sides of which seemed to be in constant conflict with each other. I was being oversensitive, but like a head-shy horse, beaten once too often about the ears, that was my instinctive reaction. It's sad, but it's based on a deep understanding of how the Jew is perceived among many people, including some Afrikaners. What can I say? We are as people the end result of both nature and nurture; our environment forms us into some strange shapes, and to use an Afrikaans expression, some of those shapes are 'krom en skeef' (skew and lopsided).

But despite all the anti-Semitism I have run into in my life there is deep within me an unbending pride in everything Jews have achieved. The Jewish genius is all around us if you have eyes to see, There is no avenue of human endeavour where Jews have not made a significant contribution – science, music, medicine, art, culture, philosophy, literature. Look at the Nobel Prize as a yardstick. The successful presence of Jews is everywhere. They have added to man's every endeavour with honour. I am proud and honoured to have some Jewish blood in my veins.

It's interesting how Jews and Afrikaners both venerate one human quality in particular. The Afrikaners wishing to pay tribute to someone will say 'Hy's mens'. The Jews will say someone is a 'mensch' – the words have the same common root, and the intention is to say that someone is fully human, a humane being, and also someone who gets things done! How many times have I heard Afrikaners speaking of someone's 'menslikheid' and Jews, in turn, speaking of 'menschheid'? Both are sentimental people, easily moved.

Growing up Jewish, and defined in my Jewishness by

Afrikaans attitudes, my feelings for Israel and Israelis were complex. I was proud of what the Israelis achieved in battle. The image of six million Jews going quietly to their deaths in the German gas chambers haunted me and gave rise to questions about why they had gone to their deaths in this way. I'd wondered if there was, contrary to everything I knew about my own Jewish family, something about the Jew that was without fight. This image was corrected on the battlefields of the Middle East.

At the same time, I was horrified at what the Israelis were doing to the Palestinians. The Israelis' crude arrogance I found unpalatable, and yet I respected and understood it too. These were not the cringing Jews of German stereotyping. Israel allowed me to feel and say, 'See, we Jews are just like you – as good and as bad.' And I could not but observe that the Israeli Jew has the same 'hardegatheid' (hard-ass quality) as the Afrikaner.

Shortly after our wedding in January 1980, Janice and I flew to Israel for a few days, en route to a new life in England. Why had I ended up with a woman from an English Irish background – who, admittedly, had a Dutch ancestor, General Janssens, who had lost the battle of Blouberg to the British? Was it that I felt too Afrikaans with Jewish women and too Jewish with Afrikaanse meisies? Could be, but there's no knowing such things for sure. England and women from an English background seemed like neutral territory – a place to which I increasingly felt drawn, a world of English novels, hunting hounds and 'gentlemanly' behaviour.

In Johannesburg, there were long delays, trouble with our El Al aircraft, we thought. The captain made himself known to his passengers in the concourse and apologised brusquely. He explained that two Israeli test pilots had just been killed demonstrating a new Israeli fighter aircraft in Zambia and he was waiting for their corpses to come on board before we could leave. When we finally reached our seats in the aircraft, we looked around nervously for two passengers who might look a mite stiff. Only El Al personnel would have made such an announcement. Any other airline would have made some anodyne excuse about technical problems, and no one would have been any the wiser, as the two coffins were discreetly placed in the cargo hold. The Israeli approach was to call a spade a spade. It felt like a very Afrikaans approach to things – crass but direct, and honest.

In one respect, the two peoples differed markedly in their approach to South Africa's future. In the years of apartheid, I could understand why so many Jews, me included, left. It was a mute protest, but nevertheless it was a cry of 'No!' I understood how Jews, for so long the victims of persecution, could not stomach the persecution of a whole population among whom they lived. Many left, especially the young. Even as Helen Suzman was fighting a brave, lonely battle in parliament, Jewish kids were slipping away, a huge loss to the country.

The Afrikaners, on the other hand, stayed – and why not? They were the masters, the lords of creation.

Now, when things are so different, when they no longer hold the reins of power and will patently never do so again, Afrikaners are leaving the country in great numbers, some to broaden their horizons, some to start again elsewhere. But many Afrikaners have once more battened down the hatches and are staying put. They have decided to bend like the grass in a storm, letting the wind pass over them, surviving with a low profile in the hope of staying on.

I realised that in writing about Afrikaners I could very well get them horribly wrong, that my view would inevitably be a partial view, and that the book might say much more about who and what I was than about who the Afrikaner was. I saw things my way; others would doubtless see things differently. As my near neighbour, Pooh Bear, the spirit of Ashdown Forest, England, once said, 'When you are a Bear of Very Little Brain and you think of Things, you find sometimes that a Thing which seemed very Thingish inside you is quite different when it gets into the open and has other people looking at it.' That's always the way, isn't it?

NEXT YEAR IN PRETORIA

I have a particular view of Afrikaners – as an inside outsider. I can see a profoundly important link between these peoples, the Jew and the Afrikaner: the mythology of land and loss of homeland. I had some understanding of the cost of becoming landless, homeless, of being a tenant people forever at the mercy of princes and people not one's own, at whose gates one sat in poverty. I understood the Afrikaners' wish to retain their land, and to be rulers in that land, for I understood how the Jews felt, forced to move on for 5,000 years, a people forever saying, 'Next year in Jerusalem.' Would the Afrikaner survive 5,000 years in the Wilderness, saying to themselves, perhaps, 'Next year in Pretoria?'

I had lived for 25 years in England with an unresolved ache in my heart for a South Africa that never was and perhaps now could never be. I would try to use the insights I had gained in my own great trek out of Africa and from my Jewish forebears to understand my mother's people. I knew that fighting for one's own place, a place in the sun, was a cause worth fighting for if one had a belief in the value of one's own culture. I thought I understood the Afrikaners and their wish for a homeland in which they were masters. Why, then, had they relinquished power?

The Afrikaners have a powerful sense of the ridiculous. They acknowledge the divisions among themselves – die broedertwis, die dwars trekkery, die veraaiers, die hensoppers (the disagreements among brothers, the pulling in opposite directions, the traitors, those who throw in the towel in the face of the enemy). Like the Jews, they tell jokes against themselves;

Van der Merwe, the butt of many jokes, is alive and kicking in South Africa. It's an honourable tradition that the Afrikaans author Herman Charles Bosman mined to good effect.

This is not to say that they did not laugh at others and scratch their heads about that great mystery, the black people, among whom they lived. They told myriad stories of the 'houtkoppe' (wooden heads) who would survive untold horrors as long as they landed on their thick skulls. Was there a touch of holding up a candle to light the dark about these stories, the belittling of a huge fear of the black man who might rise at any time and wipe the Afrikaners off the face of Africa? Quite possibly. But racial superiority was also, without doubt, a big part of this kind of storytelling. I remember one such story that illustrates the mutual incomprehension between Boer and Black. It was told to me by a farming neighbour at Blouberg. And it was told in the spirit of puzzled wonderment at how different the farmer's inner landscape was from that of his black labourers. He said he had given his black farm foreman a considerable raise after the man had worked diligently on his farm for 20 years. He said he had wished to mark this length of service with something valuable. The next day the man's bags were packed and he said he was leaving. Asked why, he explained that he felt cheated. He said that if he was worth this amount now, it meant that the work he had done for two decades had been underpaid. It was the same work. Why had his boss only seen fit to increase his salary now, after 20 years? He did not wish to work for a thief.

And so it was for all of us who grew up in South Africa. We lived side by side with each other and yet our cultures weren't available to each other in any sense of sympathetic sharing.

I recall meeting fellow army conscripts at Oudtshoorn in my first year of national service. Many of them were huge strapping lads from the Transvaal, sons of mielie (maize) farmers for whom the army was like a holiday camp. These great lumps were used to getting up at 4 a.m. or 5 a.m. to milk cows, used to slogging all day, every day. For them reveille at 6 a.m. was like a holiday lie-in, a five-day working week a joke. They told me of sisters who were quite capable of lugging 80kg sacks of mealies during harvest. Yet these great hominids trembled and fainted en masse at the sight of a doctor's hypodermic syringe when the time came to inoculate us.

There were two I recall with particular fondness. One was a tall blond boy called Johan, who had a quiet dignity and a dry sense of humour. He and I were part of a convoy, conveying half-built Land Rovers from Oudtshoorn to Cape Town, where they were to be completed. During regulation stops on the way for food and rest, he was a quiet, friendly presence by whose side I was happy to sit and chat or be silent. He reminded me of a pool of clear water in the desert. And yet I cannot say that I knew him, his innermost thoughts, his hopes, his ambitions.

A few years later I met another Afrikaans lad who became a friend in the army. We were on manoeuvres in and around Potchefstroom, hundreds of square kilometres of army terrain in which we played at war. His name was Piet and he was a dark-haired, burly rugby player with great natural authority. Like so many other Afrikaners, he was intrigued by my strange cultural duality and we had a good joking relationship.

One aspect of his behaviour puzzled me greatly. He had a great love of going to have ''n kak in die bos', (a shit in the bush), for which he always sought company. I was happy to oblige, as I couldn't abide the public humiliation of the 10-seater long-drop where many were happy to congregate while their bowels moved, chatting or reading the paper, in absolutely no rush to leave and with as little self-consciousness as horses or cattle emptying their bowels. Piet, like me, preferred some privacy for his ablutions, but he also liked to chat from a discreet distance while so engaged, joking that all he needed for complete contentment was a couple of dry mieliestronke (maize cobs) with which to clean himself afterwards. It was at times like these that I felt I was living in a Bosman story, and in a way I was.

As I grew up, I came to realise that the separate race groups lived apart from each other in theory, but not in practice. Sometimes they touched, quite intimately, but it was bad form to acknowledge this. One pretended one hadn't noticed, rather in the way one would overlook an adult caught picking his nose or farting loudly. I came to see that I lived among the seeing blind and the hearing deaf, and if they carried no white canes, their colour was sufficient symbol of their condition.

I heard a story once that seemed to be emblematic of this problem. Its setting was a small fishing village in the northwest Cape. This place started off on the seabed and, considering its subsequent history, perhaps it should have stayed there. Situated 20km from Cape Town up this cold, inhospitable coast, it had been, a century ago, a place of salt-white sand that had once been the seabed, now formed into ridge after ridge of dune, precariously fixed in place by sour-fig succulents and sea grasses. No trees grew there. This open land was tormented by fierce, wet Northwesters in winter and fiercer Southeast gales in summer, up from that sailors' grave, the Roaring Forties. It was a sea-sand desert with the bleached bones of gulls and cormorants and the occasional ostrich skeleton its only markers.

It was a good place to send an erring son caught dallying with a black servant girl – packed off in disgrace, away from society's prying eyes. There, scoured by the unforgiving winds that whipped the dry sands to a fine cutting edge, the outcasts lived or died, according to their ability to find water, catch fish or grow a few vegetables in that hostile place.

Whether they lived or died was of no concern to anyone. The Calvinist Cape expunged them from its memory when, with a few possessions piled on an ox cart, they disappeared forever into the wilderness. It was a harsh fate. Cape Town, isolated at the tip of Africa, had isolated them even farther. Proud galleons of the Dutch East India Company would appear from time to time over the horizon, beating through the last dangerous haul to safe anchorage in Table Bay.

These exiles were the 'half-naaitjies' (half-castes). Overhearing servants use the term, well-bred Afrikaans girls asked mothers who or what they were and got a slapped face for their pains. They were beyond mention, a threat to the very fabric of white masterhood and black servitude. The Bible itself condemned the sons of Ham to be drawers of water and hewers of wood for all time. To mingle the races was an abomination in God's eyes.

A century passed, but the stigma of this place of exile did not. Miscegenation, now a crime in law, came to be seen as an even greater evil, an even greater threat. Yet this place existed and others like it. The half-naaitjies and their descendants interbred further, the rare shipwreck survivor staying just long enough to inject new blood.

These people were a sentimental and superstitious lot and when the fog rolled in at the end of the summer, they said that the moaning of the foghorn was the sound of a white father mourning his lost sons.

All of this took place against the backdrop of a magnificent land. Would it have been different had the stage been a nondescript piece of central Asia? Probably; setting has its own power to inspire. Here was a homeland, tenuously possessed, that was truly worth owning. It held some of the most beautiful scenery on earth. The coasts and oceans teemed with fish. There were the majestic mountain ranges – the Cedarberg and the Drakensberg, to name just two – and the quiet backwaters of the Karoo and the Klein Karoo with their own harsh beauty. The seemingly endless tracts of the Orange Free State and the Transvaal promised a foretaste of eternity. The fecund earth threw up abundant game and wildlife, spectacular displays of flowers and forests, from small pale Karoo blooms to the flaming ericas and proteas of the Cape and the seas of Namaqualand daisies. To the north and east were the lush hills of the Eastern Cape; beyond, the subtropics of Natal; beneath it all, gold, diamonds and coal.

This was a land worth fighting for. It was a land that spoke eloquently of God's grace, power and magnificence. It was a land that humbled one and ennobled its possessor. It was a land of a hundred thousand graves: small farm cemeteries where generations of toilers lay buried; war graves beneath barren koppies; and the bones of white men and women who had set out to carve a new life here in southern Africa. Their hardships, suffering, pain and sacrifice – and finally their bodies – had fertilised this land, enriched this hard country, and, as effectively as a flag, claimed it for their descendants. Their sacrifice had ennobled these great spaces, humanised them and made them sacred to this people, this volk. This land, the Afrikaner said with some justification, was theirs by right of blood.

And as they struggled to possess it, in all its magnificence, like a python attempting to ingest a deer, they were vulnerable. Other peoples, too, looked on this land with hunger. And abroad, others who had solved the 'problem' of their own indigenous people – the Americans, the British, the Australians, the New Zealanders – pointed fingers and accused the Afrikaners of a unique crime against humanity. How that galled.

The Afrikaners, it seemed to me, were not well served by their leaders. There was something laughable, ridiculous about the Verwoerds, the Vorsters, the Bothas, something of the buffoon and the clown hand-in-hand with the bully. In a way, they were just not big enough, ruthless enough, evil enough to hold onto this magnificent land. But that is perhaps a view influenced by hindsight; at the time it seemed possible that they would hold this place for a thousand years, bolstered by the West's fear of communism.

There were cracks in the façade of invincibility – the rout of the South African Defence Force outside Luanda, and their retreat before brown-skinned Cubans. This said more than any words could – that these Afrikaners were just men after all, men who hung onto the myth that they had an exclusive right to hold this place in perpetuity, thanks to a deal struck with God Himself, sealed at the Battle of Blood River. (The battle between the Voortrekkers and the Zulus on 16th December 1838 at which the Voortrekkers vowed to God that, should they be delivered, they would commemorate the day as a Sabbath and build a church.)

Oh, how we kid ourselves, blind ourselves, find justification for horror in the most unlikely places. In churches across this beautiful land, Dutch Reformed dominees preached from the moral high ground to congregations eager to hear religious justification for control of the land.

Here, as elsewhere in the world, man called on God to underwrite and to bless the possession of a place. Here, as elsewhere, deals were done between man and God. The San paintings attest to this, a prayer in paint and stone for plenty, for game, for survival.

The Xhosa people tried too in 1856-7. Led by the vision of a girl, they slaughtered their cattle in a blood rite aimed at washing the white man out of Africa. (This vast tragedy became known as the Great Cattle-Killing.) But on this occasion God was deaf and a hungry Xhosa nation entered white servitude in a desperate effort to survive. God cannot be relied on to do man's bidding.

But for a brief moment, the sound of Dutch Reformed Church bells rang out across the southern reaches of the continent on Sunday mornings, to sing of ownership, of possession, for a people who believed that they had spent their time in the desert wisely and who now had found their Promised Land, or so it seemed to me, and perhaps to them as well.

SOUTH AFRICA-BOUND

Unbelievably, there is no one ahead of me when I check my luggage in at the SAA desk at Heathrow Airport. The place is almost calm today, 16 June 2003. It is a very important day in South African history; it is the anniversary of the 1976 Soweto uprising and is now known as Youth Day. It's 5 p.m. when I arrive at the airport after a hot day in the baking 20s and after a week of lovely weather.

I sit among the thin crowd watching for aircraft from every conceivable corner of the world and I make an internal review of my feelings. I'm not particularly excited. We've just been through a hectic weekend with friends down from Suffolk and one from South Africa who we haven't seen for years.

Finally, I board the SAA jumbo and find to my delight that it's only a third full. This being winter in South Africa, it's not surprising. I note with interest and surprise that all the cabin crew are black, not a white or brown face among them. It's years since I flew SAA and the crew reflect the changes that have occurred in the country in a very real and startling way. Where, I wonder, have all those Afrikaans girls gone? Gone to motherhood every one? I note that affirmative action has not yet reached the cockpit – Captain Hardwick sounds just like old times as he welcomes us on board for the direct non-stop overnight flight to Cape Town.

I look up and the toilet sign above my head is still in English and Afrikaans; there is no indication yet of any of the country's other nine official languages – among them Zulu, Xhosa, Tswana, Sotho.

Flight 221 roars into the twilight evening sky and shortly

I'm offered a drink. Beneath us the sheer beauty of England in midsummer garb falls away as we swing south and climb steadily on course for the Cape. I sit back and sip a gin and tonic and wonder what I will find in South Africa. I'm not absolutely convinced about my rationale for this trip. Can something that feels so indulgent really be work? I have a hollow feeling in my stomach. I tell myself that I will just have to live first and judge later, and that I should be bloody grateful for the wonderful opportunity to revisit the country of my birth, and heart and soul. One that I ran from all those years ago.

A charming air hostess serves me supper with a smile. I wash it down with a small bottle of South Africa's own unique wine blend, Pinotage, a mix of the Pinot Noir and Hermitage grape varieties. I open the book I've brought along for the flight, *A Place Called Vatmaar* by A.M. Scholtz and am soon engrossed.

I sleep fitfully and finally through the cabin windows see my first African sunrise for some time, a mix of orange, lemon and blue striations. Shortly after breakfast, the aircraft banks past Table Mountain over Table Bay, and I feel that old thrill: home, home, home again. The plane does not so much land as kiss the tarmac, so gently it feels like the best kind of welcomes, low key and warm.

Emerging from the aircraft, I breathe in the magic smell of the Cape in winter sunshine – champagne weather. I've forgotten just how seductive and mellow the Cape can be, even in the heart of its sometimes wild, wet and cold winter. Outside it's already 20 degrees, and the temperature rises as I spot my sister Jay and nephew Kirsten waiting for me in the arrivals hall.

We run the guilt-inducing gauntlet of wood and corrugated-iron shacks that line the N2 approach road into Cape Town, home to hundreds of thousands of people, patiently waiting for the miracle of the new South Africa to transform their lives. It's going to be a long wait by the looks of things, with unemployment running at around 40 per cent.

In Constantia, there are still roses in bloom, lemons on trees and guavas on bushes. The feeling of unreality I get from this fecund, fragile Eden comes upon me, as it always does, when I walk about my sister's garden.

We go up to Bishopscourt to have lunch with my father and eat delicious soup, chicken stew and pumpkin, followed by melktert. Suzie Meyer and Pieter Brill, those incredible people from my past, have spoiled me once more with some of my favourite foods. I join them in the kitchen afterwards; we talk of times past and I show them photographs of my family in England. In this house, since my mother died six years ago, it is as if time has stood still. The house is a mausoleum to her memory. I wonder how long Pieter Brill can keep fetching, carrying, cooking and driving, with his 80th birthday just seven months away?

I take my farewell of my father as his aromatherapist arrives. He climbs carefully onto the collapsible bed she has brought along with her. She smiles dutifully at all his jokes and winks at me. She's a keen walker and mountaineer, loves the outdoors, and says she has read my first book, *A Fisherman in the Saddle,* and enjoyed it. I am touched.

Down in the drive I renew acquaintance with my father's 30-year-old 300D Mercedes. It's still going 'like a donkey, not fast but steadily,' my father explains. I'm grateful, though I tease him that it might do better to span in a few donkeys to pull it. Waiting for the yellow light to disappear on the dashboard, I think for the hundredth time that this is no getaway car and that if I'm carjacked, the carjackers are going to make a very slow getaway. The engine rumbles to life and slowly I exit the house of my teens to go in search of Afrikaners and Boerejooden in the new South Africa.

The Mercedes creaks down the drive, and I wait for the electronic gates to swing open, allowing me out onto Primrose Avenue. A hundred metres up the road, we ease our way past a myriad TV support vehicles, their crews busy filming in one of the new Medici-style palaces recently built in Bishopscourt. TV is a new growth industry in Cape Town, thanks to the stunning settings and the wonderful, some say unique, quality of light.

I head back to Constantia and the room which my sister has made available in her home. I look out onto the beautiful back of Table Mountain, fissured with deep green gorges, and think of all the days I have lived at the feet of this colossus. And here it is again, anchoring me to Africa still. I draw the curtains for that ultimate indulgence, an afternoon snooze. I'm knackered.

CONSTANTIA CARJACKING

Wednesday, 18 June 2003. The talk in Constantia is all about the recent carjacking in which a Port Elizabeth sports agent was shot dead and his wife pistol-whipped in the driveway of a relative's house in Avenue Orleans. The *Cape Times* is full of it, plus a boatload of other doom-laden stories. There is enough here to make a pessimist smile.

This kind of thing is new in Cape Town's wealthier suburbs. It has been commonplace in Johannesburg for years, but in the leafy exclusivity of Constantia, such things were read about rather than experienced locally. The couple in the car were returning home after a night out. The current belief is that the killers are part of a drug mafia who do a couple of break-ins, burglaries or carjackings a day to feed their habit.

Hospital trauma units in Cape Town confirm the police statement that armed hijackings are on the increase in greater Cape Town. The medics say that victims of violent crimes have flooded their wards over the past six months.

My sister and brother-in-law have just had a burglar alarm fitted to their home. It goes off regularly at 2 a.m. with a tooth-loosening sound that at first scares me witless. The system is having teething troubles. The arrival of the rapid-response company is, as advertised, almost instant, which is reassuring, I suppose. The system is undergoing a settling-down phase, not helped by the local birds – particularly the hadeda ibis – which trigger the light beam in the garden intended for burglars approaching from the green belt, an area of open grass and woodland that abuts the houses in the area.

At a public meeting convened by concerned Constantia residents, the head of a security company tells the 200 people attending the sometimes-heated event that they are 'security naïve' and need to wise up on self-protection issues. There has been a string of burglaries in the area.

According to the *Cape Times*, Adrian Good, head of ADT Armed Security, himself a Constantia resident, says that two thirds of local people, most of them in the green-belt area, are 'sitting ducks'. Few have recently checked their security systems and burglars do not even have to break a window to gain access, he says.

The increasingly dangerous crime-and-violence situation in Cape Town is taking place within another calamity: the worst drought in living memory. Farmers are praying for rain, as lambs die by the dozen each day and the wheat fields dry out, the seed germinating only to wither for lack of moisture. It's a catastrophe.

Melanie Gosling, the environment reporter for the *Cape Times*, reports:

> The Swartland and Namaqualand are in the grip of the worst drought for 10 years. Only 50 per cent of the wheat sown in the Swartland and the Western Cape's breadbasket has germinated, with the rest in the fields lying barren. In Namaqualand, where the situation has been described as 'critical', farmers have not been able to sow at all because of the lack of moisture in the ground. There is little grazing pasture for sheep and many lambs have died. The Clanwilliam dam is only 12 per cent full. Frost has destroyed the whole vegetable crop in the Olifants valley.

Over 1,000km to the north, in Johannesburg, 22 right-wing members of a white supremacy movement known as the Boeremag are shortly to stand trial in the High Court on a charge of treason. They are accused of trying to overthrow the government with bomb attacks and attempts to assassinate

President Mandela during his tenure.

A black political group, Azapo, are reportedly objecting to the old national anthem, *Die Stem*, being included in the new national anthem. It is, they say, 'a source of pain and an unpleasant reminder of our sordid past.' They point out that the new anthem, *Nkosi Sikelel'i-Afrika*, is a complete song in itself.

The last story to catch my eye in the paper this morning is the one headed 'Afrikaans Cult Claims To Be Lost Tribes Of Israel'. The cult, named Lewende Hoop, argue that God has put the present ANC government in place to punish the Afrikaners. Jaco van der Merwe, the cult's spiritual leader, says, 'There was a time when God ordered us to take the country by force and we disobeyed His will.' Van der Merwe, who hails from the Free State farming town of Kroonstad, denies that his message is political. However, he claims that 30 congregations affiliated to Lewende Hoop have been established across the country and numbers are rising.

It sounds rather like the plagues of Egypt have descended on this benighted country – but, as a former journalist, I know that good news does not sell papers, and outside the sun is shining and most people are just getting on with their lives in the best way they know.

My thoughts and feelings as I read the paper in bed with a coffee are hard to describe. I'm thrown by the night's alarms and excursions and have not slept wonderfully well, my mind racing round the book I have come here to write. I have woken up, finally, at 6 a.m. to the cry of the hadedas and the call of wild Egyptian geese flying low over the green belt. As the first rays of the sun touch the mountain, its buttresses stand out, illuminated in gold and silver light, and my white-pink bedroom glows. It's home and it's also not home.

One of the joys of England is that it's not mine to concern myself with; I can enjoy it at one remove. It's both a pleasure and a pain that there I am and will always be a colonial incomer, not a native. Back in Cape Town I'm also not a native any longer. The cost of my living between two lands is huge, but it also brings strange rewards.

I put down the newspaper, lift my briefcase onto the bed and search for my notes. Just before leaving England, I had an email discussion with Ferdi Greyling, a much-respected senior journalist of *Die Beeld* newspaper. With typical South African generosity, he took the time and the trouble to reply almost instantly. I look now at these emails to help me prepare for a meeting I have this afternoon with Ampie Coetzee, an academic and writer who is one of the Group of 63, a newly formed, loosely based organisation of intellectuals that seeks to move Afrikaners in a new and more positive direction, as I understand it.

I asked Greyling why the Afrikaners went so quietly, when I'd believed with complete conviction that they would fight to the last man. What happened to change their minds and make them opt for peace? And how did they get the grass roots to go along with this ordered transition of power?

> It was a common misconception in the early '90s that the Afrikaners would 'fight to the end'. It was a misconception that the foreign media reporting on the constitutional negotiations served regularly. I saw it many times then – as I reported on those negotiations.
>
> Back then there was only one instance when I was scared things might erupt and that was at the funeral of Chris Hani. But it was saved by people like Desmond Tutu and Joe Slovo, who pleaded and cajoled for peace and democracy among the enraged black population at the funeral that was televised nationwide.
>
> You must remember that the negotiations for a peaceful transition were initiated by the National Party, which was the representative of the Afrikaners then.
>
> They saw that apartheid was not sustainable. Inflation went up, economic growth was negative and life was turning bleak. Democracy promised a better economic future.
>
> For the Afrikaners to fight, what would they have to do? They would have to resign their jobs, say goodbye to water and electricity in homes, cheers to cars and traffic jams and shopping centres. No more going to Pick 'n Pay to buy bread and milk. No more rugby on Saturday. No more Currie Cup finals on TV. They were

not prepared to do that.

In the Anglo-Boer War, Afrikaners were subsistence farmers. In 1994 they were suburban dwellers buying new cars, going on holiday and watching cricket at the weekend. They did not work the land anymore; they went to the gym and managed offices, sold stuff, made deals, and talked on the phone.

To fight violently would have meant an end to that. To gain what? A broken city and not knowing where your family is, if they are still alive? All this for a loose idea of ethnic pride and privilege represented by an uneducated man like Eugène Terre'Blanche who clearly drank too much and bathed too little?

To keep their lives, they had to accept democracy, which meant a mainly black government. And while they mistrusted the ability of black people – as they were taught to under apartheid – they had the example of black leaders like Nelson Mandela, Thabo Mbeki and Cyril Ramaphosa, who looked like really competent people. They surely negotiated well.

The ANC in the early '90s had a feel and a look of competence about them (they represented the best black leadership) and that helped a lot.

Choose between Pick 'n Pay and sleeping in the veld in winter with people shooting at you? No choice. They chose to give democracy a chance. This was evident around 1992 when de Klerk held a referendum about this and the white population voted overwhelmingly to go ahead with negotiations.

Quite apart from that, always remember the basic instinct of Afrikaners is to rather stop fighting when it is clear that victory is impossible. Live to fight another day, rather. That was demonstrated in World War II at Tobruk as well. This, a friend of mine, who is a military historian, told me some time ago.

Above all, remember that in spite of apartheid, Afrikaners did spend most of their time rubbing

> shoulders with black people. The nanny was black, the housemaid was black, the gardener, the manual labourers of the economy, the builders of homes and offices, the tea-makers in the office, the petrol attendants at the garage, the clients in your shop...'

I asked Ferdi, 'Where do Afrikaners see themselves now, a decade after majority rule? What do they feel about the future? How do they finesse the fear of swartgevaar? Do they feel a part of the Rainbow Nation or is there still a deep wish for a place of their own?'

> Afrikaners are well off today. They are also pissed off at affirmative action that is taking away a lot of privilege, but they are still very well employed, powerful in the economy and one of the top groups in the country in terms of wealth.
>
> About the future: I would say there is some ambivalence. They mistrust 'Africa' but they have committed to South Africa and they are seeing that it is working in more instances than it is not working.
>
> They are also confident – I would say – about the free market/state monetary discipline policy of the ANC.
>
> Swartgevaar? I would say they have apprehension at being dominated as a group by another group, but I would also say that is probably pretty normal in the world today. I would guess in the UK there are minority groups feeling the same way.
>
> But it is a new experience for us and I suspect we sometimes wrongly believe we are unique in the way (some people see a similarity between whites in SA and blacks in the US!) We are not unique, I would argue. There is probably a worry factor attached to being a minority group anywhere – specially in times of economic hardship, which is what we have in Africa. When the fight for resources gets tough, the biggest groups tend to exclude the minorities.
>
> Rainbow Nation? Look at the crowds when a Springbok team plays. See how many whites wave the

> new flag. I would say we do feel part of that nation, but many do not feel so intimately a part of it as some people may think the concept implies. They slightly misunderstood Desmond Tutu when he coined that phrase. I think so, anyway. In a rainbow, colours do not mix but each one is part of the whole thing.
>
> Ironically, that is precisely (in my experience) what many Afrikaners would object to when it comes to the term 'Rainbow Nation' – they want to make a point that yes, they are part of the nation, but they are a distinct part and would like to remain that – a distinct part of this thing.
>
> Place of their own? I would sum it up this way. If Afrikaners can all exchange their present homes and jobs in SA for equal homes and jobs in a volkstaat, the majority would probably do it. But the majority also know that that will not be possible. So they will remain in the well developed and moneyed urban centres – worrying late at night about the possibility of everything going to pieces in much the same way Americans worried about nuclear war during the Cold War.'

Following this exchange, I felt I must ask Ferdi some additional questions. I started with 'Who would you say speaks for the Afrikaner today?'

> Nobody really. The National Party turned into the New National Party and is in alliance with the ANC but probably has less than half Afrikaner support.
>
> The Democratic Alliance is trying to become the representative of the Afrikaner, but its support is much more a conservative reaction to the ANC than anything else, I would say. It surely has none of the ethnic bells and whistles that the NP always had.
>
> I would say Afrikaner business comes strangely close to some sort of leadership role at times. Even the Broederbond (these days called the Afrikanerbond and 'open to all' – 'but don't call us we'll call you') seems divided at times, although it plays a strong role in

> business and the academic worlds and as such is an influence. But there is no leader. Probably that's for the best at this stage. Let us discover principle. It is about time.

(Die Broederbond was a secret society formed in 1918, which placed key people in places of power and influence to ensure the dominance of the Afrikaner. It played a very influential role in the affairs of the volk.)

I pressed Ferdi further on Terre'Blanche. 'You are patently not impressed with Eugène Terre'Blanche. And yet I have heard from some fairly sophisticated Afrikaans friends that he is a truly mesmerising speaker, perhaps a bit florid but poetic and moving. Is that fair comment and might he have created more trouble if he'd appeared rather more credible?'

> He was an emotional speaker in a rabble-rousing way. Deep booming voice, rhythm like the old poets had – in other words, over-dramatisation. Shout and then down to the whisper and stare. That sort of thing. Many adjectives, frequent calls to blood and soil and the iconic past where all Afrikaner leaders were generals at daybreak and all black people were scheming and conniving (not too much about the treacherous English, as some of his followers were English – even some UK immigrants).
>
> Some people seemed to have enjoyed that, but I tend to listen to what arguments speakers offer, and the moment you do that, it all falls apart. No reason, no insight, no new thoughts, no reasoned argument. In fact, no answers.

What of Afrikaners emigrating, I asked. What are the emigration figures and where are they going when they leave South Africa?

> It seems there is more than one thing at work. Some leave because they dislike/distrust black people. Some leave because they have no emotional attachment to the

land but want to live comfortably and can get good jobs elsewhere. They then choose London and a nice lifestyle. Some come back. It seems there is a big stream of coming and going in the world these days. I would guess there are many Aussies and Kiwis in London as well.

Many young people go for a year or two. South Africans in their twenties can now get a two-year work permit for the UK. My one child is planning to do that. My sister-in-law's two did. They work in London, save money and tour Europe. They come back after about three years. There are a lot of people still here. I think the statistics show a levelling-off of leavers.

Finally, I asked him about the future. 'Are you optimistic about the future of the Afrikaner in South Africa? And if so, on what do you base your positive view?'

We are part of the social landscape here. Relations between blacks and Afrikaners have improved a lot; in fact, Afrikaners who are staying belong here and have nowhere else to go and many black people realise that.

It all depends (it usually does) in the end on the economic success of the country. That may be assured. South Africa is an industrial country. It has an industrial base, a working infrastructure and rule of law supported by the constitution.

In general, the trick is to get a country that ticks over in economic and infrastructure terms. That is the difficult part. It is easier to maintain it once you have it; it is a critical-mass thing. We have it, courtesy of the gold-mining industry and the price of gold in the past century. We are maintaining it. There are threats to stability like bureaucratic shit, corruption, etc, but they tend to be threats resulting from doing things too hastily or without experience rather than being a function of laziness and pure greed.

So I think the country will tick over socio-economically and in that structure Afrikaners will be able

> to live. And we have critical mass in terms of population and education. Things may change quickly but at the moment there are indications that things are going right and no clear indications that things are going off the rails. So I believe.

The future of the Afrikaners, Ferdi says, would be that of a 'minority with economic power and a vibrant culture. More and more "coloured" people and white Afrikaners will become one larger group (with two subsets – white and brown) bound by language and culture.'

Many of the issues Ferdi Greyling raised or referred to would surface and resurface in the days ahead. Looking back now, with the wisdom of hindsight, I believe he gave me a very good and accurate overview of how Afrikaners currently see themselves and their place in South Africa.

I put my notes back in my case, get up and shower. Later I go downstairs to sit in the sun, drink in that mountain-view, drink coffee and dunk karringmelkbeskuit (buttermilk rusks) made by my sister. It is balm to my soul.

The garden is undergoing a transition orchestrated by my nephew, Kirsten Louw, who is studying ornithology at UCT. His interests are, however, legion and span the natural world. There is a regular coming and going of contacts from the worlds of birds and plants and visits to strange places to view both the ordinary and the rare. His plan for the garden is to see that it boasts indigenous plants only. He's not alone in his wish to see invading species of plants removed or exterminated from this garden and the Cape in general. As a result, the lovely syringa tree that graces this garden is under threat. 'Native species rule!' seems to be his motto. God help him and his kind if the government adopts this view on South Africa's human inhabitants.

I have an appointment at a coffee shop with Robyn Cohen of the *Cape Times*. She's going to do an author profile, and a review of my first book, *A Fisherman in the Saddle*.

After so many years as a journalist, it's a strange feeling sitting down to be interviewed. Robyn is petite and vivacious and already in situ in what she describes as her office, a set of two large leather easy chairs hidden behind a pillar in the coffee shop. We order cappuccinos and poppy-seed muffins and get stuck in. Three hours later, we're still talking.

She and her husband emigrated to Australia, where they spent five years, returning to be with her sister who was dying, and have decided to stay on in South Africa. They have a young family. We share a South African culture, a Jewish heritage, and I feel very comfortable speaking to her. I can tell she is interested by my use of Afrikaans and my identification with Afrikaners.

As we finish, she offers to arrange interviews for me with a number of people, including David Kramer. He is a South African icon, a comedian, singer and playwright, and I believe another Boerejood. He is definitely someone I would love to speak to. I thank Robyn; she has given me so much more than I have given her, and her *Cape Times* article, when it appears, is half a page of kindness. It is good to be back in my old home town, despite the crime, the carjackings and those damn noisy hadedas.

RED SHOES AND GREY SHOES

There has been a spirit haunting this trip: Professor Hermann Giliomee and his book *The Afrikaners.* This massive tome - 4cm thick - is a much-referred-to document that has been a decade in the making. It's doubtless the current definitive take on Afrikanerdom, I'm told, by a number of people far more knowledgeable about Afrikaners than I. The trouble is that I have no intention of reading it for fear that the good professor's agenda, ideas and thesis will completely dominate what I am attempting to do. So I have decided to ignore it until such time as I have at least written a first draft of my own book, and then perhaps have a peek.

This decision is much in my mind as I drive to Mowbray to meet my next contact, Professor Ampie Coetzee, Head of Afrikaans and Dutch Literature at the University of the Western Cape. His qualifications to comment on the Afrikaners include his own membership of the volk and his time spent studying under the renowned Afrikaans poets NP van Wyk Louw and Ernst van Heerden. He has also taught at the universities of Natal and Witwatersrand. Besides writing on the link between literature and politics, he has recently written about the importance of the farm and the land in creating the identity of the Afrikaner of the past. He has also written extensively about and has close links to Breyten Breytenbach, whom he considers one of the world's greatest poets.

The interview has been arranged by my publicist, Karin

Cronjé, a writer herself of *Vir 'n Pers Huis* (*For a Purple House*, Human & Rosseau, 1999) and Ampie's second wife. He has subsequently remarried a third time.

As I arrive at his bungalow home situated near the open expanse of Rondebosch Common, he and his wife, Anne-Ghrette, and their two-year-old son Kobus ('Last of the Afrikaners' as Ampie describes him later) are just returning from the supermarket, where they have been to shop for a dinner party they're holding that night.

The house is securely fenced, gated, locked and barred, but climbing roses soften this security apparatus. I shout a hesitant 'hello' as the bag-carrying group disappears inside. Ampie re-emerges and unlocks the gate. 'Come in, come in,' he says and I am ushered into a small, dark sitting room stuffed with books, pictures, carvings, statues – all the stuff of an artistic, bohemian, intellectual, creative life. There are oriental carpets and beneath a couch opposite me a carved, white-eyed baboon keeps a close watch throughout the interview, from its place in the deep shadows where it is flanked by other strange creatures.

As I sit down, I notice a massive family Bible (his mother's, it turns out) by my left elbow. Later, when coffee is served, I move the Bible, not wanting to place the proffered cup of coffee on this treasured item.

Ampie laughs and says, 'It's alright, I'm not religious; you can put the cup on it.'

But I move it anyway, knowing how my own mother would have felt about it. I say, 'I don't want your mother to kom spook.' (I don't want your mother to haunt me.)

Ampie is dressed in a denim shirt and jeans with bright red, thick-heeled sneakers, which add a few centimetres to his height. His thick grey hair and short grey beard frame a face I've seen on a thousand Afrikaners: shrewd, slightly cynical, yet quick to smile, and also a well disguised wariness. I have come mentioning his previous wife and I am a totally unknown quantity; it says a lot that he has agreed to see me. He is very well known in South Africa and has many friends; the house is an hospitable one, which welcomes people from all branches of the arts. As we speak, Kobus wanders in from time to time to monitor our progress and is gently persuaded away by his mother.

I ask Ampie why the Afrikaners went as they did – 'stilletjies weggeglip,' (stole away quietly) as I put it. He begins by telling me of a visit he had at a key moment from Frederik van Zyl Slabbert, whom many South Africans see as 'the king who never was' – the brightest Afrikaans political talent of several generations who refused to get involved.

> Van Zyl was here [visiting me] just after de Klerk made the announcement about the decision to start negotiations with the ANC. It was 1990, I think. Van Zyl went and saw de Klerk. And de Klerk said to him, 'The Berlin Wall has fallen, so die rooigevaar bestaan nie meer nie (the red danger is gone, it no longer exists). It's gone. And the pressure on the country because of sanctions is getting too much. I also think that terrorism or unrest in South Africa might get worse, so let's take a chance.' That is what de Klerk said to him in private, according to what Van Zyl Slabbert said to me.
>
> And although Van Zyl did not report this to me, I suspect de Klerk would also have said, 'There is no other option; apartheid is no longer working.'
>
> I think it is a lot of fantasy, Julian, because from my angle, the angle of the writer, the Afrikaans writers had since the '60s started a protest. It wasn't an organised protest, you know. It started with Jan Rabie, Breyten Breytenbach, with André Brink, Elsa Joubert and all these people. And they actually began to create a consciousness among people, among intelligent people and among reading people, that things aren't right, that this is not the way to do things, and since the '40s or the '50s Van Wyk Louw had been saying, 'Dis beter dat 'n volk sterwe as om in onregtigheid te lewe.' (It is better that a people perish than to live in iniquity.) Liberal nationalism was the gist of his whole argument.
>
> I think these things not only set the scene, they conscientised the people. I know it is very difficult to say, but literature can actually do something. I think one should not underestimate literature.

I put it to him that today apartheid is seen as a massive failure, but it was in fact very successful in achieving its aims – keeping the various peoples and tribes separate, which led to white English speakers viewing the Afrikaners as a very unified block, when in fact, according to Ampie, there was a fertile debate going on within Afrikanerdom.

> In the '60s, apartheid worked so well that the country's economy was at a peak. The irony was that during this time the Afrikaans writers who became emancipated, especially prose writers, picked the fruit of the powerful Afrikaner hegemony and then they turned against it. That is why censorship had to start, because the government had to censor its own people. This was the most effective way of silencing their own people; they were naughty boys, you see.
>
> Banning books like André Brink's *Kennis van die Aand* in the '70s caused one helluva noise among the people. You know, there was a court case about a novel and this hadn't happened before.
>
> OK, black people's writing was banned but the Afrikaner didn't care much about that. There were only a few of us academics and intellectuals who cared. The banning of black writing was not important to most white people. No white writing had been banned, then *Kennis van die Aand* and *Burger's Daughter* by Nadine Gordimer were banned. Now this brought the attention of readers and intelligent people to the fact that these things were happening in the country. Why were they happening? They knew why they were happening but now it was on paper. Now it wasn't ministers saying, 'Dit gaan regkom. Dit gaan goed wees.' (It will come right. Things will be good.) People became conscientised, and also there was the role that de Klerk played.
>
> Now Hermann Giliomee says de Klerk sold out. They [the Nationalist government] sold out to a certain extent; they did not negotiate enough [with the ANC]. In terms of language, they did not get enough assurances.

> They got the constitution protecting 11 languages but that's not happening. English is basically the language of administration in this country. So it is the language of government.
>
> Giliomee also says they did not negotiate enough for minority rights. I really think the ANC overwhelmed them, the ANC were too clever for them. I'm not that much in favour of Thabo Mbeki anymore but who can argue against this guy? I mean, he is a bloody good man! And Thabo and Mandela, Here, jong! (Good heavens, man!)You can't...'

He leaves his sentence unfinished, perhaps not wishing to articulate just how badly the white Nationalist politicians were outgunned by ANC blacks.

> The right wing of the Nationalist Party feel they were outnegotiated; people like former Nationalist cabinet minister Connie Mulder say this. You know who you should speak to is Karel Boshof IV, the young guy, he lives in Orania. (Orania is an attempt by a small group of Afrikaner purists to create a whites-only homeland for themselves in the Northern Cape.) Boshof's brilliant and he's a philosopher. And you get the angle of the minority-group idea from him. And I think the only Afrikaners who will really survive are the Afrikaners who do that. It is not a ghetto they live in. But the Afrikaner who can withdraw and practise his language and culture... 'There is already an Afrikaans diaspora taking place. You can see it from London, and it's also not only a physical diaspora but a spiritual, a cultural diaspora. My concern is that the Afrikaner as a group with a definite language and a definite literature is going to dissipate.
>
> I feel pessimistic about the future of the Afrikaner. Afrikaans made the Afrikaner. OK, it also made Afrikaner nationalism, but if it weren't for Afrikaans there wouldn't have been an Afrikaner today. It started round about 1875. There was an organisation set up then, Die Genootskap van Regte Afrikaners, in 1875.

> Before that Afrikaans was spoken by the slaves, the coloured people, the farmers. It is doubtful how it developed, but it broke away from Dutch because Dutch is too difficult. Afrikaans has Malay words and Portuguese words. So, formally, one can say it started in 1875 as a movement.
>
> And then it became a national movement and developed a literature, which in a sense one can almost say began undermining it, because it began undermining the hegemony of the Afrikaner. There is a poem by Breyten called *Taalstryd (Language fight)*. 'Taalstryd' is what they called it in the nineteenth century. We are talking about a taalstryd now again. Now this poem of Breyten's, he wrote it in prison, it's about Soweto of '76 and the killing of Hector Petersen, about Afrikaans being forced on blacks. The poem is an attack on Afrikaans, in Afrikaans. And it's a beautiful poem. But it's very vicious.

Ampie points out that Afrikaners tried to do to blacks exactly what the British did to Afrikaners: they tried to force them to speak the language of their political masters. The cost for Afrikaans could be terminal, he says:

> Afrikaans as a tertiary medium of instruction is being broken down. Not systematically, but definitely it is being destroyed. The University of the Orange Free State is practically an English-language university. The Rand Afrikaans University has more instruction in English than in Afrikaans, and there was one big fight at Stellenbosch University about two months ago. We were there, Groep 63, a group of Afrikaans intellectuals. Stellenbosch is transformed, it is changing. For instance, if there are three English-speaking students in a class who cannot understand Afrikaans, Xhosa students for instance, then the class will be in English.
>
> There were letters in the paper from students and from their parents about this. Now they [the university authorities] say that they have made a compromise, that it is not necessarily going to be like that, but it is going to

be like that, because the new Education Act of Asmal (Kader Asmal, former minister of education) says that it is unthinkable that there can be an Afrikaans university. There cannot be an Afrikaans university anymore. Just as he says there cannot be a Xhosa university or a Zulu university or a Venda university ... but he does not say that there cannot be an English university! He leaves that out because it's obvious what is going to happen.' [Later, when I check this, I find that what the minister actually said was: 'Language should not be a barrier to university access.']

During apartheid, the white people from Natal sent their children to Stellenbosch because it was safe. And it's a good university and it didn't have that liberal image like UCT and Wits. So the anglicisation started already. And then, since 1994, when the universities opened to all, the Xhosas started coming to Stellenbosch. The university where I teach, the University of the Western Cape, used to be an Afrikaans-speaking university. OK, it was an apartheid university for coloureds, but that's OK.

When I came there in 1987, we had one thousand first-year students in the Afrikaans department. Now we have 70! The university is totally English. This is not because of the coloured students but because of the Xhosas. I can understand that: why should they learn Afrikaans? English is an international language.

Now the coloured people from the platteland are suffering. They have nowhere to go. They can't go to Stellenbosch; that's becoming English. They can't go to UWC because that's English. They come to us. The law students, they come to us and say, can't we help them? Because they are sukkeling (struggling). They come from Riebeek Wes and from Koekenaap and from these places, where they don't hear English.

So you see no one can convince me that Afrikaans will survive in the universities. It will survive as a language that you speak in your house, that you speak with your friends, but it has developed an infrastructure – it is a

> language of philosophy, it is a language of science, it is a language of literature. If the universities don't use it, who the hell writes in Afrikaans then?
>
> Now, at the moment, Brink writes his novels in English and in Afrikaans; he writes simultaneously. Rachelle Greeff has decided to write in English. Breyten is writing prose in English; he can't write poetry in English, thank God! But he is frustrated. He's not publishing in this country anymore because they don't sell his books. Anyway, that's another story.
>
> Coetzee has gone to Australia because – one of the reasons was – in his book *Disgrace,* a black man rapes a white woman. The Boss [President Mbeki] himself objected to this. The Boss is very sensitive and very paranoid about this. If you criticise him, you are branded a racist.
>
> So you see, to me, the future of the Afrikaner is dependent on the language. If the language does not exist as a language of tertiary instruction, as a language of academia, as a language of thinking, I don't see much hope for it.'

Returning to the key days of change between 1990 and 1994 and the move from white to black rule, Ampie says:

> One thing that happened to us that was fortunate was Mandela. Because I know a lot of Afrikaners of all kinds, working-class Afrikaners like my mother, who died four or five years ago. No one that I know ever said anything bad about Mandela. That man really controlled the transition because of his personality and because of his power; because of the fact that he was not bitter, he was not angry. I think that was very important.
>
> There was a small percentage of the Afrikaners who knew that the blacks were not going to kill us and rape us. To a certain extent, some people in the church had influence, like Beyers Naudé, and other younger theologians of his calibre. Although to me, the church could have done more. I'm not a supporter of the NG

Kerk. And there was also a feeling at the time of defeatism. You know? 'Here, ons kan niks doen nie. Hulle is die meeste in die land, ons kan hulle nie altyd onderdruk nie. Ons moet nou maar voort gaan en kyk wat gebeur.' (Oh God, we can do nothing. They are the majority in the land, we can't continually keep them down. We might as well go forward and see what happens.)

The English did not want to have anything to do with it. They had their own political party... and, talking about political parties, you can see what has happened to the National Party. It's basically disappeared. Hulle praat die ANC na (they speak like the ANC). There is no more opposition.

I think that they [the NP] did this for reasons of survival – that is the big thing. You could say that apartheid was about survival and the leaving of apartheid was about survival. I'm not concerned about the survival of the Afrikaner as a distinct ethnic group because that's not important. But the survival of the language is important to me; the survival of this language of ours in its fullest flowering.

But there is no togetherness anymore. We have broedertwis (brothers fighting); but to have broedertwis, you still need to have broeders, who are together, who are a clearly defined group. You always have broedertwis, it goes throughout Afrikaans history. But now you don't even have that anymore. We don't even argue against the right-wing Afrikaners like Connie Mulder; it's pointless. They have a good point sometimes but it's pointless arguing.

These Boeremag people are totally stupid, not an inch of heroism about them, nothing, nothing at all. So I think it could be fatigue or it could be that we are transforming into another nation, a bigger nation, without necessarily having Afrikaans as the cohesive strength, becoming bilingual, say, and not having this sentimental attachment to Afrikaans as in the past. I think actually that is what is happening. I think it is only groups like

> those at Orania who can maintain a culture to a certain extent, but limited, and they are not a threat to anyone. They are living in the desert and are not a threat to anyone. But I won't join them.'

I asked Ampie how the National Party bosses had convinced grassroots Afrikaners to accept such a radical change as black democratic government.

> The Broederbond had already started softening up the grass roots. I know this because my previous wife's father was a Broeder, a conservative nationalist, and he said long ago that the Broederbond was talking to its members about having a black president. But that would be just a token president. But even so... I think the Broederbond should not be underestimated in this process of change.
>
> And, yes, there is also this thing, it also comes from Van Wyk Louw whom I mentioned before, the concept of 'die openbare gesprek' (the open public debate). Afrikaners like this, to sit and talk about things. You go to someone's house and you have a topic for discussion and then you talk about the topic. These Broederbond meetings were also a form of oopgesprek (public conversation), but they were not open, of course. But that idea of sitting and talking through a thing was important in the process of change and persuasion, I think.
>
> Another thing which could mean the end of the Afrikaner is our gemoedelikheid (agreeableness). At those first meetings with the ANC at CODESA [Convention for a Democratic South Africa at which the official negotiations took place between the ANC and the Nationalist government], I think things were much too gemoedelik. This is perhaps a weakness of the Afrikaner, or perhaps it's a good thing, I don't know. They become buddies, man. Afrikaners become buddies very quickly – you know, slaan mekaar op die skouer, drink 'n dop saam (Clap each other other on the shoulder and have a

> drink together) and talk and talk and talk. And eventually they can't be serious anymore.

He laughs.

> The Afrikaners are very sentimental, and gemoedelikheid [agreeableness] goes along with this. Another thing worth mentioning is my son Marko. He's 18 and at Westerford School, an English-medium institution. He is sometimes called 'Boertjie', although he's a big guy, and he hates it. He hates being called a Boer. He's had fights about it, not physical, but fights. He never talks about the Afrikaner. He has no consciousness about it, and when I carry on about Afrikaans dying, he just laughs at me.

Ampie returns to the issue that most concerns him, saying that all that holds the Afrikaner together is his language. He says that he shares a similar culture to the Scots South Africans across the road:

> We have koeksisters and melktert and biltong. OK, but that's not culture. City-based Afrikaners don't have a great sense of cultural identity anymore. And if you look at the National Party, it's become weak, it's not important. There are no Afrikaner leaders anymore. There are no strong leaders. I may not have liked the apartheid leaders, but they were powerful. In that sense the Afrikaner is like the African: an African wants a strong leader. A traditional African looks up to his leader. You respect your leader. It's weird in a way that we saw Mandela as a leader and Mandela is black. I think that the only thing that Afrikaners will get together about is the language.

Ampie tells me that a group of people had tried to start an Afrikaans university in Oudtshoorn a few years ago, led by Nick Barrow:

> He's like the boss, the tycoon of Oudtshoorn. He's a big shot, a man with a tremendous image. And he started the Oudtshoorn festival and a youth festival there. The idea of the Afrikaans university, to be based in the old army camp in Oudtshoorn, took form in a few people's minds. We got together twice about this and then Kader Asmal saw me at Stark Ayres, the garden centre here in Cape Town, and he said to me, 'Why are you starting a ghetto?'
>
> So I said to him, 'In the Bible there's this thing about waar twee of drie in My naam vergader.' (where two or three gather in My name') That is good; but if two or three Afrikaners get together, then suddenly it's a ghetto? Its bloody kak, man, it's total shit!
>
> And so I said to him, the point is to have an Afrikaans university. And now Jakes Gerwel has been appointed to head a commission to investigate the position of Afrikaans at universities. And he came out with the suggestion that there should be two Afrikaans universities in South Africa, Potchefstroom and Stellenbosch. And Asmal and them just discarded that. Now they've started a Technikon, and that's OK, that could ultimately develop into a university, but the Higher Education Act states that there shall not be an Afrikaans university.

Ampie looks both angry and forlorn as he says this. At that Oudtshoorn meeting, he says, one of the group was the political scientist Jannie Gagiano, whom he describes as 'a devil's advocate'. Ampie says, 'Everything we suggested, he countered, saying, "Julle's mal, julle's mal, julle's stout, julle's kwaad, julle's kwaad katte, julle kannie argumenteer nie." (you are mad, you are all mad, you are naughty, you are cross, you are angry cats, you can't argue). The next day, he wrote a piece for the press headed "Kwaai Katte?"' (Cross Cats?).

I file this bit of information away, knowing that in a few days' time I will be interviewing Jannie Gagiano. Ampie speaks about the shortage of Afrikaans leaders, and I ask him about Breyten Breytenbach, whom he so admires. He replies:

> Breytenbach is very powerful and a very good speaker and a hell of a good poet, but he is not a politician. But he could put in words what is in our hearts, because he has got the language. I think that he is one of the greatest poets in the world. The irony is that he writes in one of the smallest languages in the world. He is translated now into English and French but it's not the same because he uses Afrikaans metaphors that just don't translate. 'Hy kyk die kat uit die boom.' How can you 'look the cat out of the tree'? 'Die aap is uit die mou' (The secret is out) – 'The monkey is out of the sleeve'. It's surreal, totally surreal. 'Die koeel is deur die kerk en die dominee is dood' (It's too late for tears) – 'The bullet is through the church and the vicar is dead'.

He laughs with delight. He goes on to talk about the use of Afrikaans by coloured people. 'They speak Afrikaans but they prefer English,' he says. 'That is mostly urbanised coloured people; they speak English to their children. Afrikaans to them has no romantic or sentimental value; it's purely a medium of use.'

As I listen to Ampie, the words of the Dylan Thomas poem *Do Not Go Gentle into That Good Night* come to me. Here is a man doing just that on behalf of his language. His language was seen as the language of the oppressor. The attempt to force it on blacks as an education medium lit the fuse of the massive internal unrest in 1976 that marked the beginning of the end of white rule; yet it is Ampie Coetzee's language and he loves it. For a writer, it is his medium and its loss is terminal. I think I understand a little of what Ampie feels, as it's my mother's tongue too; I'm with him all the way on this desire to see Afrikaans have a future.

He mentions Dan Roodt, who has started his own group, Praag, [Pro-Afrikaans Action Group] to save the language. And the singer, Karen Zoid, who takes the opposite view, that it's all sentimental nonsense. This younger generation of Afrikaners who are less concerned about the future of the language call people like him 'old grey men in grey shoes'. He says that

Afrikaners and their language are becoming marginalised, and that he must learn to accept that. 'I don't mind too much,' he says. But he does, he does.

We speak of the Afrikaner's mythology and mythmaking and I ask how much importance one should ascribe to the current interest in Siener van Rensburg, the 'Boer Prophet' as he is known, who lived during the Boer War and whose sayings are being reinterpreted to cast light on the issues of the day in South Africa. Ampie is emphatic. 'Of course they have completely misunderstood him, those people. He was prophesying about the Boer War. It's all nonsense.'

He pooh-poohs any talk of a Third Boer War. Instead, he raises a much more relevant subject, that of Imagined Communities as outlined by the writer Benedict Anderson. Ampie says, 'You make the community yourself; you imagine it. I know the Afrikaner was a construct made through the language of Afrikaans. Now one has to begin imagining the community.'

We speak about the international Afrikaans diaspora, and I suggest that maybe the internet will provide a vehicle for the Afrikaners to create such an Imagined Community – allowing the Afrikaners to exist as a community, at least in cyberspace. Ampie seems taken with this idea and fascinated to hear about the many Afrikaans-medium websites for expat Afrikaners round the world.

Ampie's wife Anna-Ghrette comes in to say goodbye. She's off to Cavendish Square for some retail therapy with Kobus and their house guest. A few minutes later, the phone goes. It is Anna-Ghrette, phoning from the car to say keep an eye and a nose on the springbok haunch in the oven, the centrepiece of their dinner party that evening. 'As jy 'n boud ruik, set hom net sagter,' (If you smell the haunch, just turn down the oven), he reports his wife's words and laughs delightedly. Here is a man still in love with words, with meanings, with his young but expressive language.

Ampie sums up the concerns of Afrikaners. The list is headed by affirmative action, hugely hated by all and particularly by those who have lost jobs or whose jobs are threatened. But there is no fear of any night of the long knives – unlike in 1994, when some people went in for hoarding tinned foods in their cellars against perceived mayhem:

> Crime does worry people, but it's a general sort of fear, a feeling that it's wrong and it should be stopped and that the government is too soft, that they are trying to fight crime in a democratic way. You must remember that the Boere were brutal, man. They were bloody brutal! It's my feeling that the government should be harder on these criminals and frighten them. But there's no feeling among the Afrikaners of 'kom ons kom in opstand teen die regering omdat hulle nie die diewe vang nie'. (Let us stand up against the government because they are not catching the thieves), There is no feeling like that.

Finally, I ask Ampie to describe the Afrikaner as an imagined patient on a psychiatrist's couch. What does he say about this person, the personification of the nation? How would he describe such a mythical person's mental profile, currently?

He says that this is very difficult, not only because there are so many different kinds of Afrikaner but also because the very concept of Afrikanerdom is being dismantled – not consciously, but inevitably, it is happening, it is dissipating:

> If you have an Afrikaner capitalist on the couch, he would most probably be quite happy because the economy isn't all that bad, the rand isn't all that bad. And he wouldn't be concerned about politics anymore. He would even try to do his affirmative action bit, to see that he has enough black, previously disempowered people in his service.

He then considers the response of a lower-income group of Afrikaners, and says:

> I think that in their heads they're living their domestic lives, and they're not really concerned about what has happened. I think – and this is the first time that I've said this – but I think that they're becoming apolitical – except

for my Afrikaans friends who're mostly writers or intellectuals. But the rest are increasingly apolitical and the older generation is still to an extent racist. But not blatantly racist. They're not afraid of the government because they see that there are efficient guys like Trevor Manuel, like Mbeki and [Penuell] Maduna. Yes, I think that they are going on with their lives.

And that in a sense is how Giliomee ends his book. I think he's a bit sentimental, [says Ampie as he reads from the doorstopper.] 'They no longer spoke of themselves as a separate volk with a special calling on destiny, but accepted a common South African identity and a duty to address the challenges that confront the country. Yet they were not attracted to the nation-building creed of one history, one public language, one patriotic party. They were without strong leaders or organisations, but were rediscovering their own particular identity, one that was forged by their own complex internal history and the love of the language that they spoke and the harsh but beautiful land in which they lived.'

Ampie says, 'I don't really think that Afrikaners are rediscovering their own particular identity. I think that is romanticising, but to a certain extent what Giliomee is saying here is probably true.'

I thank him for his generosity in seeing me and in speaking so freely. He walks me back to my car saying, 'Let's see if it's still there.' I doubt that anyone in their right mind would want to steal the old Mercedes, but then I suppose that if Afrikaans is starting to disappear within a century of its birth, an old Mercedes could easily vanish in just two hours. Happily, the car is where I left it. We shake hands and Ampie turns for home, where a haunch of venison is demanding his attention. Tonight there will be guests and roast springbok and red wine, and to me it seems that the Afrikaans culture of hospitality is in remarkably fine form in this the Year of Our Lord 2003.

EDUCATION IN BLACK AND WHITE

It's hard for those of us not personally involved to realise the huge changes in South African education. A man who exemplifies this change is Anton Meyer, the headmaster of Laerskool Groote Schuur, a junior school in the Cape Town suburb of Claremont.

Anton's white Afrikaans Calvinist background didn't prepare him for what was to come, yet he has coped well with change – in fact, he has helped to lead it. He is remarkable in his way. He is a big man physically and also in terms of enthusiasm. Enthusiasm defines Anton – enthusiasm and energy. Although he's now 53, he's still an arm-waving windmill of vitality. I liked the man immediately when I spoke to him from England, setting up an appointment.

His school was the first Afrikaans-medium state school in South Africa to open its doors to all race groups, in November 1989, after 98 per cent of the (all-white) parents voted in favour of this change. As a result, Anton Meyer was at the cutting edge of educational change, his school (today 50/50 black and white) becoming a model for others across the country as he became a spokesman for change.

I have reached him through Karin Cronjé once again – he was headmaster to her and Ampie Coetzee's son, Marko. She describes Anton as 'a very unusual Afrikaner'. He says he will be happy to see me when I explain my mission and is emphatic about the change Afrikaners have made. He says he's 'gatvol' (pissed off) about the ongoing perception of Afrikaners as narrow-minded racists. I like his unexpectedly frank openness.

The appointment with Anton is for 9 a.m. on Thursday, 19 June. When the morning rolls round, I'm the last out of the house. My sister Jay has been up the mountain to walk the dog Monty, a German Schnauzer whose breed name is Rommel. Monty keeps a beady eye on all who approach the house from the unusual vantage point of a happily brown couch in the TV room, over which he drapes himself in a sort of hanging position, the better to get a long view, I suspect, under and beyond the overhanging branches of an enormous plane tree which shades the drive.

As Jay and Monty take their exercise a few hundred metres above the house in Cecilia Forest, my brother-in-law Guy is already on the way to work at 6.45 a.m., aiming to beat the traffic on De Waal Drive. I cannot help but smile at this, thinking about the bloody English M25 motorway traffic, which has shortened my life by months if not years. Guy, too, is part of the new South Africa. A civil engineer by trade, he's had a tough few years, but has recently started a new job with a civil engineering firm with branches in a number of cities across the country. My brother-in-law is a big man, but a quiet one, your typical strong, silent type, but with a very keen sense of humour.

Guy is an anglicised Afrikaner with a fantastic full name: Johannes Guillaume van Helsdingen Louw (a literal English translation would be John William Thing-From-Hell Louw). It's an impressive moniker. His father Alec was a highly respected SAA pilot in his time and served with the RAF in North Africa during the Second World War, putting his plane down once between two lines of Allied army tents when he missed the runway in a dust storm. The plane's wings neatly lifted every guy-rope of the tents along his impromptu runway in a terrifying wake-up call to all the soldiers inside, sleeping peacefully just seconds before they woke in terror.

At the school, I park under some shady oaks. The place looks from the outside like a privileged one in this middle-class and largely white suburb. I make my way inside; on this glorious sunny day, the cool beneath the oaks is already beginning to feel welcome.

Anton is a robust man, and in good shape, casually dressed in an open-necked shirt and slacks. Later I hear he's a keen tennis player, once short-listed to represent South Africa at the game. But, he says, 'I jolled [partied] too much.' He is currently captain of the veterans' team for Western Province.

He has a large office dominated by a round table. He indicates a chair and I sit. On the table is a jokey card that reads, 'People who think they know it all really annoy those of us who really do!' There's a huge painting of District Six (the vibrant coloured and cosmopolitan area of the city which the government declared a whites-only area in 1965 and subsequently destroyed) given in lieu of payment by a parent who couldn't afford the school fees. On the other wall, tellingly, is a big collage, a colour picture of each child in the school and their names and the class they're in. I'm impressed and believe him when he tells me he knows each child by name.

The office walls also carry a number of other photographs: Anton with pupils pictured in *Die Burger*, entitled by him 'The Long and Winding Road'; one titled 'Ebony and Ivory' shows him with the school's first black pupil. It becomes clear in a very short time that he has an encyclopaedic knowledge of pop music, which he loves. He also loves to dance – 'And, man, I love to party!' he says with an engaging smile.

He is not what I expect a headmaster to be. He is a very menslike mens, very much a people person, with a huge personality that seems to run away with him at times. His ebullience makes it hard for him to keep still. There is a great wish to talk, to communicate, to be understood, to connect. Unlike me, he moves constantly and comfortably between English and Afrikaans.

In the first few minutes he tells me that he has not always been a good man. 'Ek is 'n stoutgat outjie,' (I am a naughty chap) he admits with a sense of chagrin. But he says, with disarming simplicity, 'I've come to God and Christianity now. God has accepted me.'

He tells me that he and his wife Madelief have been married for 29 turbulent years. His religious conversion two years ago has given them a new and better relationship, he says. The family has had some tough times recently. But, he says,

'We are taking a step together in faith.' There is a childlike simplicity about these statements that helps me deal to some extent with my cynical response. He is patently sincere and speaks from a deep emotional level that indicates some great pain, which relates to his immediate family, although he doesn't wish to discuss it.

Then, as if on cue, Madelief arrives. She's younger than her husband, and with her cropped blonde hair, silk shirt with a bow at the neck and a tailored suit, looks like a Parisienne. She has popped in specifically to meet me, she says, as she and Anton enjoy making new friends. Picking up where he left off, she says the two of them began praying together two years ago and this has enriched their lives and strengthened their marriage. Their two sons have both been abroad; one is now back, the other still working in London.

She tells me a story that illustrates her new spiritual awareness:

> I was conducting a choir and I saw such pain in the eyes of one of the girls. I took her aside afterwards and found that she had been raped at the age of seven. She said that as she sang this song we'd just done, she was having flashbacks to this terrible incident. It was frightening how easily I might have shouted at her for what could have been interpreted as simple inattention.

Anton says that he and his wife have become charismatic Christians, that 'there is a new song to be sung' and that there is 'a need to invest in people's emotional bank accounts' and that sometimes it is necessary to give emotion reign over the intellect.

All this is still very new for him, Anton says. He describes his youth growing up in Mossel Bay, where his father worked as a manager for the menswear firm Hepworths. He recalls with some pride that his father was unusual in addressing coloured men as 'Meneer', an honorific title not usually bestowed by whites on blacks.

He says that he would have loved to study law, but as the family didn't have the financial resources, he opted for a career in teaching and went to Oudtshoorn College, where he got a bursary. He quickly adds, 'Everyone got a bursary, it wasn't a merit bursary.' He didn't like it there, it was too conservative, but his father insisted that he stick it out.

Things did not proceed smoothly after teacher-training college. Anton recalls that he left his first teaching post in Grahamstown – PJ Olivier Skool – because his work conflicted with his role as a disc jockey at Rhodes University dances in 1971. He speaks of his departure from his first post after getting into some kind of scrape. The first he knew of the trouble was when his then headmaster knocked on his door on the Monday morning. It was not a good start to a teaching career. 'I was living two lives in Grahamstown – 49 per cent of the teachers at PJ Olivier Skool enjoyed me, but 51 per cent didn't like me.' And he laughs with gusto.

Despite this unpromising start, he moved to a teaching post in Upington and worked his way through the ranks, becoming vice-principal before coming down to Groote Schuur as principal in 1987 at the tender age of 37.

I begin by asking him why the Afrikaners gave up power so quietly: 'Hoekom het hulle so stilletjies verdwyn?'(Why did they slip away so quietly?)

He answers this by explaining that the Afrikaner has on the one hand, a profound belief in Christianity and, on the other, is also desperately stubborn. 'I think there was a real feeling of religious change. A feeling of, "Well, we stuffed it up, we have to repent, and change is the way to go". To my mind, the Afrikaners have accepted change better than English-speaking South Africans.' The Afrikaner underwent a form of a conversion on the road to Damascus, he believes:

> I remember very clearly, after we opened our doors to all races in 1989, how I and Madelief went to speak at other Afrikaans schools in the Western Cape – Ceres, Saldanha and many others, twenty in all. We went there by invitation to chat about what we did at this school. You could see such antagonism and aggression when I spoke there. I'd say to them, 'You don't have to change your school. I'm just giving you the Groote Schuur perspective.'

> And then somebody would stand up from the audience eventually and say, 'Listen, boys, we've now heard what that man has said, we've got no option.' It was like walking north and turning south.
>
> I found this everywhere I went. There was, I remember, a guy in Saldanha who was alcoholically propelled. He was standing at the back. He'd come from his golf club. He was a navy guy, a parent at the school, and he gave me a hard time in Afrikaans, saying I was so clever and stuff like that. I just replied that he and the school could do what they liked; I was simply there to tell them about my experience at Groote Schuur. I wasn't saying integrate; they could choose to stay as they were or integrate, it was their choice. I said, 'You can choose to take the ossewa (oxwagons) over the Drakensberg mountains; we're taking the Concorde.'
>
> At every school I went to, someone would eventually stand up, someone brave enough, and in a firm voice say, 'We've got no choice!' 'I remember one day a man from the Koue Bokkeveld, a very conservative area, a very tough and typical Afrikaner, he stood up and said, 'Meneere, Dames en Here, ons het geen keuse nie, ons het gehoor wat daardie man gesê het.' (People, Ladies and Gentlemen, we have no choice, we've heard what the man has said.) 'We must change course!'
>
> One night I was asked to visit a guy's home in Cape Town. I was very suspicious about it, but when I got there, I was asked to speak for 10 minutes about what had happened at this school. This was prior to '94. And when I came in, I saw government ministers sitting there. It was obviously a Broederbond meeting.

People at all levels were clearly very interested in the model Anton was developing at Laerskool Groote Schuur.

He says he believes change came to South Africa because the world has become a global village. 'Sanctions were biting, people aren't dumb; change was inevitable. People didn't want another Boer War. They said, "We must change." The Afrikaner is, after all, very pragmatic.' Anton speaks of the changes in his own life, how he now attends a mixed-race church group each Wednesday, and adds, 'I will not attend a whites-only church group. The time has come for everyone to make a difference.'

He speaks of a dance he organised at the school before 1994 to which he invited a black woman and her husband. 'I was dancing with her. I did it on purpose. I was bum-jazzing with her,' he says, and describes a bump-and-grind routine that I imagine must have raised some eyebrows at this otherwise all-white event.

He says that this black couple spent the night as guests at his and Madelief 's home just up the road. 'I didn't want to look back and think I didn't do enough,' he says. 'So I said to her, come and sleep at our home.'

He refuses to call himself 'headmaster'. 'I hate the word "headmaster". I call myself a learning person. Who wants to be a headmaster?'

He has recently invited his multiracial staff to join him at teatime for a glass of wine and some rock 'n roll for 30 seconds as 'a token that we are free'.

Anton is hugely uninhibited, something of an eccentric, and I ask him how he came to be a headmaster, a man who admits that he can dance with a glass of wine on his head, a man who breaks every convention?

He shrugs and smiles, then returns to the issue of interracial relationships, and tells this story:

> With the older black and coloured folk, they still don't know how they stand with you as a whitey. So this is what I say to these people. I say you have a spirit. I don't know what colour it is. I've got a spirit, you've got a spirit, and your spirit is going to live forever. And the spirit is something that is colourless and colour-blind.
>
> Let me put that story into context for you. When I got here, this was an elite Afrikaans school. Very arrogant. Many of the parents here were parliamentarians. I made a rational decision to change all that because I didn't like to compartmentalise people. That's why I see Christ as a very liberated figure. So when

> people came here with their Afrikaner clichés I tried my best to break them down by doing things like driving into the assembly hall with a motorbike, or saying something controversial in assembly. And I didn't get the flak that I expected.

He contrasts this with his time in the Upington school where, he says, 'If you spoke English there, they thought you were a communist.' He giggles in a very un-headmasterly way at the thought.

His work towards a broader vision for his new school in Cape Town included bringing in a black newspaper seller to an all-white meeting. He asked all those gathered there to put their hands together to welcome this man, including white parliamentarians, and he laughs with glee at the memory. The man was an ANC cell leader, he says, whom he got to know at the nearby set of traffic lights where he sold his newspapers.

Anton contradicts all my perceived and received ideas of the Afrikaner. He's a living testament to the fact that one generalises about a people at one's peril. But he's not without prejudice, he freely admits. He has recently got into hot water for speaking against homosexuality to his pupils. As he puts it, 'I'm still a bit old-fashioned, I suppose. I believe in Adam and Eve, not Adam and Steve.'

The following day there were complaints from two or three parents and Anton then backtracked, telling pupils, 'I'm off-track on this issue. Follow your own ideas.

He has a pupil currently at the school who is something of a celebrity – the junior horse rider Bongani Mvumvu, 14, an international dressage champion. This lad's remarkable story warms the heart. He was discovered living rough in a Phillipi pigsty, among the market gardens and dunes of this outlying area of Cape Town, and today is representing South Africa at equestrian events round the world, thanks to his adopted white family. In 2003, he was named the PSI/FEI World Children's Dressage Challenge Champion in Germany, despite only being in the saddle for three years. He has been a pupil at Laerskool Groote Schuur for three years and Anton is full of praise for this young man, whom he describes as self-confident and intellectually very sharp. It gives this headmaster huge satisfaction to have played a small part in the phoenix-like rise of this child of the new South Africa. It's just another everyday miracle – a black boy being taught by a mainly Afrikaans-speaking staff, and blossoming. Bongani is a symbol of what is possible when people of good will work together.

At the end of our meeting, I take Anton back to his analogy of the colour-free spirit and ask him white South Africa's defining question: 'How will you feel if one of your sons comes home with a black girl whom he wishes to marry?'

Anton looks at me with a big grin and says, 'You've got me now!' He has helped to bring about change in this wonderful country, a 'major paradigm shift', as he puts it, but he's still not free of his history as an Afrikaner. In the end, we're all a product of our hard wiring, our conditioning, and it is the next generation that will move further away from racism in South Africa.

So would he cast out his son if he came home with a black wife? 'I would sacrifice a lot of things for my son. But it will be very difficult, like the Benguela Stream meeting the Agulhas. There is rough water there. That's a tough question,' he says and laughs hugely – in part to hide his embarrassment, I suspect. But I respect his honesty. It would have been so easy to lie.

Anton takes pleasure, and not a little pride, in the fact that black and coloured people have approached him to be their mentor, including one who was sexually abused as a child. He advised this man to find his father and tell him he forgave him 'because it is a great release to forgive someone'.

We talk about how the mass of Afrikaners was persuaded to join in the liberalisation of the country and Anton surprises me once more. He says he was invited to join the Broederbond when he was 42:

> I was intrigued by this, and excited by it, because I knew I would meet parliamentarians there and hear the inside story. I decided that I would join for a year, without telling them this. My father had told me years ago, 'Don't change your bank, stay with the Standard Bank, and

> please never join the Broederbond.' But I decided to go ahead and join them then, 11 years ago, because I saw change coming. There was already talk of big change in that Broederbond cell in '92. There was a shift in thinking, a change in thinking about people of another colour.

Anton now touches on the sore issue of affirmative action and the wish, expressed by many Afrikaners, that a line be drawn under the inequities of the past – something that blacks are understandably reluctant to do. He says the Afrikaner has accepted the status quo:

> Honestly, I think the Afrikaner is prepared to share most of the things in this country. I and other Afrikaners are delighted to see a black man come through on merit, say, for instance, in rugby. We are delighted. But somehow the nation has to leave behind this bias in favour of blacks and be on par with one another again. We have forgotten about the past; now they must forget about it too.

He accepts that while apartheid survived for 40 years, there has only been 10 years since its demise, but in those 10 years, he feels there has been a lifetime of change:

> Through evolution, 10 years is like 40 years to my mind, you know what I mean? We are living faster, quicker, Future Shock tells you that. Technology has changed everything and the last 10 years have been fast-forward. So it's been like 40 years already.
>
> So get real! Give me the same chance as you have. We've been leaning backwards to change. OK, there are still Afrikaners who moan, who speak about not trusting blacks, we cannot deny that. But I also see people wanting to catch up, especially blacks. So when I see a black guy playing cricket for South Africa I'm so happy, I want him to be there. I just want us to become a normal society, everyone the same, with the same chances.

We move on to his new Christian thinking. He tells me that next time I come to the school, there will be an Israeli flag on display:

> There's a new wave of Christians coming. I go to listen to what they say. They talk about the Israelis from a prophetic point of view. You must see the movie *The Rape of Europe*. The new wave of thinking of modern Afrikaner Christians about Israel is that Israel must be blessed. I was with people yesterday who blessed Israel and the Jews. I'm still 'n bietjie dom oor dit (a bit ignorant about that) but I'm learning. The movie is about the Daniel story, where he prophesied the Four Kingdoms. In this he foretold that the Roman Empire would come together again. Now, if you watch the trends in Europe, why does Europe want to unite? In Salzburg there's a building erected that looks just like Babylon. Now Babylon is seen as evil, as satanic. The symbols there in Salzburg, a lady riding on a beast, you see them everywhere. The legend goes that the beast raped the lady in the sea. But I cannot articulate this, verbalise this. There is a new way of thinking about the Bible, but you must watch this movie. Christianity is taking the Afrikaner on a new journey.

All of this charismatic Christianity stuff makes me distinctly nervous. I understand what's driving it, the sense of disorientation, the sense of loss, the need to belong, but frankly I'm not comfortable with it at all and don't trust it one iota. The mix of insecurity, emotion and religiosity makes for an intoxicating spiritual cocktail, in a manner of speaking, with consequences that can be just as dire, I suspect, as overindulgence in the real hard stuff.

Anton says he is for change, but not just following the stream. 'You know, they say that the only one who likes change is a baby with a wet nappy. But a swimming pool that doesn't get stirred goes green with algae. "Love" is a verb. We must change through action.' He says he wishes 'to live from the heart', that he has a vision of his books 'in a great heap with the cross on the top' and, finally, that his reading will stand him in good stead.

He talks about one of his teaching staff:

> She was very angry with whites, she threw stones. She is now in my school. I had an interview with her and I said to the rest of the panel, bugger the rest, I'm going to appoint you because there's something to say for a rebel too. She sings a song from the heart. I prefer that to one who does it from correctness.
>
> She invited me one day to come to Blue Downs, to her house. My Here, was jy al daar gewees? There were just blacks and I was scared. I carried a revolver with me. I ate at her place, but next-door was a shebeen. So I went in there with R10 and they asked me to buy a drink for them and they were playing – can you believe it, the irony – Satchmo's *What a Wonderful World.* 'I see trees of green, la-la la-la...' And so I bought them a nippie (a dram). And when they were finished, I had to drink some of it too, just to show them that I was there in good faith, which is a good ritual you know.'

He goes on to explain how physical factors can bring change – the time he got into a white colleague's car uninvited and, putting his hand on his shoulder, told him he was aware of this man's bad-mouthing him behind his back. The man changed overnight, he says.

He tells of the coloured teacher who had caused him a great deal of trouble and whom he finally addressed by sitting back to front on his chair and asking her to do the same, saying, 'We are not going to keep going in opposite directions. Now, like these chairs, we are going in the same direction. We are both going to face west now.' That, too, brought its reward, he says.

He did a similar thing during assembly when he reversed the normal seating plan for pupils and then spoke about renewal and about new perspectives. 'It's easy for people to understand then, because they can see what you mean, right there in front of them. Sometimes you have to be a little creative.' He's not afraid of the unconventional, and in these unconventional days maybe he is the right man in the right place.

Speaking about change and leadership, Anton raises his blood pressure significantly by commenting on the New National Party and its leader, Marthinus van Schalkwyk:

> 'Kortbroek'? (Shortpants) Aaagh! No man, he's a nothing! I tell you, and Leon is an a nothing too! But Kortbroek is everything that we don't want in this country. Ons soek liewers 'n ou wat se hare deurmekaar is en wat 'n bietjie rof is met 'n rowwe uitspraak, maar wie is diè klein kat? (We would rather find a chap whose hair is a mess and is a bit rough and who speaks in a raw way, but who is this little cat?)
>
> You take the charismatic black leaders... I mean, some of them look strong, you know, hulle hemde hang 'n bietjie uit maar (their shirts hang out of their trousers), but this guy will never form a New National Party. He's enough to upset anybody's blood pressure!

Anton is a man who speaks to people in elevators. He's not afraid to reach out. 'The other day I hugged a black guy in church,' he says and, laughing, he shows how he overwhelmed this short black man who was somewhat taken aback, it appears. I'm not surprised; being hugged by Anton must be something of a total experience.

He repeatedly makes the point that while there is a lot of racial tolerance in the liberal milieu of Cape Town's southern suburbs, Rondebosch, Newlands, Bishopscourt and Constantia, this is not necessarily the case in Upington, a town in the remote Northern Cape, and other areas in the boondocks. Older realities linger there. Speaking of the future, he says there are a lot of insecurities:

> You can't deny that. I think people don't care about black majority as long as it's fair. If whites can be in a contest for a job and have a fair chance, then OK. Jobs are important, because if you ain't got a job, you ain't got money, and if you ain't got money, it kills the dream. My son has stopped dreaming about this country because of this. I also think there's no place to hide anymore,

> because there was a mass exodus of our young people to the UK about 10 years ago. People said, 'Fantastic, spread your wings.' But you want to live in the same country as your grandchildren.

Tougher times in South Africa have brought positive things too, he maintains. It has forced whites, and Afrikaners particularly, to be much more innovative:

> They've come up with some fantastic ideas. There are two kinds of Afrikaners, the one who has given up on this country and talks about the crime and how they haven't got work; and there's a second group, a pragmatic, innovative group, who say there's no place to hide anymore; we have to make it work in this country. So there are two definite roads. But sure, the future looks bleak to a lot of people, because if you haven't got work, well, that's that. And there are so many people who haven't got work in this country. The crime rate is high and you can understand it somehow.
>
> But there are also a lot of white people bridging the gap, leaning towards blacks, and maybe it's artificial at the moment; it will take time to become natural – visiting blacks in their homes and having them in yours and getting over feeling a little bad because you still have more than them. I still think there is a lot of goodwill. It's just a question of integrating more, negotiating more, talking more, communicating more. Breaking down walls. Trying to get the emotion that we have to do something for somebody else.

His school is 'adopting' another school of 1,500 pupils in Atlantis, the tough settlement north-west of Cape Town. 'Half of them come from shacks. They have nothing. I sent a letter to the parents of our own pupils, asking them to lead this initiative. You have to reach out to others. It's coming back to Christianity again. Walk the extra mile. It's better to give than to take.'
He's tired after three hours of talking. He leans back in his chair and invites me to dinner at his home on Saturday evening.

There's something about this man that touches me, his African physicality, his energy, his simplicity, his role in change, his honesty, his energy, his limitations, his passion, his naïveté, his hospitality. There's wisdom here, and also a desperate search for meaning. It feels to me as though Anton is a good symbol of the Afrikaner - still trekking, still in search of something, making a not inconsiderable contribution as he goes.

Almost Behind the Boerewors Curtain

The press is awash with the ongoing debate on racism. Democratic Alliance leader Tony Leon has accused President Mbeki of using the race card every time he wants to silence his opponents on any sensitive issue.

Leon says that on President Mbeki's watch, the country has moved from the politics of the Rainbow Nation and reconciliation to the politics of race-labelling and race-baiting. Leon describes the president as 'flaming' critics – using a barrage of intimidating, hostile, derogatory messages to silence his accusers and end dissent. Leon says Mbeki has done this on issues of poverty, AIDS, Zimbabwe, joblessness and crime. 'We need to get out of the cul-de-sac of racism and return to the inspiring vision of a Rainbow Nation,' argues Leon.

The President has not taken this lying down. In an article in the *Cape Times*, Mbeki turns on his accuser by quoting a white Afrikaner professor from Stellenbosch to make his case on racism for him. Professor Amanda Gouws of Stellenbosch University's politics department says:

> We have not yet moved beyond the politics of the past (to) where we can have open debates about the past and students can formulate their own positions on reconciliation. Students have not progressed beyond the us/them divide – clearly because white and black students do not share the same interests and have not developed a collective voice. Reconciliation is the status quo. A

> consequence of this perception is that white students can remain passive – they have to do nothing to change the status quo, while black students have to be politically engaged to change it... Thus the challenge remains: how can reconciliation be brought down to the grassroots level?'

The President says he quotes the professor because what she describes at Stellenbosch is in fact true of the whole country. He adds that he also quotes her because if he said this himself he would be accused of playing the race card. He adds, 'We did not achieve liberation in order to perpetuate a master-servant relationship in our country. Let me make this clear once and for all: there is nobody in our country, or anywhere in the world, who is going to stop us from confronting the cancer of racism and continuing to struggle to build a non-racial South Africa.'

'Whites,' he says, 'are keen to forget the past, while blacks neither want to nor will forget the past. Persisting racism and racial disparity constitute an obstacle to the goal of national reconciliation.' This, it seems, is an unwinnable argument for either side; it is an issue that will run and run.

It seems like a good time to take a look at what is described as Africa's greatest shopping experience – Century City, Canal Walk – on the edge of Cape Town, where I am to meet Eben Cruywagen, of Radio Sonder Grense.

Canal Walk is immense, described by some as Boere-Kitsch-Gothic. Its halls and malls are crammed with hundreds of shops, fast-food joints, restaurants – every imaginable commercial transaction takes place here, and all of life is here too. One could easily get lost in this place. I'm early, so I stroll the halls till just before 7 p.m.

Eben has suggested the Canal Walk venue to save me a trip from the southern suburbs out to the northern suburbs of Bellville and the surrounding area popular with Afrikaans speakers, which he describes as going 'behind the boerewors curtain' (the farmer's sausage curtain.) I'm much taken with this description, which I've never heard before, and rather sorry that I'm not to be invited behind this culinary dividing line.

Eben is a slight figure. His wife, Theresa McArthur, is a

distant relative of the famous US war leader, General McArthur, she says. Both are actors, or were actors for many years. They make an unusual couple and they intrigue me.

After some discussion about what to eat – steak or fish? – we head for a restaurant, a not-too-distant walk away. We're shown to a table with a view and order. Theresa wants hake, fried not grilled (they usually grill it, the waiter says, but a quick look at the set of Theresa's jaw and fried it will be); Eben asks for calamari and sole, and I have kabeljou, which is delicious, with the bottle of local dry white that Eben orders.

Eben broadcasts and also lectures in media theory at Stellenbosch. Theresa works at a factory that produces wooden pallets. She runs a developmental course on the side at this factory to teach some basic skills. The place is staffed by some very tough black and coloured workers, she says, so she uses her acting experience to show them, among other things, how to use a toilet. That is how basic some of the skills needed are, she says. Many of these people have never seen a piece of equipment like it before.

The staff come to her with some very personal problems, including sexual ones, asking for her advice. She tells the tale of a black male worker who believed his ex-wife had put a spell on him, making him impotent. Theresa sent him to a GP who also specialises in toormedisyne (traditional magic medicine) to take off the curse. This is, she says, an everyday African reality, as real to blacks as the Bible and Christian faith are to whites.

She says with pride that her black staff call her 'Mama' and say to her that when God made her, He had obviously run out of black skin so she had to make do with a white one – the inference being that she's a good black woman under that white camouflage.

By the end of the evening, it emerges that this is another couple who pray together just before going to bed, sometimes in English and sometimes in Afrikaans. They don't say which is more effective.

It is Theresa who taught Eben his near-accentless English by getting him to talk with his mouth almost closed, and she shows me how she achieved this by pushing on his cheeks, compressing his mouth. She then demonstrates on herself how the characteristic sound of Afrikaans comes from a much more widely open mouth.

Theresa, it is soon clear, is a formidable personality. She told Eben at the outset of their relationship, 'The marriage won't last a year if you try to change me.' But, she says, she has also had to make allowances, getting used to Eben's one great fault, for example. It would appear that he has no sense of time at all, while she is punctual to a fault and compliments me on being five minutes early for our meeting.

The fact of the matter is that she and Eben have a good thing going; their 30 years together says it all.

As our food arrives, we get to the point of the evening – politics. Theresa says that there was a point at which she wished to leave South Africa. She used to carry a panga in a sheath down her back and wielded it once in anger when she found three black men in her car. She laughs, recalling the incident: 'They ran for their lives, and that changed my attitude to the situation here. I decided we should stay.'

They agree that the Nationalist government began using American TV, which featured middle-class black actors, as a means of 'preparing us for change'. Personally, I am not sure about the accuracy of this view, but it is Theresa's considered opinion.

Like all South Africans, they speak well of Nelson Mandela and his pivotal role in change. 'The Madiba magic was that he said, "The past stops here. Whites have as much right in the new South Africa as blacks." He saved the country.'

The handover phase – the Government of National Unity – was, they say, crucial. 'It gave us a process, instead of an umbilical cord being cut off.'

They are optimistic about the future of the Afrikaans language. I prick up my ears; this is not what I've been hearing from Ampie Coetzee. But this couple agrees that 'the language is secure.' In fact, they believe that the language has been liberated. 'The brown Afrikaners, the coloured people, will keep the language alive. The richness of the language comes from them.' They also point out that there are now departments of Afrikaans at Russian and German universities. And blacks are speaking Afrikaans, they say.

Change had come to South Africa, they explain, because 'a generation of Afrikaners had arrived who were prepared to do business with blacks'. Afrikaners had not been given much credit for this, they felt.

I ask how the Afrikaners feel now, after nearly a decade of black majority rule. They reply that two-thirds of Afrikaners feel there's light at the end of the tunnel, and a third feel all is lost. There will be no complaints, however, provided Afrikaans and the Springbok emblem are retained, they say. 'As long as people speak Afrikaans at home, dream in Afrikaans, write Afrikaans and get emails from Afrikaners overseas in Afrikaans, things will go well with the language. Afrikaners have learned that you don't have to be dominant to be Afrikaans.'

They speak about integration of black and white and coloured on the country's playing fields and the number of mixed-race couples you see today.

Theresa says that, without doubt, there is a sense of loss among Afrikaners, 'a sense of heimwee, but largely it is a good life, better than we expected.'

Eben points out that the area of the country in which you live can skew your view of the political realities or the success of the new South Africa. 'Cosmopolitan areas aren't the same as the platteland. There, things are still much as they were. But the kids do think differently now. That is a very big change.'

And he makes what I think is a very important point, that in the days ahead I will hear confirmed by other people I meet: the fact that the Afrikaners are not alone in their fear of cultural and language loss; black parents are facing the same issue. 'Their kids are growing up with new values, a new language, a new culture. We are now all part of a worldwide culture, a global 'Americanisation'. So blacks, too, are facing a future in which their own cultures are under pressure; the Afrikaner is not alone in this.'

We talk of the resurgence of interest in the Boer prophet, Siener van Rensburg, and Eben and Theresa do not discount his impact on modern Afrikaners. In fact, they point out that the 1994 elections were as peaceful as they were, in terms of Afrikaner participation, because many believed in Siener's prediction that all would be well with the volk.

On that note we call it a night and I spend far too much time trying to extricate myself from the mall.

Serendipity

There are times in one's life when things go so right they scare you. This trip has been a bit like that and one day in particular is really astonishing, as much for what had gone before as well as for what was to come. This is how it is on Friday 20 June 2003.

I have an appointment at Stellenbosch University to see Professor Albert Grundlingh, chair of the history department. I read that his particular specialisations included the Boer War, the history of ideas and War and Society – perfect for what I am seeking.

As I drive, I pass many men, pushing supermarket trolleys along the road into Stellenbosch. They are loaded to the hilt with 3m lengths of wood, no doubt for building shacks or for firewood.

Stellenbosch is basking in a mellow 23 degrees of winter sunshine, the branches of oaks dappling the white and green architecture. On the steps outside the history department, there are half a dozen black students, so dark they look blue-black; they appear to be from other parts of Africa, and so it proves – the building also houses the department that deals with foreign students. In the lobby, a group of blonde Afrikaans girls, looking like Barbie dolls, stand and chat about the end of term and the forthcoming holiday. I look from one group of students to the other, amazed that all this has happened, and without the total meltdown I expected.

These two student groups remind me that while I have a number of senior academics who have agreed to be interviewed, I haven't lined up anyone young at all. A Stellenbosch student would be a good idea and, taking a deep breath, I march up to the group of young women rather hoping one of them will invite me for coffee and a chat. When I explain what I've come seeking, they're unanimous: 'Gaan praat met Yvonne Malan.' Yvonne, they say, is finishing her Doctorate of Philosophy and has served on the Student Representative Council; she has a lot to say for herself and isn't scared of controversy. She sounds ideal.

I make my way up to Professor Albert Grundlingh's office, finding it easily enough and knock on the door. Professor Grundlingh welcomes me. He has been head of the history department for two and a half years. He has shrewd eyes, is in his fifties, I reckon, has artistically long hair and a moustache. He looks a bit like an older French musketeer. In a movie, he'd be well played by a ruffled Gerard Depardieu, I think to myself while making small talk. Albert Grundlingh looks comfortable in a navy double-breasted blazer, a zigzag navy and white tie and baggy grey slacks. He tells me that his wife is a psychiatrist.

We get cracking on my reason for being there. He says that the Afrikaner did not 'just go quietly':

> In the 1980s, a real stand was made. I don't think one must underestimate that. This was the time described as one of 'Total Onslaught', which saw the introduction of a full conscription campaign, the setting up of the Civil Cooperation Bureau and all those dirty tricks. That did represent a stand. That's also when the Afrikaners' search for justice and survival played itself out. You've got to survive in justice. This made a moral difference, the need to survive in justice.

I can hear the echo of Van Wyk Louw. He says, 'Becoming a republic in 1960 was the fulfilment of a dream. The thing, though, got out of hand when the Afrikaners got rich and they could afford these excesses. If they had to choose between BMWs and swimming pools and ethnic identity I think the BMWs had a head start.'

But that wasn't a choice they had to face just yet. 'The economy grew hand over fist and farmers were getting £1 for a pound of wool. Things were booming. We were doing almost as well as Japan or California. The Afrikaner became part of the early global growth pattern. This, of course, was on the back of repression of trade unions and repression of political activity.'

There were other factors that began to change things, brought about by a questioning of the values associated with domination, he says, and points to a thesis on the End Conscription Campaign (an attempt to stop the call-up of 18-year-old conscripts). 'Even popular Afrikaans music like that of (well-known Afrikaans performers) Koos Kombuis and Johannes Kerkorrel in the Voelvry Toer (Free Bird Tour) carried this message, mocking the laager mentality and the army call-ups.'

I suggest that few people outside that laager realised just how fertile a debate was going on. He makes the point that even now there are those who don't want to understand the significance of that debate among Afrikaners. 'The longer you can demonise the apartheid government, the more it suits current politicians: the comparison with Nazi Germany, which I don't think apartheid can be compared to; all that talk about genocide. In fact, the black population actually grew during the apartheid years.'

However, he adds, 'I think white people should refrain from expressing an opinion on what apartheid did to people, as we didn't experience it for ourselves, didn't experience the pain and the human suffering.'

Afrikaans youths increasingly questioned military service, as they bore its ever-greater weight, being called up for an initial two years, followed by frequent camps, he says. The consequence of national service was that young Afrikaners were increasingly wondering what it was in aid of, adding to the debate within Afrikaans circles.

Professor Grundlingh says it began to be clear that South West Africa (Namibia) would be 'given to SWAPO' (South West Africa People's Organisation) when that country got its independence:

> In the townships, there was a civil war. The military began to worry increasingly. The generals also became

> aware of the fact that you may have a military victory but you'd never have a political victory. The military could have staged a coup and Constand Viljoen did think about that. He was the one general who commanded a lot of respect, among both military and civilian leaders. But eventually he came to the conclusion that you could have a military coup, but you'd still have the same problems the following day. You'd still have the same political problems. So that scotched that idea.'

But, I ask, you still have the fear of swartgevaar (black danger). How do you move from an intellectual assessment of an insuperable problem to an emotional acceptance of your wives and daughters being in the hands and the power of the black masses?

Grundlingh says that one must look for the answer to this question in the referendum of March 1992, when 67 per cent of whites voted for dialogue:

> Not [he emphasises] for an ANC takeover – that is a crucial distinction. They [the white electorate] voted for cultural rights to be maintained. That was the assumption, for weights and counterweights, for cultural space to be protected, and for language to be protected. So what that 67 percent voted for was South Africa as they experienced it at the time, minus apartheid. That is what De Klerk and the National Party promised. It turned out, of course, that in the negotiation process, the ANC were much more adept than the Nationalists, and of course also the Boipatong massacre was useful for the ANC.'

Ultimately, he says, the Nationalist government didn't give up power; 'they were pushed'. (The Boipatong massacre on 17th June 1992 came at a critical stage of the Codesa negotiations when armed Zulu hostel residents enraged by attacks on the largely Zulu Inkatha Freedom Party supporters, killed 45 men women and children in the Vaal Triangle township of Boipatong. ANC politicians argued that the massacre was carried out by a 'third force' of police and soldiers, though this failed to stand up in court.)

Grundlingh goes on to speak of the weakness of the National Party negotiators. Roelf Meyer, the lead negotiator, was at the University of the Orange Free State at the same time as Grundlingh, though he didn't know him personally:

> Meyer grew up through the ranks of the ASB, (Afrikaanse Studente Bond) you know, student politicians, and the Nationalist Party. These people only spoke among themselves. They never had a broad exposure to any hard negotiations with people from a different sort of culture and background. Meanwhile, the ANC had people like Joe Slovo, who had international experience. Our guys were very parochial; they never had any heavyweight training in negotiations like the ANC, who had more international diplomatic contact than the South African government had at the time. The government had been frozen out internationally.

During the subsequent Government of National Unity, the Nationalists didn't realise that everything, including cultural issues, had to be renegotiated, he says. 'Things went well the first year. There was none of the bloody transition that everyone had feared. Then the Rugby World Cup came along in 1995. This had a major impact, showing that South Africa can be a normal country. Afrikaners exchanged rugby for ideology and it wasn't a very good deal.'

I find it hard to believe what I hear, and a month later, in summery Sussex with bees buzzing in the July roses, I listen to the tape again and again to make sure I heard right. Bloody rugby! Who'd believe it? Selling your birthright for a mess of pottage, as the biblical story of Cain and Abel has it, sounds a good deal by comparison. The rugby thing has always been something of a mystery to me. But then, I never played it. Grundlingh speaks of Mandela with faint cynicism – the only person I spoke to who does this:

> Mandela, he of the studied stoop of humility. I've

> watched this guy and how he operates, you know, shuffle, shuffle. You know, you can't buy that. You know, they put this guy in jail for 27 years and he comes out and seems very agreeable. He's a smart politician, a very good actor. He's remarkable. I'm not saying that he's cynical, but once he'd found this role, and found it worked well; then he carried on with it. After a time, I'm sure he didn't even realise that it was a role anymore. But he had to find that. He's a different generation, mission trained. The African bourgeoisie produced people like him: black anglophiles.

I ask what Mandela's range of fancy and formal shirts worn loose over his trousers say to him. 'They're African chic put onto the body of a black anglophile. It's not a real African jungle type of design either – it's very sophisticated.' For once I'm speechless, and thankfully the good professor moves onto a new subject.

Grundlingh says of the Christian revival that's making its presence felt on the Stellenbosch campus:

> This charismatic Christianity started locally in the 1990s – while the Dutch Reformed Church was losing so much of its flock, the charismatics were on the march. It's a sort of feel-good religion; you don't have to worry too much about what you've done wrong in the past. Here on campus, the students flock to it. The Dutch Reformed Church is losing members. It can't hold onto its youth and is worried about how it's going to survive.

Later, speaking to my cynical old father, he says this is what lies behind the NG Church's sudden warm welcome of its separate sister coloured church. It needs the numbers. He could well be right.

> Afrikaners have four choices [says Grundlingh]. They can buy into Mbeki's nation-building; they can make money; they can emigrate; or they can find a safe, nostalgic past to live in. Those are the four basic choices.

> [I refrain from mentioning a fifth option – the Boeremag route, violent white opposition to black domination.] Religion can fit into any of those four but it doesn't have to be dominant, because material circumstances now dominate to a much greater extent than before. People are trying to maintain the position they have been catapulted into since the 1960s. So that's where the real challenge is: the material rather than the spiritual.

Sticking with things spiritual and material, I ask about the Boer prophet. On the issue of Siener van Rensburg's prophecies pacifying the Afrikaners, he says this is fanciful:

> The atavistic 'lurid rurals' like those of the Boeremag are the only people who pay this stuff any attention. Siener was a bit of a conman, a spin artist, and he suffered from epileptic fits during which he 'saw things.' He lives by crises. Every time there's a crisis, some people will turn to stuff like this. It is in part because of the setbacks the Afrikaner has suffered, decimated during the Boer War and pauperised by the Depression.

The conversation becomes more general and we talk about people we know and, as is almost inevitable in this small white society, we find someone in common. One of those amazing moments occurs in which history becomes personal, and your worldview shifts slightly; it's another instance of serendipity. I mention a few names from my South African past. At one name, he looks up and smiles. 'Van die Vrystaat. Ja, 'n ou skelm, wat Basutoland toe gevlug het in die oorlog. Hands-uppers,' he says. (From the Free State. Yes, an old crook who fled to Basutoland during the Boer War. One of the hands-uppers, the surrenderers.)

Hands-uppers? I ask, knowing he's referring to Afrikaners who gave up in the face of British might. These were no hands-uppers, I say blithely, sure of myself; this family provided the country with a president, for heaven's sake!

Grundlingh smiles that smile again, and says, 'Yes, the person concerned was a very good politician. But the family was hands-uppers all the same. They farmed outside Bloemfontein and when war broke out they just moved themselves and their stock across the Basutoland border, where they waited out the war.'

Now it's my turn to smile and shake my head. I say to him, 'God, you Afrikaners are hard, unforgiving people, with very long memories! You're worse than the Jews.' The professor likes that; he laughs delightedly.

We move on, after a time, to speak about where he feels the Afrikaner is today. He says:

> There's a great sense of disillusionment and ambivalence. But there's also a re-emerging sense of tenacity. Afrikaners feel that this country is still theirs also. They are still learning their politics in the school of hard knocks. This includes a desire to retain places that they feel are theirs, like the University of Stellenbosch. Free State University is about 65 per cent black; at Pretoria the numbers are approaching that, as are the others. So Afrikaners feel that they're entitled to a university for Afrikaans-speaking people. These are the issues that Afrikaners organise around today – maintaining cultural spaces.

The arts festival in Oudtshoorn (Die Klein Karoo Nasionale Kunsfees), he says, was set up as a deliberate attempt to establish an Afrikaans cultural space, not only for white Afrikaners, but for coloured Afrikaans speakers too.

He says that the arrival of black students at Stellenbosch was very difficult at first, but today it's taken in stride by everyone. I describe the two groups, black and white, male and female that I saw on my way in, and he says, 'They're very polite to one another. Maar hulle kry nie vatplek aan mekaar nie,' (they can't get to grips with each other) and he laughs as I do, at the unintended double entendre. And as if on cue, there's a knock on the door. It's a student from Gabon asking for a quick word. Politely, the professor asks the student to give him just a few minutes more and then he'll be with him.

Stellenbosch, Grundlingh tells me, is much like a

university in the Midwest of America – essentially conservative, though catering to people from very different ethnic backgrounds, and trying to reach out, trying hard not to be too parochial. He's very concerned that Afrikaans will be lost:

> If the language doesn't fulfil any higher-order functions, scientific functions, academic functions, then obviously it's going to lose a lot of its impact, a lot of its compunction, for people to learn it. It's a real threat. English is such a powerful language, when you run it alongside Afrikaans it just swallows it up. And these youngsters, these kids, they see that as a plus, they want to learn English, they realise that if they want access to the wider world they need English. They realise their futures are limited in this country.

Does he see new Afrikaans leaders emerging?

There is no one with any charismatic appeal, he says. 'They will not easily forsake the comfort of middle-class existence for the uncertainty of politics under the dominant and autocratic ANC rule. You need a political platform, a political programme, and you need to appeal to black people. It is a tall order.' It is indeed.

I tease him gently about the Afrikaner's new 'weddedness' to BMWs, swimming pools and shopping at Pick 'n Pay, and suggest that within such a view, Raymond Ackerman, the company's chairman and founder, surely deserves a medal for helping to stave off Afrikaner unrest.

He laughs and says, 'He staved off the revolution! And provided a consumer revolution instead!'

I add that my 11-year-old daughter likes to wind me up by saying, 'When the going gets tough, the girls go shopping!' Is this what has happened to Afrikaners? They're avid mall strollers today. Have they given up on the ververlate vlaktes (the distant lonely landscapes)? He does not disagree.

He says, vis à vis Ferdi Greyling's comment about Tobruk, that at least 50 per cent of the enlisted South African men during the Second World War were Afrikaans. He laughs and adds that Ferdi Greyling also comes from Oudtshoorn, 'though he is a bit younger than me.'

'The Oudtshoorn Clan,' I tease, as I'm finding that there are so many links to that town among the people I'm randomly speaking to. Why is Oudtshoorn becoming such a cultural fulcrum? I ask.

There's a very practical reason, he says. The place has many halls, venues for performing arts, standing empty. It's as simple as that.

When he hears some of my own mixed family background, Grundlingh directs me to a book by Karel Schoeman, *Die Laaste Afrikaanse Boek* (*The Last Afrikaans Book,* Human & Rousseau, 2002), set in Paarl of the '50s and '60s. He describes the writer as having a good recall, though the book, he says, is self- indulgent.

'That's what I specialise in!' I tell him, laughing. 'Self-indulgent books. Self-indulgent isn't a bad word in my lexicon.' What else is there? What keeps you tucked away in a room, typing for months, talking to yourself? The first rule for a writer, it seems to me, is a certain amount of self-indulgence and inward focus. Not easy for others to live with, though.

I tell Professor Grundlingh that I'm off now to find Yvonne Malan. He nods emphatically. 'Very articulate; you'll find her very interesting.' I thank him and bid him farewell.

Outside Grundlingh's door I pass a group of black students. They're from all over Africa, something that would have been unthinkable just 20 years ago. Things change; the only constant is change. That is what my life has taught me.

I consider the loss of Afrikaans and accept that it would be a little like losing my mother a second time. But when I compare that small loss with the huge loss of potential suffered by blacks in Africa through the worst of colonialism, and in South Africa in particular, through apartheid, it seems a small price to pay. After all, there are other languages, other songs to sing.

Turning round in my head, as I do from time to time, to look into my second ethnic mirror – the Jewish one – I think that the Jews lost their language after the destruction of the Temple 2,000 years ago which preceded their departure into every corner of the world. It didn't cost them their essential identity, though, and today, once more, Hebrew is being spoken in Israel.

This, then, is the crucible that now faces Afrikanerdom. It will forge a new, stronger Afrikaner identity, or burn it to a crisp. Time will tell.

It is bad of me, because while I like to tease, I'm not too keen on being teased myself, but I can't help it – I find myself throughout the trip passing on this comparison with Hebrew, and suggesting that if Afrikaners are patient and strong, they, too, may be speaking their mother tongue once more, in its full literary, intellectual and scientific glory, 2,000 years from now. This thought gets a mixed reaction.

I make my way down the road to a rather more modern building with a set of lifts and go up to the sixth floor to meet Yvonne Malan. She's a slight, boyish figure, with short brown-blonde hair, dressed casually, and it soon emerges that she has run the Comrades Marathon three times. Last year, she came 33rd in her age group. She also plays soccer.

She's an unusual philosopher. Behind her hangs a mock-up of a *Time* magazine cover with a picture of George W. Bush, below it in bold type the words 'We are fucked'. Here, it seems, is a new generation of Afrikaner. It quickly becomes obvious that she's not averse to breaking taboos.

She sits with her arms crossed, almost hugging herself, a little shy, cautious, unsure just who I am and what I want, but there is a staunchness there, a bravery. She is petite but strong, like a finely wound-up steel spring.

She was born in Pretoria, she says, but grew up in the Cape's Overberg region and went to school in Somerset West. Her doctoral thesis is titled 'Deconstruction and the Ethics of Resistance'. It will doubtless not be light reading.

I explain the central theme of my book and again serendipity strikes. She tells me that she too is a Boerejood! Her mother's people arrived in South Africa from Germany in the 1930s. Her mixed religious background isn't an issue for her, it seems:

> I grew up with a fairly open-ended view of identity. My family never enforced any specific identity on me. The

> fact that a third of my family doesn't even speak Afrikaans and others are Afrikaans writers was never a problem – just a great way to make interesting connections. And even though I'm related to Andrew Murray, the Scottish missionary, through one grandmother, there was never any sendingsdrif (mission drive). Rather, my family tried to teach me to stand up for the underdog. To be a bystander was just not on! They also taught me that one is a South African first, before any tribal loyalties.

Her Malan ancestors were Cape rebels in the Boer War, she tells me. This war once again casts a long shadow. Here is the offspring of Afrikaners who might have sat out the war in the comfort of the British-controlled Cape Colony, but who opted to go north to fight alongside their brothers and cousins, putting at risk all they had in the Cape. Somehow, I'm not surprised to hear this. Yvonne has the look of eagles about her.

We begin to talk about the Afrikaners and she describes them as 'a very authoritarian people, who follow what their leaders say.' This, she indicates, is now changing fast in the reality of the new South Africa:

> Today the young aren't focused on the language and the church. Identity is more about which soccer team you support and the kwaito music you listen to. Culture is much more broadly based. Mixed schools ended the fear of the 'Other'. Now the swartgevaar are one's friends. We've grown up with interracial dating.
>
> I guess the two generations differ markedly in this. The older generation's sense of Afrikaner identity was produced by fears, fears that my generation no longer have.

A few weeks after my return to Britain, I receive a number of emails from Yvonne about aspects of her life she feels might be relevant to Boerejood. One reads, 'Our soccer team is the only team in our league that has players of all race groups. One of the many upsides of that, no matter where we play, is that we're sure of group support. If we play one of the "black" teams, all the "coloured" crowds cheer for us, and vice versa. Our team finds it very funny.' She adds another snippet that casts a curiously powerful light:

> Something else I found really interesting was Madiba's 85th birthday. To PW Botha et al he might have been the enemy, but today he is everybody's favourite grandfather. On his birthday people could SMS him messages which the SABC screened throughout the evening at the bottom of the TV screen. And the messages came from everywhere, from blacks and whites, from Guguletu and from the van der Merwes in Boksburg!

She adds to my sense of the 'commercially comfortable Afrikaner' by saying, 'Afrikaners like M-Net, cell phones and their creature comforts today.' But they are not comfortable with everything, it appears. 'The older generation is confused, not sure which battle to fight right now. The language issue is a big thing for them, while young Afrikaners see language as a creative force, rather than as a bastion of culture.'

Some young people, she admits, are bothered by affirmative action and they go abroad, but generally come back after a time. AIDS and corruption are two issues that 'we also get upset about,' she says.

Ultimately, though, young Afrikaners want to be part of a bigger South African picture, she says, rejecting the vision of a breakaway Afrikaans group. 'The Orania people are seen as a bunch of complete idiots. They are a standing joke. No one will move there.'

Yvonne is irritated by President Mbeki and Tony Leon's ongoing debate about racism. 'Let's play with the possibilities of the future,' she pleads. And she says something that instantly stops me and my flying pen: 'The old men with grey shoes, the decisions are no longer with them. We no longer rely on identity politics. This is simply not an issue for my generation.'

I realise that by some incredible piece of luck I have found myself sitting before Ampie Coetzee's accuser.

Serendipity rules! Yvonne explains how she got up at the recent openbare gesprek (public meeting) at the university and gave the Group of 63 – 'their average age, not their number,' she says, scathingly – a piece of her mind. As a result, she has taken considerable flak.

She says, 'You do know that my name is mud around here? In *Die Burger* the next day there was a huge piece by Hermann calling me a rude youngster who should know my place. This triggered letters to *Die Burger* and to me personally, calling me a volksveraaier' (a traitor to the folk).

She is not without support, though. Poet and author Antjie Krog and philosophy professor Willie Esterhuyse both intervened and defended her in the columns of the newspaper.

I think to myself: 'Who would turn a butterfly on the rack?' Not that Yvonne is a butterfly in any way, more like a tiger, admittedly. But, dammit man, she's 25 and a young woman and brave. Why not pick on someone your own size?

Yvonne suggests that I make a point of seeing the theologian Professor Jaap Durand. 'He's my hero,' she says. 'I hope I can be half as brave as he is one day.'

In a tribute to the man she calls 'Oom Jaap', she says: 'Do you know the saying, "The soul of one good man is worth as much as all the earth?" Oom Jaap is one of those guys. He has this absolute instinctive sense for justice and this utter outrage against injustice.'

Later in the trip I will see a photograph that goes some way to explaining Yvonne's homage to Jaap Durand. It's a newspaper picture taken of Oom Jaap on the University of the Western Cape campus in the heart of the 1980s turmoil. It shows a huge crowd of people running away from the cops after being tear-gassed, sprinting away, climbing over fences, desperate to put as much space as possible between them and the forces of law and order. Against this backdrop there's a lone figure, academic robe flapping behind him, with a look of pure outrage on his face, waving his fist at the cops and walking towards them determinedly. It's Jaap Durand. I guess that kind of sums him up. No wonder he elicits loyalty from those who understand the courage it takes to stand alone.

It's recommendation enough for me. Jaap Durand is

currently the Stellenbosch University ombudsman. He also serves on the University Council and was formerly the vice-chancellor of the University of the Western Cape and much involved with student politics during the darkest days of apartheid. He is an old opponent of the previous regime. I make a note to set up a meeting if he will agree to see me.

I'm greatly impressed by Yvonne. I'm impressed as much by the sense of integrity and intellectual honesty that emanate from her, as with what she says. I believe South Africa will hear more of this young woman. If Afrikaners are to have a future here, she is definitely going to be part of that future. Yvonne, you may or may not realise it, but you are already running in your fourth Comrades Marathon (the big one, called Life) and you are well up in the lead pack.

As I leave, she puts out her hand and I shake it warmly, when in fact what I want to do is hug her, this Boerejood girl who makes me proud of my mixed heritage. I ask if I can buy her lunch, but she declines graciously and I take the lift down from the sixth floor. It seems a long way down.

I feel flat and also hungry. I find a spare table at De Dros. The place has a sunny piazza where students congregate and a TV crew – from the university's media department, I suspect – is busy filming. I eat a steak roll and sip a beer. I feel old. Too much damned serendipity for one day. It knocks you out.

Ontspan (Relax)

It is Friday night, 20 June and I'm meeting Karin Cronjé for supper. I'm taking her out to thank her for the great publicity she has helped to generate for my first book and for the invaluable leads she has given me for my second.

We have chatted on the phone and e-mailed each other, but we have not met as yet in person. I may have mistaken the time we'd agree to meet and I'm there at five to seven. Our table has a window view of the courtyard garden and the bar on the other side of it. I can also watch customers arrive and play the game of wondering which one she might be.

I order a gin and tonic, write up some notes from my day in Stellenbosch and at 7.30 p.m. Karin arrives. She is tall and has astonishing eyes, blue, and slightly slanted. She is an attractive woman, with a fragile glamour about her. I have sent her a first draft chapter of *Boerejood* and after we are comfortably seated with drinks she gets down to business: 'Ag, you know we've heard it all before, how terrible the Afrikaners were. I think you must explore your reasons for leaving South Africa more deeply.' There is no beating about the bush here.

She means well, there is a far-off look of 'writerly' preoccupation as she says this. She is herself just finishing her second book. How she finds the time to be a single parent, promote other people's books and still write amazes me. But I know that writing is like a weed, it will come up through the cracks in the paving stones; there is no stopping it once it gets hold of you. I make notes of her thoughts and we move on to possible titles other than *Boerejood.* I suggest 'Liewer bang Jan as dooie Jan' (Rather cowardly John rather than dead John), only half joking. I know only too well that the costs of cowardice are legion.

Over supper we move between courses to the bar across the courtyard, to allow her to indulge her nicotine habit. She has started smoking again nine months ago she says, when she sat down with the manuscript of her second book, which she began six years ago. She smokes hungrily and we continue our peripatetic dinner between two poles – the bar and our dining table in the restaurant.

She is uncompromising about emotional intelligence and speaking the truth to an almost uncomfortable degree. And is as open and insightful about her own life as she expects you to be about yours. It's a level of honesty and communication that cannot be sustained by me, it is too exhausting, but for one evening it's like holding your hands to a blazing fire – warming body and mind.

We talk of writing and she says that she finds it an agonisingly slow process. She recognises that extraordinary feeling that one gets when one is writing well – that it comes from somewhere beyond you. Her work as a publicist – promoting the work of other writers – is not always easy. But at least it keeps her in a writerly milieu.

We talk of shoes, Ampie's red shoes and the accusation that he was an old grey man in grey shoes. She says the red shoes are post-divorce, so she doesn't really know why he wears them. I am touched by the unexpected kindness with which she speaks of Ampie, her former husband.

She talks of her first book, *Vir 'n Pers Huis*, described as perverse by some, brave by others, and tells of an old flame who read the book and has now reappeared in her life saying that having read it, he now understands her. She smiles a sphinx-like smile and I feel a moment of pity for the old flame.

As we speak, I understand that this is a woman walking round with the thin skin of a writer and the artist's savage soul. Her new book *Alles Mooi Weer* (Everything Beautiful Again) should, with luck, be out next year.

We talk of land, loss and identity. She speaks of how she has felt herself to be an Afrikaner in internal exile. She describes how this feeling abated one day in a sudden warmth she felt for her two nieces and their friends, recognising their Afrikaansness, loving them and their mutual culture, having once rejected it, having a sense now of 'my mense'. I feel a powerful recognition of that moment.

At five past midnight we are the last guests there, still talking animatedly, when we are asked, not to leave, but to move to another part of the bar while they wash the floor and stack the chairs. We take the hint and I walk her back to her car. It has been a remarkable evening.

The Dinner Party

At the Alphen Hotel I meet up with Fiona Archer, a longstanding friend from my horse-riding days on the Cape Flats. She is an ethnobotanist who studied at Stellenbosch University and has worked with the San and the Nama peoples for many years on developmental projects. Despite her very Scottish name, she is a true Afrikaner and, surprisingly, an early member of the United Democratic Front, when to be such was not a comfortable option for anyone, least of all a blonde Afrikaans girl. I respect and admire her greatly and count her among my best friends.

Fiona has arranged a number of contacts for me to speak to, including her sister, the actress Elizabeth Archer, and her brother-in-law Johan van Jaarsveld, a playwright. It is years since I have seen Fiona but our friendship, like all the best friendships, allows us to simply pick up from where we left off.

Fiona tells me that she's comfortable with the political changes in the country. 'I'm free of the guilt of living under the apartheid regime and free of the influences it had on my choices. And, although it's very difficult to make a living now, at least you know that you, and only you, are responsible for your survival.'

She adds, 'Of course, it is distressing to see that those who always spoke of acting fairly and justly, may, after all, have rather more selfish and greedy objectives.' But she is optimistic:

> I love the new South Africa because I've been freed from guilt and the sense that I have to make up for what my family and ancestors created here. And it's joyful to

> discover my own people, not as the enforcers and the oppressors but just as people. Now that we are the oppressed, I can explore the poetry of the language and the cultural aspects I enjoy – no longer spoilt by any sense of our being oppressors.

In these words, she speaks of the reasons, the many reasons, why I call her a friend.

Before I know it, we are driving up an almost vertical road to reach Elizabeth and Johan's home. A boisterous black and white bull terrier comes bouncing down the steps to the gate to meet us, making some fairly scary noises till he recognises Fiona and turns into a wagging machine.

As we eat, we talk about South Africa, a country that for them has changed beyond recognition. For them, Elizabeth and Johan, the political changes are devastating, because in effect their livelihood disappeared with the axing of so many Afrikaans TV programmes. Currently, the language represents only a tiny fraction of TV coverage, not enough to provide a living, they say. The result is that they have had three tough years as the literary sea in which they swam dried up. Now both are working in English or directing productions in African languages.

They believe that black South Africans feel strongly anti-Afrikaner and certainly associate the volk with all things negative. Johan and Elizabeth appear resigned to an extent and feel the volk has been abandoned to the ANC.

They tell me that Pik Botha, the former Minister of Foreign Affairs, is still very bitter about de Klerk relinquishing power. Pik, it seems, wanted the Government of National Unity to run much longer than it lasted. Then they say something that leaves a little silence: they believe that the Afrikaner is a law-abiding citizen 'up to a point'. I am a guest in their home and I let it go.

Despite this fighting talk, they don't see many options for themselves. Orania, they say, is about avoiding reality. Tellingly, they point out that many farmers still think they are little kings on their farms, although many are being killed, especially the old and the vulnerable.

And then those strangely South African phenomena,

sports and politics, come round once more. Johan says, 'Our lack of success on the sports field – in rugby and cricket especially – is having a really depressing effect.' This, he says, could increase the Afrikaners' sense of grievance against the regime.

Meanwhile, times are tough. On the surface, things look good. Elizabeth still rides her own horse each day, but this good life seems fragile now. Then Johan comes out with a stunner. We're talking about why the political change occurred in the way that it did and he says, 'FW basically lost focus because of his affair with that Greek woman.' The 'Greek woman', Elita, is now his second wife. His first wife, Marika, was murdered.

Elizabeth falls around laughing and says, 'You know, Johan never says very much, so when he does open up it amazes me, some of the stuff that circulates in that mind of his,' and she slaps him lovingly.

Johan adds that the Nationalists didn't exactly field their strongest negotiators against the ANC. 'We put up all the lightweights, like Roelf Meyer, who was basically told not to rock the boat.'

Later, after coffee, Fiona and I take our leave and drive round the mountain to Constantia. I think that Johan and Elizabeth may simply have been unprepared for the scale of the changes confronting them. Maybe they believed such change in South Africa was impossible? They aren't alone in this. But the new South Africa is a reality now and the tough economic choices it brings with it are not easy to reconcile with their previous life or expectations.

Both Fiona and Elizabeth still live what may seem an enviable lifestyle. To anyone on the Cape Flats it would seem incredibly luxurious. But for these two women, struggling each in her own way to come to terms with the huge changes in the country, it is not easy to cope with the financial implications of survival. They see how far they might fall and how easily it might happen and it frightens them, I suspect.

The survival of Afrikaans would not only mean a great deal to many; it would also help a people to survive culturally and economically. But if a language is to be crucified what of English, of German, of Spanish? Do these, among so many others, not also have blood on their vowels, metaphorically speaking? Should we justify the disappearance of a language because of what was done in its name? I fear that there are people who would say 'yes' to that. But they do not speak for me.

Johan and Elizabeth's struggles, like fish gasping for oxygen in a dying river, are not something I can feel neutral or calm about. Some would say the world has lost hundreds of languages and loses more each year – so what if Afrikaans goes? This is no argument. Every human artefact, tangible and intangible, has value, for each illuminates our world. The language of the only white tribe of Africa deserves saving, for it is part of our common African heritage. We will all be the poorer without it, without its writers, artists, poets, singers, playwrights and actors, without its vitality, humour and ingenuity.

I am not as sanguine as Yvonne Malan, but then I am old enough to be her father. In the UK, the National Trust spends billions saving and restoring old homes that are seen as part of the national heritage. Is Afrikaans not part of South Africa's heritage?

Nelson Mandela's place in history is secure for all time because of his generosity of spirit, his capacity to forgive, his leadership. He is what we all aspire to be, a great human being. That is why he inspires love. Can his inheritors meet that standard? I would like to see the ANC do all it can to save Afrikaans. This act would place the new regime in the hearts and minds of Afrikaners more securely than anything else.

It is not politically necessary to do this. Afrikaners are, after all, just seven per cent of the population, Afrikaans speakers just 12 per cent. But what an ornament this act would be, speaking as it does of moral breadth of vision, of cultural generosity, of bigness of spirit, of wisdom. And let it be said, this act would be more generous than that of the Afrikaners, who tried to force their language on others, creating an explosion from which they are still reeling. Is that not the very reason to do this? To be better than them; to act justly?

Where is the black or brown poet, the new Van Wyk Louw, who will say, 'We must rather die as a nation than live unjustly'?

I find that there are times when there are no English words to describe my feelings, and then I turn to Afrikaans. 'Laat ons taal lewe so dat ons van julle geregtigheid kan sing!' (Let our language live so that we can sing of your justice.)

'SUBVERSIVE' LITERATURE

Many people have told me, 'You will like Professor Louise Viljoen,' and despite this, I do, instantly. You'd be an odd fish if you didn't. There's much to like about the chair of Afrikaans and Nederlands at Stellenbosch University.

To meet her at Stellenbosch, I decide to take the coastal route from Muizenberg and then over the N2 via Baden Powell Drive, avoiding the early-morning rush hour traffic over De Waal Drive. It's a lovely route that allows me to see all my old fishing haunts – Strandfontein, Swartklip and the cliffs of Seagull Beach where I once buried a cache of lead sinkers. It's a bit like riding the big dipper, giving me a very strange feeling in my gut. I'm unprepared for the emotion aroused by this road, cutting as it does across many of my former paths to the sea – first with my father and his friend Pascoe Grenfell, to fish, and later, on my own, on horseback, from Wetton and Philippi down through the dunes to these beaches. The road takes me effortlessly along the coast and over my past life. But for the odd car, all seems quite deserted, just one solitary black jogger on the beach at Strandfontein who has the look of a boxer in training. When, an hour later, at 10 a.m. sharp, I walk into Professor Viljoen's sunlit office in the Arts Building with its views of the surrounding mountains, I'm greeted with a warm smile and a firm handshake. How could I not like this woman? I have the almost instant feeling of 'hier is een van my mense' (here is one of my people). She has that effect on many, I suspect. She is tall, in her late forties, capable looking, and has an air of competence about her. She is known as a very good literary critic, besides being a leading academic in her field.

I ask her what I have asked everyone else: why the Afrikaners relinquished power, seemingly without a struggle, when I had expected decades of blood and guts. She replies frankly that it's a question to which she does not know the answer. However, she says, Afrikaans literature might have had an impact. 'The Afrikaners are a difficult group to define. They're not as unified as people from outside believe them to be. There were critical voices from very early on.' How, then, did Afrikaans literature affect South African politics?

> At first, before the 1960s, Afrikaans literature was used by the regime as a tool, appropriated in a certain sense by Afrikaner nationalism, to help it establish the Afrikaner as a separate nation with a separate language, a worthwhile literature. The early Afrikaans literature, before the 1960s, was, you could say, nationalist literature. Going back now to that literature, you see all sorts of ambiguities in the texts.

The professor makes the point that Afrikaners had always embraced their writers and artists rather in the way the French do. This is in stark contrast to the way in which the English regard their writers and artists – as a suspect bunch of bohemians, probably up to no damned good. So when Afrikaans writers began to write subversively and against the idea of Afrikaner hegemony, a literature that was critical of the excesses of Afrikaner nationalism, as the Sestigers did – Breyten Breytenbach, Etienne Leroux and André Brink, for example, who made their names in the sixties – they were still writers and so they were still respected. These writers, despite their ethnicity, helped to articulate the moral argument against apartheid.

This subversion was boosted when young Afrikaans writers did their national service, often serving on the border during the war against communist forces in Angola in the 1970s. They came back even more determined to oppose what they saw as the imposition of an evil system. The effect of conscription was to create a counterculture. This army literature, known as die Grens Roman (the Border Novel) by Etienne van Heerden, Alexander Strachan, Koos Prinsloo and George Weideman, among others, spoke out strongly against the then Nationalist political thinking. These young national servicemen were extremely critical of the role of the government.

This particular genre was assisted in its aim by another kind of novel, die Plaas Roman (the Farm Novel), which started out with a romantic view of the farm in the '20s and '30s but which later, in the '60s, turned against this view, seeing the farm as a microcosm of the larger society, where a patriarch dominated his wife, children and servants. All were placed in a hierarchical order, the baas at the top, the women submissive, the black and coloured people peripheral. This new kind of Farm Novel showed how the reality of the farm culture bolstered the status quo, strengthening the white Afrikaner male in his position of dominance. The effect of these books was to undermine and subvert this farm culture and its under-strutting of the regime.

Two works stand out in this genre - Etienne van Heerden's novel *Toorberg* (Tafelberg 1986) and Etienne Leroux's *Sewe Dae By Die Silbersteins* (Human & Rousseau 1964) - the first of a trilogy known as *To A Dubious Salvation* in the English translation.

Thus, subversive border literature and farm literature paved the way for change, Professor Viljoen believes. Its effect was magnified by the powerful place Afrikaans writers had in the affections of their readers:

> Writers were public figures, even if they were very critical of the status quo. Look at the figure of Breytenbach, an enfant terrible, extremely critical of the apartheid government, yet still embraced by the literary system, getting literary prizes from his first volume of poetry onwards. They may have despised his politics but they celebrated him as a writer.

This celebration of Afrikaans writing gave writers a platform and a status that the government couldn't effectively counter.' 'It was quite a sturdy literary system, perhaps the strongest in South Africa. The whole system of Afrikaans publishing – writers, critics and publishers – was a powerful lobby for change.'

Louise also points to the huge impact of the book by Elsa Joubert, *Die swerfjare van Poppie Nongena (The Long Journey of Poppie Nongena)* in 1978. 'This book exposed the structural violence of apartheid and in effect conscientised Afrikaners. The book relates the story of a black woman born in Upington, who grows up speaking Afrikaans. She moves to Lambert's Bay, where she is married, and then goes to Cape Town. There the Group Areas Act and the homeland policies force her to move to the Ciskei where she has never been in her life. This was the Afrikaans book that truly opened the eyes of Afrikaners; it was a very human story. They said, 'We didn't know this was happening.' A lot of Afrikaans people who felt very comfortable in their farmhouses or suburban homes and who thought apartheid wasn't such a bad idea were shocked when they were confronted by the nuts and bolts, the reality of apartheid.'

And now Louise Viljoen makes a statement, which was said to me in many different ways by many others I spoke to. 'The Afrikaners are a very pragmatic people and they could see that apartheid wasn't workable anymore; something had to be done.' This feeling was echoed and emphasised by their leading writers, she says. The combined effect, she believes, brought some pressure to bear on the government. Just how much, it is impossible to say.

As she speaks, the perhaps unworthy and uncharitable thought comes to me: Now, in retrospect, was the effect of these young Afrikaans writers being reformed into some kind of intellectual and moral fig leaf for Afrikanerdom, giving Afrikaners today the freedom to say, 'Look, we were never the monsters you made us out to be. Look at what our writers, artists and intellectuals were saying at the time.' But Louise is not seeking to duck anything. She says to me, speaking about the Afrikaans identity:

> You explore the effect that certain elements have had on your identity. Some of them are appalling but you cannot

> really argue them away. They are there. You are resigned to the fact. Some of the symbols of Afrikanerdom, [the former national anthem] Die Stem, certain very nationalistic songs that were part of your upbringing, and of course, Calvinism. But you're quite resigned to it. You know that you can't really change it. I cannot deny my roots; some of it was positive, some of it was negative.'

Young Afrikaners, on the other hand, she says, are simply not worried about preserving things. 'They tend to be more dynamic, make new connections, move to new spaces. This is something that is perhaps difficult for older Afrikaners to envisage.'

She says that during the 1980s she was very pessimistic. 'I thought, how can we solve this without a revolution or a bloodbath? The relief when things went the other way was enormous. It was so unexpected and so strange. For such a determined group of people to hand over power like that... it hasn't happened elsewhere in the world. It was a huge shock.'

We touch on the issue of the relationship between Jew and Afrikaner and she says:

> There is an identification between the Afrikaner and the Jew because of Israel, the Israelites entering the Promised Land, and the Afrikaners entering what they saw as the Promised Land. That is one of the parallels that often gets drawn. But then I think that Afrikaners were not free of all the prejudices about Jews. But on the other hand, they lived in such close contact with them.
>
> I grew up in die aangrypende lelike dorp van Vredenburg (the arrestingly ugly town of Vredenburg). Such a dried-up and ugly little town, but that's it, that's where I came from and it's something that you don't deny. And Jews were an intrinsic part of the community, a respected part. You lived with them, you dealt with them every day. My father was a chartered accountant and he often had dealings with Jewish attorneys; they were good friends. And I had Jewish friends, very gracious and well-educated people. Today, of course,

> many of them have gone, but for me, my generation, we lived intimately with Jewish people. And there, in Vredenburg, I found that familiarity bred respect, not contempt.

The thought warms me. She does even better then: she makes me laugh. She tells me a joke. 'What is the difference between a Jew and an Afrikaner?' I shake my head, braced for the worst. 'Wel, hulle se 'n Boer maak 'n plan, maar 'n Jood maak 'n plan wat werk!' (They say that a Boer makes a plan, but a Jew makes a plan that works!) And she laughs like hell and I join her.

I have been wrestling with internal devils as Louise speaks, because she moves me greatly. In her tone I hear my mother, her kindness and generosity. As I listen to her, the cost of my 24 years abroad is borne sharply in on me. All the things I forfeited by leaving, the sense of belonging, the sense of community, the almost-instant connectedness with people of like mind. I find I have to hold hard to control my emotions. Imagine what she'd think if the tears began to roll! I say to myself, 'Bloody hell, get a grip!' And I hear England in those words. The lip stiffens. In the end I manage, though only just.

Louise speaks about the changing nature of Afrikaans identity and says, 'Orania doesn't appeal to the majority of Afrikaners. It's just not an option. People are too comfortable as they are.'

The impact of globalisation on young Afrikaners is a great reality, as it is for English-speaking South Africans. And this affects identity, which is not static. 'The Afrikaner is constantly evolving. Young Afrikaners going abroad hasten this process. They are becoming world migrants and in the process they see different cultures, different perspectives. It changes them and they return to South Africa with different views.' Once again, literature is ahead of the game, she says. 'So much of Afrikaans and other writing wrestle with the problem of identity and how to define it. I have roots which I cannot deny, but I personally feel that I'm still evolving.'

Black parents, too, are concerned by the changes they observe in their children, she says. 'Black South Africans my age are appalled by the fact that black teenagers don't know about

1976 and frankly don't give a damn about it; they have moved on. Life does move on. New formations of identity emerge.'

Something that saddens her is a coping mechanism she has seen compiled by those who leave the country: 'A lot of my kids' friends and their parents have emigrated to the USA. Quite a number of these families have made scrapbooks that list the horrors of South Africa to help them cope with homesickness. I think that's terrible. It's like defiling your own mother, taking these negative images with you.' It's the first time I've heard this and my own experience perhaps makes me more sympathetic. I know that had it not been for my wife, I'd not have lasted more than one winter in Britain. So, if people are serious about leaving, a scrapbook of South Africa's gothic horrors may be just the thing to see them through the dark night of the soul that is facing them abroad.

Louise adds, 'We are migrating again. For my generation, this is strange, that we are becoming emigrants again.' I interject, 'A second Great Trek?' and Louise says:

> Ja. It makes me sensitive to the fact that I'm the descendant of people who also migrated. That is also a part of my history, because I'm descended from Dutch and French settlers in the country. So my forebears have been here for about 300 or 350 years and I had a very settled feeling. I still have a very settled feeling. I have no wish to go. I will stay here, for better or for worse. It's not that I think South Africa is perfect or the best. It's in a sense like your parents: it's what you have, and you just cope with it. I'm fairly fatalistic. But then, I'm not a very scared person. I just live my life and what comes to me will come to me.

I tell her I envy her, that I'm rather more wedded to the idea of 'liewer bang Jan as dooie Jan'. She laughs and says, 'But what people find if they emigrate is that they have not escaped all problems.'

I can only agree. I tell her that recently London was expecting a biological attack on the underground tube system and that police have been patrolling the perimeters of Heathrow

Airport to prevent terrorists from using missiles to shoot down aircraft. Perhaps South Africans who are staying on should compile those scrapbooks from the overseas press?

We talk about what it is to be Afrikaans and Louise says:

> In a certain sense, we tend to withdraw into a laager. Sometimes I think, though it may sound silly to say it, that Afrikaners are shy. That withdrawal into the laager – maybe that's 10 per cent of the reason for it. There was also the idea, of course, that we have to be pure and are best on our own, the whole apartheid thing. But on the other hand, they have this principle about hospitality, being good to the stranger who comes through your door – and that seems to fight, in a sense, with this laager mentality. The moment this poor person steps through your door he is entitled to your hospitality. But today I think the Afrikaners have given up the idea of being in the laager. They are now part of a larger world and surviving quite well. There are still some people out there who are uncomfortable, but they are getting used to it.

We gossip for a moment about Karin Cronjé's book *Vir 'n Pers Huis*. Was it well received? I ask (professional curiosity on show).

'Yes, it was well received,' says Louise. 'I wrote a review of it. I thought it was quite a gutsy book, especially in its exploration of certain feminist themes. I thought it was a brave book, very frank about sex and women.' And now I get another surprise. Louise adds:

> Afrikaans literature goes very far, in fact it goes the whole hog, with sex. You wouldn't believe it. You have gay writing in Afrikaans that is the frankest that you can get. I think a lot of people don't know that. It has all happened since the 1980s. The most explicit gay writer is a poet called Johan de Lange. Very explicit gay poetry. Then there is the short story writer, Koos Prinsloo, who has now died. He was very controversial – explicit about gay sex in his books. He also wrote about real people and

> brought them out of the closet. There was a furore about his books.
>
> Outsiders think Afrikaans literature is fairly dowdy, stodgy, Calvinist, Nationalist literature. But from the '60s onwards it has been exploring politics in South Africa, the army, the border, the farm, sex and gay literature.

It seems that the more I learn about the Afrikaners, the less I feel that I know them. As always, the simplistic stereotyping of people is shown to be wrong. The truth, it seems, is always a disappointing - or, for that matter, an exciting - grey, not entirely one thing nor the other.

David Kramer – Another Boerejood?

I'm happy. I'm on my way to meet David Kramer at a café at the Cape Town Waterfront. He is a hero of mine and a South African icon. He is a singer, playwright and entertainer whose down-home music – a strange Cape crossover, a mix of English and Afrikaans – has tugged at my heartstrings for all those years in Europe. He, like me, is a Boerejood, I believe, who grew up among Afrikaners, in his case, in Worcester, on the other side of the mountains.

As I drive, I think of the changes in fortune of Jews and Afrikaners in the last half century. The remnants of Auschwitz starting from scratch in Palestine, who today are seen as a brutal force themselves; and the Afrikaners, once lords of all they surveyed, now a little-tolerated minority in the country they once owned, 'bywoners in die land van hul vaders' (tenants in the land of their fathers). It is a strange inversion.

Having found the café, I sit in a quiet spot. I wonder if I will recognise Kramer in the flesh. Just then I look up and meet the eyes of a slight man walking past, his hands in the pockets of his baggy trousers. On his head is a small, incongruous, pork-pie hat. I'm fairly sure that it's David, but never having met him I hesitate and stay seated. Then I get up and look down the mall at the retreating figure. There is something of Charlie Chaplin in the walk, feet out sideways, neck in, hands in pockets. Upright and aware. Of course, it's him!

I get up and wait for him to come back to the café. After a few minutes he returns and I introduce myself. We order coffee and begin to feel each other out. There is something cautious about him, something of the hurt child about his eyes and his slightly stiff body language. He bends from the hips, holding his upper body still. When the odd passer-by notices him and smiles a greeting he half bows, formally, from the waist, smiling.

He is nattily dressed in corduroy. A wheaten jacket, chocolate trousers, and (damn!) brown leather shoes. The trademark red shoes are just for the stage, he says. He wears a white button-down shirt done up to the neck and that brown pork-pie hat with a guineafowl feather, which he keeps on throughout the interview.

We speak first of his family history and he says that he and his wife Renaye are both from Worcester. He says that he doesn't really qualify as a Boerejood, that it's 'a bit of mythology that has built up' around him. But he explains that he does have a mixed South African background that goes back to his grandparents.

> On my mother's side, my grandfather was an Afrikaans Jacob Muller, descended from a butcher or a baker who came from Germany in the 1700s and worked at the Castle in Cape Town. Jacob Muller was a hairdresser who called himself a 'Professor of Hairdressing' and he went to London and did the Queen's hair at certain points. He met and married my grandmother there in London. She was British.
>
> On my father's side, my grandfather came from Lithuania, as a 17-year-old, just before the turn of the century in 1899. His name was Karabelnik, but he adopted the name Kramer here. He had two brothers who went to America who also called themselves Kramer. All this family history is rather vague, as it was never spoken about.
>
> He started out in Namaqualand and then ended up in the Klein Karoo, in Oudtshoorn, working for a feather buyer. Oudtshoorn was a bloody El Dorado. He met my grandmother there, a Miss van der Vyver, and got married, and I suppose he kind of adopted the

> Christian faith. My impression was that at the end of his life there was a huge yearning for him to go back to what he was.

He continues to explain his identity:

> For the Afrikaners, what is it about them? It's kind of important for them to know if you are Jewish or not. What usually happens in interviews with Afrikaans journalists is they have the impression that I'm Jewish and will ask me, 'Jy is mos Joods, nê?' (You are actually Jewish, aren't you?) And I would never deny or confirm any of that stuff. So it became generally thought that I was Jewish, which is fine by me. But I'm not anything really.

I tell David about being described as a 'fokken Arabier' by an Afrikaans sergeant in the army during my national service, a man who was as confused as I was about my correct religious appellation. David Kramer laughs. It is a good moment.

Where does one fit in? We agree that the Jew and the Afrikaner have a somewhat conflicted relationship that makes it far from simple. He says:

> There is some kind of tension in terms of the 'Tribes of Israel' and 'God's People' and then wanting to bring people to the Christian faith. Which is what I think happened to my grandfather.
>
> Being a teenager here on his own, he must have been in a household where they kind of persuaded him to accept Jesus. What happened then was that a much younger brother came out to South Africa and there was a big argument, because the younger brother was very frum (religiously Jewish). And ja, so the family split up. My grandfather never mentioned to us, my father or me, that we had any other relations in South Africa. It was only through my own research with my brother in the late '70s that we found there was some family in Johannesburg. I had also discovered some family in Israel. We traced my grandfather's brother and sister in

> Jo'burg and then through the Internet found we had family in Israel and even my father's cousin who lived in Lithuania until after the Second World War. He survived all of that.

David grew up among Afrikaners. He says it's hard to remember what he thought of them during his childhood and teenage years:

> I went to Boys' High in Worcester and there were three Afrikaans classes and one small English-speaking class in each year. So within that school environment we were slightly isolated and different, a mixed bunch of people, the sons of Greek and Portuguese café owners, Jews, the sons of the English, Scots and Irish who worked in the Hextex factory and the sons of English-speaking farmers. And Afrikaner nationalism was on the ascent. We were taught by some aspirant Nazis. There were volkspele (folk games) and folk dancing, people grasping for some kind of white culture.
>
> It felt terribly confined and suffocating to be in Worcester in a school environment like that. Most of the teachers were bullies. And then there was the army experience. So when I came out of that, the last thing I wanted to do was speak Afrikaans. I had absolutely no interest in anything Afrikaans at that point of my life. At home we switched between English and Afrikaans, you know, that whole Boland code-switching thing. My Lithuanian grandfather only spoke Afrikaans, by the way. But I distanced myself from that.
>
> Then I went to Leeds University and was confronted by the British folk music scene. I became quite active performing in the folk clubs. I was quick to realise how ridiculous my situation was. I'd come out of Worcester with my repertoire of late-'60s popular songs – Donovan, Simon and Garfunkel, Joni Mitchell, Randy Newman, the Beatles and various other things, I suppose, and of course the big one at the time was Cat Stevens. So, I realised that this was not going to work for

> me, a South African trying to sing in these voices. So I became aware of voice and I became aware of South African identity, of how different I was. You know, you suddenly see yourself through someone else's eyes. And you become very aware of your difference. What most people do then is run from that identity, suppress that identity and try and merge as quickly as they can. And I also did that. I did a lot of that.
>
> But two things were happening at the same time. On the one hand, when you came back to South Africa, you wanted to sound as British or foreign as possible; but meantime, in Leeds, I was becoming more and more South African – particularly in my writing. I had started to write South African songs in matric already, a whole hotchpotch of stuff – on the one hand trying to sound like Procol Harum and on the other hand I wrote a song that I could still perform today called *Annette van der Wa*. I was 18 when I wrote that song. She comes from Koekenaap. And it is in the essential David Kramer style. Maybe these things are sent to you.

And he laughs. 'Look,' he says, 'there is a pirate ship!' He chuckles with delight. And ghosting past us, there is, indeed, a pirate ship, with brown sails and a Jolly Roger flag. David continues:

> I'm a reluctant writer. I find it quite hard to put my bum on a seat and song writing isn't quite like writing a novel; it's inspired at first and becomes a craft after a while. The big thing is to recognise a fresh idea and then hang on to it for dear life. Ideas used to come to me much more easily when I was younger, but then I did not always do something about it, I suppose. There is a certain laziness and reluctance to put things down. I'm more dedicated now.

I ask if he sleeps with a notepad by his bed. He says not, though he does wake up in the night with what 'seem like brilliant ideas. And then I can't remember them in the morning and when I do remember them they don't seem so wonderful,' and now he laughs from the belly. He talks passionately about the things that trip his creative juices.

One such is Koos Sas, a San whose skull sat in the Montagu Museum for many years, with the name 'Koos' written on its forehead. He wrote a ballad about Koos Sas in 1982. 'I felt that the spirit of Koos just wouldn't let me go, you know?'

He kept a notebook about Koos that he wrote using his left hand, although he is normally right-handed. It was an attempt to connect to the right side of his brain. He'd also been drawing with his left hand in the art class he was taking at the time. 'So I wrote in a very childlike hand. And one morning I woke up and wrote a song, which was about a dream. It was called *Ek het gedroom van water.*' This whole episode left him feeling that he was a vehicle for another's voice. He speaks about being in therapy. I ask specifically if he is comfortable about me writing this and he says, 'Ja!' He continues:

> They put you into this kind of semiconscious state and then you have to imagine who your spirit guides might be – that sort of thing. And one of the images that came to me was that of a Bushman. And then I was reminded that when I was a child I made a diorama in which I used model Bushmen. I always wanted to be a Red Indian in the 'cowboys and Indians' thing. So for me there has always been an identifying with those kinds of cultures. Their stories have more appeal to me than anything else.

He has an endearing way of talking. He thinks and then he talks and then he thinks some more and then he talks some more. It is evident in what he says that there is a mind at work, a good mind, and that he and it are in discussion before its product is committed to speech. There is a definite hiatus that makes notetaking (and, later, downloading the hours of tape) easier than usual.

He says that he was one of the first national servicemen in 1970 to be called up for a year rather than nine months. He confirms that he is 52, just a year younger than me. 'We were told that if we did a year, we would not have to do camps.'

In 1971, he went to Leeds University in England to study textiles. On his return, the army tried to get him to do camps but he managed to scotch that. 'If they had made me do camps or tried to send me to the border I would not have come back to South Africa from England.'

In 1977 he and Renaye emigrated to America. He explains, 'After the 1976 uprising our vision of the future was pretty pessimistic; we did not see any future here for having a family. The long-term future looked really bleak at that point. So we went off to America to try to make a new start there. I got a job down in North Carolina at a place called Raleigh, in textile and tobacco country.'

Before this, he had worked for three years as a textile designer at HEXTEX in Worcester, who had sponsored his original trip to Leeds University. He had not had any interest in textiles, he says, but managed to get a bursary from HEXTEX and so went off to England. He became a weaving designer for menswear cloth, arranging the necessary engineering.

He technically deconstructs the Harris Tweed jacket and the shirt I'm wearing and explains that knowing how to make different cloths, how to actually engineer this on machinery, was his particular skill.

So, while Renaye stayed behind in New York, he went to Raleigh, where he applied for a job in a furnishing fabrics factory, but he soon discovered that the owners of the factory liked him for an odd and unacceptable reason. 'It was quite a shocking experience for me,' he says. 'It was like I was going to join the Ku Klux Klan. I'm sure they gave me the job because I was a white South African and in their minds we had the right idea about what to do with black people. So I came back to New York and said to Renaye, 'I can't do this. We are going from one situation to another that is even more unpalatable.'' So they took a trip across America instead to have a look at this new continent. They bought an old VW camper van and travelled for three months, after turning down the Raleigh job:

> In those three months, I did some serious thinking about what I wanted to do with my life and I decided that what was most important to me was writing my songs. If I

wasn't going to be doing that, I was going to be a pretty unhappy person. And I felt so foreign in America. Our ideas were focused on having children and a family life and we wondered if we wanted the kids to be American. So I said to Renaye that I would really like to go back to South Africa and take our chances there. I needed to write about South Africa. That is what I understood and those are the stories I needed to tell. I couldn't see myself doing anything in America. It wasn't like I could suddenly adapt and write American stuff.

So then we came back. I can't explain to you why I always had a feeling that there was hope in this country. I think it's to do with my sense of the people. I understood the politics but I never felt that there was a hatred, that we had a kind of bloodbath situation here potentially. That might have been naive. There's certainly rampant racism here and the apartheid politics then, but somehow this negative stuff didn't look to me as if it had a long-term future. The forces of isolation that were working on South Africa, economically and culturally, I thought would not take effect. What was amazing was that it took so much longer than I expected. But I'll tell you there is only one reason why it ended when it did, and that was when the Berlin Wall came down. That was the turning point. That was the end of it. The future of this country was very much in the hands of the generals in the army and they had more political foresight than the politicians. And they knew. They were telling the government that a political solution had to be found. Not that I knew this at the time, but with hindsight I can see this. Hindsight is the most wonderful thing!

He laughs.

But when the Wall came down, you could no longer scare little white Boere-boys into saying that we are fighting communism. And then there was Christianity – communism was what gave Christianity a reason to fight the black man. When there is no communism, then it's

> just rampant racism, isn't it? And that doesn't sit too well with the Christian bible. And that's the kind of stuff that I think influenced de Klerk and those people. With their Christian Calvinist background, they had to do some real soul searching about that, and realise that they no longer had any justification for trying to hold out. So the pressure must have mounted enormously from Britain and America, who before might have said, 'Right, you are holding the fort for us.'

He raises a question: 'Won't South Africa go the way of Zimbabwe?' and he answers his own question with an emphatic 'No!

> Absolutely not! People overseas forget that South Africa has a very sophisticated economy, unlike so many countries to the north of us. I mean, Zimbabwe has the economy of Worcester, I think. That's about it – a few factories and some farms, and not much else. I think South Africa is so integrated into the world economy now that it's almost impossible for that kind of Zim political stuff to take place here, although farmers are very scared of that. I spoke to one over the weekend and he said that if the ANC starts to lose support they would turn to the land issue to gain votes. That is a real fear in farmers' minds.

He returns to the story of his upbringing:

> I was very disdainful of everything that was happening at my school in Worcester. The only thing that was of any worth to me was that I was going to art school. Art was one of my subjects that I felt I learnt something in. And I also went to the public library and there I found the Sestigers who were coming out then – André Brink and the poetry of Breyten Breytenbach, and what was most exciting for me was the poetry of Adam Small. There was that kind of voice – as in his *Kitaar my Kruis* (My Guitar, My Cross) and those kinds of things. Etienne Leroux's

> *Sewe Dae by die Silbersteins (Seven Days at the Silbersteins).* They seemed to wish to liberate themselves from Calvinism.

The Worcester library had one more surprise for him. There was, he said, a book by Bishop Trevor Huddleston about what was happening in Sofiatown, about the forced removals of the late 1950s. Books as bombs, I think. 'That started to make me aware of what was really going on,' he says. The books of Abraham de Vries also struck a chord, and then there was Herman Charles Bosman:

> Now, let me just talk about Bosman, because that was the start of it for me. This is how it happened. I was in Standard Nine in Worcester, I was 17 and I was playing the guitar in a rock 'n roll band. All I was interested in was the Beatles and the Stones and Dylan and that stuff. And then Percy Sieff came to the Little Theatre in Worcester and he did a show on Bosman, a one-man show. The first act was Bosman's Jo'burg lifestyle and the story of him shooting his stepbrother and his incarceration. And the second act was Oom Willem Prinsloo's stoep stories. And that was mind-blowing, because for the first time I heard a South African accent on the stage and basically what it said to me was that it was legitimate to tell a South African story.
>
> My brother was at Art School at Michaelis, studying painting, and Neville Dubow was one of his lecturers. Dubow switched him on – he came home with this idea that artists in South Africa needed to look at their own world, the world around them, not to paint in the style of overseas artists. The conclusion that my brother came to was that the world that you know can be more interesting than the world presented to you in magazines. And he came to me and said the most radical thing I'd ever heard. He said, 'Worcester can be more exciting than New York if you look at it properly!'

David said that he had just written a song, which, 30 years

later, said the same thing. 'The chorus of the song says, "Maak jou oë net oop dan word jy gedoop. Elke oomblik word jy weer gedoop." (Just open your eyes and you will be baptised. Every moment you are baptised again.) And the verse goes, "Daar is plekke wat met jou praat, 'n kloof, 'n koppie, die hoek van 'n straat".'(There are places that speak to you, a gorge, a hill, the corner of a street).

There is a long silence following that. I think of all my years away and David's time abroad and how South Africa and the Cape in particular, has called and called to us. There are indeed places that speak to you, and having spoken, echo forever in your heart. We look at each other and then we look away, acknowledging the emotion, and watch seagulls swooping and screeching, boats manoeuvring in the harbour. It is a moment of great poetry for me, of feeling touched by someone and also something universal. I feel deeply grateful to be sitting with David Kramer.

I talk about being an outsider and he says, 'That is important. It was the same with me.' I tell him how I work alone, write alone. And how, having met him, I feel how enriching it would be, perhaps once a month, to sit round a fire with a few like-minded people and talk. 'I think we all feel that, you know,' he says. 'Maybe it is a bit of a romantic notion, the idea of the café society and all these okes (guys) sitting round. But hell, it is a lonely occupation.'

We talk about the Afrikaner and the Afrikaans language. He says:

> Language was the unifying force that created their identity. I came to a point when I had to ask myself why I did not want to speak Afrikaans. And what was I going to sing? I asked myself, was there a South African folk-music culture? If so, what is it? The only Afrikaans folk music that I could think of was the stuff I grew up with – *Suikerbossie* and *Bobbejaan Klim Die Berg (Sugarbush* and *The Baboon Climbs the Mountain).* Simple Afrikaans songs that were sung around campfires.
>
> But when I started looking more closely at this Afrikaans folk music in the '70s it was a revelation to me.

> As I looked at the lyrics, I realised that this has not been written by white people. No one had suggested this to me before and when I began to scratch into the history of Afrikaans I was gobsmacked to realise that Afrikaans was never the language of whites. As it was taught to me, three men got together at Dal Josafat one night in 1875 and invented or proclaimed the Afrikaans language. Nonsense!
>
> So that was completely liberating for me, understanding the roots of Afrikaans, and that is when I started writing Afrikaans songs. The thing for me was to make a connection to the folk tradition so that there would be some reason to move into the future, to reconnect with an Afrikaans folk tradition. I was influenced by the kind of thing Dylan did with Woody Guthrie.
>
> I suppose the most political thing I did in my work was not the content but the form. Political messages are sought in the content and there is a lot of innuendo and politics but the really radical stuff was in the style and the form.

I ask him to explain this. He says by 'the form', he was adopting:

> a style of singing that was obviously not white and a way of playing the guitar that was influenced by farm music. My purpose was to pull together South African influences into a kind of melting pot that would form a South African sound. Now when Johnny Clegg (another half Jew) does it, it's all very obvious to people. When a white man sings Zulu, it's obvious. When a white man sings Afrikaans, it's not. When I started it was the time of the hugely popular Afrikaans singers Gé Korsten and Sonja Herholdt. And that kind of Afrikaans, it was 'Omo Afrikaans' – whiter than white. Then came two fresh voices. The one was Anton Goosen and the other was me.

We talk about David writing his own story one day. 'I see myself as a storyteller and I've written musicals. I keep meaning to write my story; I started a chapter about my life, very much tongue-in-cheek, told in a humorous way. I tend to lean towards the serious but I'm better at humour,' – and once more the laughter comes that lightens his face and his body. When he laughs, he seems a different person, less intense.

Returning to the issue of the Afrikaans language, he says some people are very paranoid about it and this is why there has been so much cultural activity at arts festivals like the annual one held at Oudtshoorn:

> It's supposed to be just an arts festival but it is very much about the celebration of language. And it's supposed to be very inclusive as opposed to exclusive, and the debate rages every year to try to get more coloured people involved. White Afrikaans speakers realise that for the future, the language needs to embrace all Afrikaans speakers, of which the majority are brown and black, always have been, and this is something that was not acknowledged a few years ago. I don't know what the figures are, but when I travel around this country, most people speak Afrikaans. Probably much more Afrikaans is spoken than English. That will change now because of what's happened within government.
>
> These festivals have particularly been sponsored by Naspers (an Afrikaans media group). I think they realise, being in the magazine industry, that if there aren't people speaking Afrikaans in the future, who is going to buy the magazines?

He flags up another change happening among Afrikaners that he sees as important:

> Younger people, young white Afrikaans speakers, are travelling to London in numbers for the first time in the history of South Africa. What we did 30 years ago they are only starting to do now. This generation is much more open to the broader world. These people come back and there is a cultural intercourse happening as a

result.

I agree, and tell him about the mountain bikers I met near my home in Sussex just three weeks previously, who came belting down a hill towards me and my horse, one shouting to the others behind him, 'Pasop, daar is 'n ou toppie op 'n perd hierso!' (Be careful, there is an old man on a horse here!) They nearly fell off their bikes when the 'ou toppie' stopped next to them and said, 'Jou bliksem, wie is jou ou toppie?' (You bugger, who is your old man?) You can no longer use Afrikaans in London as a private language. Those days are gone.

He says that the new generation are also finding new Afrikaans icons and he mentions Koos Kombuis, Karen Zoid, Valiant Swart, Akkedis, Kobus – the new alternative voices. He adds, 'They are just enjoying being young, liberated, Afrikaans speakers, who also speak English. They are much more international now.'

I am very comfortable on the café deck this sunny morning, but I see that David is shivering. I suspect that this is the temperature, to some extent, which is cooler than for the past few days, but it may also be the tension of speaking so passionately about his subject. I suggest we go inside where it is warmer, but he says he's happy where he is. We talk on. He says:

> In the '80s, opposition politicos encouraged people to stop speaking Afrikaans, just at a time when I was rediscovering Afrikaans. And so, today, you find in the metropolitan areas the younger generation of brown people speak English now. So there was quite a sea change. They had no historical perspective. The facts of the history of the coloured people in Cape Town were completely suppressed; it was hidden history. History is always written by the ruling power. There is a tremendous difficulty now to find out about the original inhabitants of this country. The only records that exist are court records – this Bushman or that one appears in front of a magistrate. Records of misdemeanours and stuff like that. You can't really piece together anything.

> But that is where the research is being done now.
>
> The history of the ruling power describes the history of the underdog or just doesn't describe it at all. One of the subjects of humour in this town is the way in which coloured people describe their backgrounds. They will always tell you about their German grandfather or their Scottish grandmother. No, not grandmother, that's wrong, it's always the male side, of course, so it would be a Scottish grandfather too. And that's it. People laugh a lot when that is raised because they know what that means. So there is an inferiority complex associated with indigenous people or slaves or whatever. But that's starting to turn around now. Now it's becoming very fashionable to have non-white ancestry.

He says he is beginning to see an investigation of the past by coloured people:

> And through that, they're discovering aspects of their history that make them feel proud and enable them to embrace their own history and identity. But it's quite shocking when you speak to young, coloured people, and I've worked with them for quite a number of years with the musicals I've done. You ask them anything about their background and they haven't got a clue about who they might be.

We talk about the threat to history, culture and language, created by the process of globalisation, an establishment of an almost universal homogenous culture. But David is not despairing about this:

> Smaller cultures and traditions can't remain static either. It's not a bad thing to modernise and move forward; that isn't bad. So when I start to think about these intellectual concepts of what culture is, for example, then it becomes complex and confusing. At the end of the day I have a statement that I like to make to throw the cat among the pigeons. I like to say, 'There is no such thing as culture.'

He puts on a gruff voice and says in response to his last comment, "'What do you mean? Of course there is! What is culture?" This is a question that upsets people a helluva lot. Some people tell you culture is these books and this music. I tell them no, those are its artefacts. Culture is a state of mind. I don't know much about this. There is a commonality, I suppose, but on an individual level, culture does not exist.'

The bang of the noon cannon makes me jump. I don't know quite what I expected from David - a musician, a playwright, a poet... so why am I so surprised to find an intellectual? We talk about another Boerejood, Pieter-Dirk Uys - the other great South African humourist and satirist - and David says that he has known him a long time. 'He is a nice man, but not one who suffers fools gladly. He makes some brave and outrageous statements and takes a lot of flak for it, but he does not back down. So he doesn't care about what you think of what he thinks. He's not trying to be diplomatic.' I put it to him that he, on the other hand, does seem to suffer fools gladly. He laughs and admits it. 'I suppose I do, really.' I tell him of the occasional obituary that I will read in England about someone who had a great spirit and of whom it is said, 'He suffered fools gladly.' I add that I would rather live among those who suffer fools gladly, having a personal stake in the issue, as it were.

I ask how he deals with fame. He shifts uncomfortably, as though the question has touched a nerve:

> When I come out to shopping malls like this, I know... Well, it's not so bad anymore but when I was on television you know that people are going to come up to you all the time and say the same things to you. And I'm quite prepared for that, because it just has to be like that, if you are popular and you want people to know about you. So I don't expect any kind of privacy when I'm out in restaurants. So you just have to find ways of creating your own spaces. Which means travelling overseas for my holidays.

We return to my main theme, the Afrikaner, and he says this is a loaded, complex word, rather like 'culture'. 'Which Afrikaners do you mean?' he asks. 'Because there is such a wide spectrum of Afrikaans speakers. And people tend to throw lassos around things that suit them.' I tell him I am interested in knowing about the Cape Afrikaners, white and brown. He points out the numbers of black Afrikaans speakers in the Karoo:

> Do you know how black the Karoo has gone? And it's all Afrikaans. Go to the wine farms in Paarl and Worcester and De Doorns – I went looking for guitar players – and who is working there on the farms? Black people, speaking Afrikaans. It is the language of work. They are migrant labourers, I suppose, who came in and learned the language of the farm.

I try to localise the Afrikaner for my purposes and ask him to look at the people he was at school with. 'I didn't have much contact with them, actually,' he says. 'I bump into some of them occasionally. Look, after school I wanted to get away from that, those people were in the army with me, not my school friends but those kinds of people. I moved into Cape Town, an English-speaking environment. I live in Camps Bay now and I never hear Afrikaans.'

His old schoolmates have found ways of adapting to the new reality, he says, by working in Afrikaans-controlled companies, or government institutions, or taking on new black partners. 'People know what the new rules are and they are learning to play them. They are conducting their business in English but they are also very keen on immersing themselves in Afrikaans culture, like rugby and ou boeremusiek (old country music) and festivals. You just have to go to the Klein Karoo Kunstefees (Small Karoo Arts Festival) to see the interest in things Afrikaans, and of course there is a tremendous nostalgia.'

He says he knew this new interest in Afrikaans culture would occur and that there would be a resurgence of interest in his work 'because it describes a South African experience rather than a 'blommetjies en voeltjies – hoe mooi is die Kaap' (Flowers and birds – how beautiful is the Cape) kind of song. It has been incredibly interesting to me, that my two biggest hits till today – the most popular ballad that I ever wrote, a song called 'So Long Skipskop', about forced removals, and one called 'Meisies Sonder Sokkies' (Girls Without Socks) – have been discovered by the next generation.' The latter song became the biggest 'sokkiejol' (disco party) hit, he says, 13 years after he wrote it:

> It is very much in the coloured idiom. What I think appeals to white people about it is the rhythm of the song combined with a kind of clever playfulness of rhyme, in which one is speaking the new Afrikaans. And there is a new Afrikaans, which is not that Pretoria University Afrikaans. There is an Afrikaans of the streets and once again it is the idiom of the Cape where the double negative is absorbed into the words.

He gives an example of a double negative. 'In Afrikaans you'd say, 'Jy moet dit nie doen nie.' (No you must not do that). That becomes, 'Djy moenie dit doenie.' So the double negative is absorbed.'

He speaks the words of 'Meisies Sonder Sokkies', as it illustrates this play on the absorbed double negative with an attractive and playful rhyme.

> 'Iewers hie binne in, my bokkie, Met my hart soos 'n tok-tokkie,
> Ek droom van 'n warm Kersfees dag En 'n meisiekind sonder haar sokkies.
> Bokkie ek willie vir jou jokkie Of jy my lief het weet ek okkie.'
>
> (Somewhere inside, my darling, With my heart like a tok-tokkie,
> I dream of a warm Christmas day, And a girl without her socks.
> Darling, I don't want to lie to you. Whether you love me I also don't know.)

The new popularity of his music amuses David. He recalls an incident 25 years ago when he went to play in Calvinia and some of the farmers walked out. 'Some people working with me heard the farmers say, "Nee God, man, hy sing soos 'n blerrie Hotnot".' He repeats the jibe: '"Hy sing soos 'n blerrie Hotnot." (No God man, he sings like a bloody Hotnot) And now, today, that is what they want to hear.' (Hottentots were one of the original indigenous peoples at the Cape. The use of the word in the mouths of whites was generally derogatory).

He tells me of the joy Afrikaans brings him in its descriptive, robust, coarse power.. This, he says, reminded him of Namaqualand.

> I always loved the Namaqualanders because they were always vulgar, both white and brown; that's the interesting thing about them. My ears nearly fell off when I first went into their homes. It was 'fok dit' and 'fok daai' (fuck this and fuck that). I was shown a little succulent there called pieletjies' (penises) [and he now puts on the voice of an old crone who also has the distinctive Malmesbury brei (accent) and he mimics] 'Ja, jy weet, maar as dit eers reën hierso, dan word daai pieletjies trille.' (Yes, you know, when it first rains like this, then those little dicks get to the size of horse pricks).

I nearly fall off my chair laughing and spend the rest of my time in the Cape repeating this story, eliciting varied responses. This gem, he says, comes from the Garies area. He says it's a life's work writing down these sayings and songs.

He is optimistic about the future; in fact, he says, 'Now is the best time to be in South Africa. It is the best time I've seen in my lifetime. The economy has never been so buoyant.' But he is deeply disturbed by the AIDS pandemic and he pays tribute to the work of Pieter-Dirk Uys in fearlessly promoting AIDS awareness. AIDS, David says, could turn everything round in South Africa, from hope to despair, and then to disaster.

David Kramer is a mirror reflecting our society here in the Cape. In him we see ourselves. Is it not strange that in his mix of German, Lithuanian, English and Dutch genes we find a new, true flowering of the beauty and strength of Afrikaans, and stranger yet, that it comes to him through the prism, the view, the accent of a brown people whose indigenous ancestors were derogatively labelled Hotnots?

The white Afrikaner would do well to remember that they speak a Hotnot taal, and that a Boerejood brings them this gift (for whatever David feels himself to be, one Jewish grandparent was enough to condemn you in Hitler's Germany).

David would be the first to blush and splutter at being called a poet-prophet, but that is what he is, for he shows us how we are, and how we might attain a future together. He certainly speaks for the Cape.

If we could just see with his eyes we would, in the words of his song, be once more 'gedoop' – be baptised, have a new beginning, a truly new beginning. I like the irony of that: this great gift brought to us by a 'wit-Boerejood-Hotnot-boetie' (a white-boerejood-hotnot-brother).

I think, too, that the black peoples of South Africa no longer need a champion; they are now the champions, the victors. It is the half-forgotten, most disregarded of our ancestors, the Khoi, the Griquas, the Hottentots that now need our embrace; that need celebration. For was it not Christ who said, 'For that which you do to the least among you, you do unto me?'

David Kramer is giving voice to this lost people in his modern musical amalgam, in the stories he tells and the sounds he unearths. And he is doing it in Afrikaans! In this there is hope for us all.

The View From the Other Side

There comes a point in this journey when it becomes obvious that I need some more perspective, an alternative view of the Afrikaners than the one they offer of themselves. To see the Afrikaners in the round I feel it would be helpful to see them through the eyes of brown and black Afrikaans speakers. And, as usual in South Africa, the names flow in, and the help with it. What is it about South Africans of every colour that makes them so openhartig, so open-hearted and generous? Not all and not all the time and not to everyone, but when you feel this warmth it blows you away.

I write to Professor Hein Willemse who heads the Afrikaans Department at Tukkies, the University of Pretoria, and he replies almost instantly. I am away, into a world I know little of.

Hein Willemse studied Law and Afrikaans literature at the University of the Western Cape. He has the following academic qualifications: BA (Hons) (Cum Laude), MA (Cum Laude), MBL and D.Litt. He has published widely on Afrikaans language, literature and orature studies. He also taught for extended periods in Mexico, the USA and Namibia. He was editor-in-chief of the multilingual African literary journal *Tydskrif vir Letterkunde.* His books include the award-winning *More Than Brothers – Peter Clarke and James Matthews at 70* (Kwela, 2000) and A*an Die Ander Kant – Swart skrywers in die Afrikaanse letterkunde* (*On The Other Side - black writers in Afrikaans literature*), (Protea, 2007).

As a young academic, Willemse played an active role in the opposition to apartheid and along with other Afrikaans authors - including Andre Brink, Breyten Breytenbach, and Etienne van Heerden - attended the historical Victoria Falls Writers' Conference in 1989, where various Afrikaans intellectuals met with banned South African authors and members of the ANC. The man has impeccable credentials for viewing the Afrikaner in his own language, but from a black perspective. I wonder how does he feel about white Afrikaners and about himself as a black Afrikaans speaker?

I start, as usual, by asking why the collapse of apartheid's values had been so sudden. Professor Willemse says:

> Apartheid as a system had run its course. Since the late 1960s, the nationalistic justification for it had come under increasing pressure from within its own quarters. The call for verligte (enlightened) Afrikaners was a clear sign that the system as envisaged had run into problems. Obviously, those problems were exacerbated when, in the '80s, even Afrikaner intellectuals closely linked to the ruling party could no longer justify apartheid, neo-apartheid or the mutations of racial separation. They could no longer justify it to themselves or to those still supporting them outside the laager. And let's not forget the pervasive impact of the cultural boycott and sports boycott. For the first time, the Afrikaners had a considerable class of intellectuals who could only go to fellow pariah countries or institutions:
>
> By the end of the '80s, the National Party had very few intellectuals who were prepared to prop it up - its last major intellectual exercise, namely the development of the tri-cameral system (creating a three-chambered parliament for whites, coloureds and Indians) and the doctrine of 'total strategy', (read total repression) had failed or disintegrated miserably.
>
> My own observations suggest that the fact the Afrikaners were regarded as the polecats of the world had a major impact on them, especially the class of intellectuals and business people. In the post-apartheid

> phase, Afrikaner public commentators often comment on how great it is not to disguise their origins when they go overseas, or that nowadays their South African passport is acceptable everywhere.
>
> One shouldn't forget the impact of apartheid on the economy: in the '80s, the South African economy was an economy of siege. The government was debt-ridden, had debt rollovers and for almost a decade growth was negative. It's therefore not surprising that some of the first sections to speak to the ANC were the business leaders, followed closely by Afrikaner intellectuals, writers and - lo and behold! - the rugby administrators. By the end of the '80s, Afrikaner intellectuals knew that they could not sustain apartheid in any shape, manner or form. Some of them still tried at CODESA (Convention for a Democratic South Africa) but the system had lost its moral justification.

When I ask Professor Willemse how he thinks Afrikaners feel today, he says with impeccable tact that he won't presume to speak for the feelings of Afrikaners. Instead, he lists individuals and their writings as people who provide useful insights into the mind of the Afrikaner today. He mentions Dan Roodt, a conservative commentator; Danie Goosen, *Groep van 63 (Group of 63),* moderate to conservative; Chris Louw, *Boetman en die Swanesang van die Verligtes (Boetman and the Swansong of the Enlightened);* Van Zyl Slabbert, *Afrikaner Afrikaan (Afrikaner African);* and major newspaper columnists JC Steyn, Hermann Giliomee, Leopold Scholtz, Max du Preez, JP Landman, Antjie Krog, Johan Rossouw, Tim du Plessis, and Christi van der Westhuizen. They mostly publish in *Die Beeld* and *Die Burger.* Max du Preez's autobiography, *Pale Native,* is also instructive. All of these writers and intellectuals provide valuable insights today into who and what the Afrikaners are and where they are going, he believes.

'What do Afrikaners hope for from the future?' I ask. Again, Professor Willemse says it isn't for him to say, but then adds:

> My own criticism of many of the spokespeople or commentators is that they do not really envisage a secure future for Afrikaners. Quite often, the future that is suggested is one of relative isolation with an overriding Afrikaner-centred perspective – see the documentation of Dan Roodt's group: the so-called Afrikaner Forum. People like J.P. Landman, Max du Preez and van Zyl Slabbert seem to think of a more overarching 'South Africanness'.

Many Afrikaners are emigrating, he says, but then he qualifies this:

> Yes, many are going, but I think the numbers are exaggerated. This is often used for purposes of propaganda. There are situations of severe pressure that force professional people to seek out new possibilities. Similarly, there are also situations where people have not adapted to the new South African situation. The issue of rationalisation of emigration is a mixed bag of impressions, propaganda, economic and social pressures, and political orientation. I don't think there is one Afrikaner-specific rationale for emigration.

'What of the language, Afrikaans?' I ask. Many white Afrikaners seem really concerned for its survival, and some ironically look to the brown and black Afrikaans speakers to keep it alive.

> Yes, that's true, Especially at the level of cultural politics, many Afrikaner intellectuals and culture brokers are seriously concerned about the future of Afrikaans. Gradually, at the level of official language or at the high end of the economy, Afrikaans is downgraded. The same process is happening at institutions of higher learning where Afrikaans used to be the primary language of instruction. This has real consequence for Afrikaans as a language of higher-order activity: the publication of academic texts, instruction at universities, as a language of record in the courts, the business world and the state.

> The latest census figures indicate that 42 per cent of Afrikaans speakers are white; the majority, about 58 per cent, are black Afrikaans speakers. Within the next decade those figures will continue their respective trajectories: the figures of white speakers of Afrikaans will diminish further and probably more rapidly, while those of black Afrikaans speakers will increase at an accelerated rate, given the projected population growth rates.
>
> This is a situation where the long-held myth of Afrikaans as the 'possession' of the Afrikaner is coming home to roost. Afrikaner commentators realise that the future of 'their' language is very much a case of shared commonality – it cannot be sustained through old-style insularity.
>
> Overall, there is a need for a language dispensation that does justice to the demands of a country like South Africa. The latest language policy makes provision for the use of six languages in the business of the state: Afrikaans, English, one Nguni (Zulu, Xhosa, Ndebele, Seswati) and one Sotho (Setswana, Sesotho) language and, on rotation, Shangaan and Venda. This policy is probably closer to the needs of our population. The greatest need is for justice – also in matters of language. Quite often Afrikaner ideologues tend to overemphasise their concern for Afrikaans, and in the process they forget that other South Africans might have similar concerns about their own languages.

As perceptive as Willemse's thoughts are on the survival of Afrikaans, I am equally fascinated by his response to my question about the emergence of new, credible, Afrikaner leaders.

> Some random names that come to mind: Johan van Zyl, Sanlam's new boss; Koos Bekker, the CE of Naspers; Whitey Basson, the CE of Shoprite; Coenie Burger, the moderator of the NG Church in the Cape; Theuns Eloff, the rector of Potchefstroom University; Chris Brink, the

> rector of Stellenbosch University; Tim du Plessis, former editor of *Rapport* newspaper; Arrie Rossouw, the editor of *Die Burger* newspaper.

And how do black Afrikaans speakers feel about their own position today, I ask. Do they feel that they are Afrikaners - whatever that may be? Are they hopeful about the future?

> There is no one position for black Afrikaans speakers. Some of them are from slave extraction, others from south Indian extraction, others from indigenous South African extraction, still others defined as Xhosa or Sotho or Tswana or Indian or coloured. Very few would self-identify as 'black Afrikaans speakers'. Should they be put to the squeeze, they would probably choose the well-worn ethnic appellations.
>
> There might be people who would refer to themselves as Afrikaners, associating themselves with the 'white Afrikaners'. There might be those who would argue that the term itself was a matter of usurpation - naming yourself after the continent - and, in any case, the term was also used for purposes of group identification by the Hôa-aran [the Afrikaner of northern Cape and Namibia - there are quite a number of black people with the surname 'Afrikaner' with this particular family history].
>
> In general, I suspect that there is very little political or social identification with the Afrikaner from these quarters. If anything, there is the expressed need for the acknowledgement of people's own histories [slave, Muslim, Griqua, coloured, etc] and their own trajectories into the future; securing a political and economic path that would not discriminate against them in the new South Africa. Most of these people have probably dealt with the issue of Afrikaans and overall it is not a major part of their struggle for a secure future.'

As I read Professor Willemse's responses, my instant and overwhelming feeling is one of sadness and loss. Here is this sensitive, intelligent, cultured, insightful man giving his view of his world. His voice is being heard, but how many like him had been forced by apartheid to remain mute?

Horses in the Franschhoek Mountains

I feel tired and a little jaded after almost a fortnight of constant interviewing, and so decide that some 'horse medicine' is needed. This is my failsafe pick-me-up, more reliable and effective than any stimulant.

I had seen an article in *SA Country Life* about a man called Pieter Hugo who runs a riding operation – Paradise Stables – in Franschhoek. He takes clients horse riding across country in this most beautiful part of the Cape, on routes that also offer wine tasting at the many estates in the valley. I decide to forgo the wine tasting; my wish is simply to head for the hills, to feel a horse beneath me once more, carrying me away from thoughts of books and interviewing. Pieter's horses sound good: fit long-distance competitors who do well in a variety of endurance rides, much better than the usual riding school mokes provided for the casual rider.

Between the lines of the article, it sounds as if Pieter is a bit of a character too and this adds to my expectation of fun. In the event I am not disappointed. I call and find that on the day in question he has no other engagement and I arrange to take a two-hour ride with him. The price, he says, would be the same if I brought a guest so I call my friend Fiona Archer, who is happy to join me on this jaunt.

The morning is another perfect one as we drive out to

Franschhoek, the sun shining on mountains and wine farms, the few clouds gleaming pink in the winter dawn, backlit and stunning. There is not a spare ounce of flesh on Pieter's light frame and he looks just as fit as the three grey Arabs his grooms lead out. To my surprise they are wearing bitless bridles – there is absolutely nothing in their mouths, nor is there any sign of the disc-brake effect of a hackamore. The bridles are, in effect, head collars or halters with reins attached to the noseband. I've never seen anything quite like this in 45 years of riding. But as he seems eminently competent, we get on board and walk out of the stable yard.

It is a strange feeling. I'm six foot two and used to riding Irish hunters or Irish draughts and this little beast feels tiny. His head seems much too close to me, and, as I'm perched on a military saddle covered in sheepskin, I feel even more awkward – and there are no brakes.

Pieter talks non-stop. He is a fund of local lore and also hugely knowledgeable about horses. He speaks fluent if heavily accented English, with a Malmesbury brei (twang). I ask how he acquired this particular rural accent and he says he picked it up from the sons of his father's farm manager many years ago.

We amble along on a dry gravel road, heading towards high ground. As we talk, the conversation moves into Afrikaans. Most of his clients are overseas visitors sent to him from a couple of the top hotels and restaurants in the area. I can imagine the effect this landscape must have on such visitors, particularly after a few wine-tastings. It must feel as though they have died and gone to heaven and are now riding through the Elysian Fields; it is that beautiful. Pieter says he has not as yet lost anyone overboard, but there has been the odd bit of fun. I can imagine. We turn off the gravel road into Port Jackson and pine scrub; the path turns soft and sandy and away we go. We have told Pieter that we are both fairly competent riders; in fact, we have both signed a document to this effect, so he lopes ahead. His horse knows the route and sets to at a slow canter, which soon picks up speed. I work at finding a comfortable position on this active little horse and do not succeed too well, but as we move up to higher ground I finally find a rhythm and the feel-good factor begins to kick in. I'm at the back; Fiona is in the middle, riding easy, as I'd expect. The horses – all three – have no mouth contact and work freely without any sense of 'collection', so to all intents and purposes Pieter is riding all three, because they take their lead from him.

We have a brief walk and then he sets his horse at a gravel road that climbs the side of a mountain and away we go at a brisk canter. I weigh around 80 kilograms and plus the tack this horse is carrying, it hardly breaks sweat. There certainly is no laboured breathing; we simply float up that mountain. And these horses are not clipped – they carry their full winter coats. It is remarkable, a tribute to both them and their owner.

Below us, farms unfold amid vines, white-fenced paddocks and dams. When we pull up to a walk again, Pieter tells us that many of the magnificent homes in this valley are British-and German-owned and that they provide an income for a new breed of young women who for R50 a night are happy to house-sit while the owners are abroad.

Now we move into a new landscape, riding between blue gums, pines and fynbos. The going is a mix of sand, gravel and rocky bits. The horses are surefooted and never seem in danger of stumbling, never mind falling. I know my own horse, a 17 hand Irish draught, would be like a drunk man on a Saturday night over this ground.

Pieter charges R1,000 a month for stabling, inclusive of shoeing, which he does himself. In Constantia it is nearer R3,000 a month, Fiona tells me. In England, livery charges are around £100 (about R1,200) a week, exclusive of shoeing, so it is not that much more expensive than Constantia at current rates of exchange. The trick is to look after them yourself in your own stables if you can, as that brings down costs considerably.

Pieter talks a blue streak about horses. You get the impression that he would do this job as much for the geselskap (the chat) as for the money. But it may in part be a way of disguising an innate shyness. Fiona agrees that this could be the case.

Horses have been the salvation of his farming operation, he says. He has had some tough years having to buy out his siblings, but today he says he makes much more from riding and stabling than he ever did from exporting proteas. That business, flower farming, did well at first but latterly it has been in decline, he says. Today he is firmly locked into tourism and the Twin Towers tragedy in New York has brought him a bonanza, as Americans increasingly discover the delights of South Africa. I hope, for him and for so many other South Africans, that the tourism boom keeps booming; a slowdown in the leisure business would prove a disaster for a lot of people.

Now, at the highest point of our ride, the views of the surrounding mountains are stunning. We are strung out along the path; talk is difficult and for a few moments all I can hear is the sigh of the breeze in the treetops and the click of the horses' steel shoes on the rocky outcrops. I feel recharged, energised and at peace with the world all at once. The horse medicine is doing its stuff.

The mountain path finally widens and we manage to ride three abreast at last. The horse Fiona is riding is no longer able to intimidate mine with a threatened kick, causing mine to keep back, and we ride up alongside Pieter. He has relaxed and has been telling us jokes in Afrikaans. He turns to me and asks who and what I am, born in the Cape but living in England for 23 years and yet speaking some Afrikaans?

I tell him, 'Ek is 'n Boerejood.'

Pieter laughs fit to bust and shouts, 'Die ergste soort!' (The worst kind!) and hoots across his horse's neck. I grin, feeling the muscles in my cheeks ache. Fiona laughs hesitantly and I laugh to reassure her. It is one of those situations. What does one do?

A Turbulent Priest

Refreshed by my ride in Franschhoek and a good night's sleep, I head out to Stellenbosch the next morning to meet two men who might offer me rather different perspectives on the Afrikaner. They are Jaap Durand, a theologian who bravely opposed the nationalist government at the height of its power, who is currently ombudsman for Stellenbosch University; and Jannie Gagiano, a political scientist, a politician and also, by all accounts, an unbridled force of nature. It promises to be an interesting morning.

It is a crisp, sunny day and Stellenbosch is beginning to feel like a home from home.

When I called Gagiano to set up the meeting, he said he was the main cook at home and had various meals to prepare, but that 11.30 would give him enough time to manage his culinary engagements. His voice is a big one and ultra macho, so his cooking responsibilities seem unusual - or is that me being sexist? After all, I also cook at home.

I stroll across a municipal car park to the Lutz building, where Professor Durand has his office. Professor Durand is one of the handful of Afrikaners who took on the might of the Nationalist monolith, a man who stood outside the laager and dared to criticise it. Beyers Naudé led this grouping, but there was also a 'loyal resistance' led from inside by writers such as Van Wyk Louw, he says.

Durand could easily be mistaken for a Spaniard. He is formal in manner at first, which accentuates this impression. He is first a theologian and then a philosopher, he says. He studied at Stellenbosch and then did his Doctorate of Philosophy at the

Free University in Amsterdam.

He says it was clear from his doctoral dissertation that his path and that of the Afrikaner establishment were 'going in different directions'. In fact, he was at loggerheads with the Nationalist government from the offset. He has never been a member of the white Dutch Reformed Church. Instead, on his return from Holland he went to the black church in the Transkei - the Dutch Reformed Church in Africa (DRCA) - and from there to Port Elizabeth where he served as a minister in the black township of Kwazakele.

He spent eight years in the Eastern Cape, which served to intensify his opposition to government policy, writing a book about his experience in the townships called Swartmanstad en Toekoms in 1970 (Black man city and the future). The *Argus* called it a 'devastating blow for apartheid'.

The coloured Mission Church then called on Durand to take on a role at the theological faculty at the University of the Western Cape (UWC). Not surprisingly, his separation from white Afrikanerdom grew ever greater. 'As the years went on my isolation greatly increased, especially in the '80s. It was very difficult, not only for myself but also for my family, for my children,' he says.

Desmond Tutu, speaking at the inauguration of the Beyers Naudé Centre for Public Theology at Stellenbosch University in November 2002, had this to say about the ostracism of Naudé:

> He was ostracised and vilified by his own Afrikaner community which regarded him as a traitor, a veraaier, a turncoat who had betrayed the volk. Social ostracism is harsh and painful and particularly for Afrikaners who, like Africans, are a very communal sort of people deriving nurture from the intimacies of corporate existence. To be banished from the community was a living death, an experienced hell.

Thus spoke Tutu of Naudé. But Jaap Durand may have had it harder. He did not enjoy the high national and international profile that Beyers Naudé had; he and his family were subject to even greater pressure and the real possibility of physical danger as a result. Jaap Durand stood alone in the face of all that his hostile community could throw at him. But he stood and he did not bend.

Not that you would hear this from Durand. He says he was much supported by Beyers Naudé when he first came back to South Africa from Holland. As the years passed, he had meetings with Naudé in the Transkei, and from there, the religious organisations Pro Veritate and the Christian Institute developed.

He found 'the University of the Western Cape, UWC, was under the complete control of the Broederbond and the white establishment.' It was, in effect, an apartheid institution and he was very reluctant to go there, but he felt he should go where he was needed. He became dean of the theology faculty and during this time, he says, 'We were in the forefront of the resistance in the university itself.

'There was an ongoing struggle,' he laughs, 'between the faculty of theology at UWC and the people in control. When Dick van der Ross became rector he had a lot of opposition and we fell in behind him to support him.'

Then 1976 arrived and the school boycotts, and he says it became clear that finally things were changing as a result of this opposition. How did he survive these harsh years? I ask. He was a man who loved his country, he was an Afrikaner and yet he was a pariah.

He says that while his children – a girl and two boys – were young in the '70s it wasn't too bad, but when they became teenagers, it became very difficult.

But the toughest test lay ahead, he says, 'when I became deputy vice-chancellor at UWC in 1980. I became Dick van der Ross's deputy and those became the really difficult years. The '80s were tough years.' Because of the Group Areas Act, Durand could not live near the university, and he did not want to live in Bellville, so he made his home in Stellenbosch, where his children attended local schools. 'My children experienced subtle and sometimes not such subtle innuendos at school. They had a feeling of constantly being under attack because of their father.'

He says that despite this pressure at the Bloemhof and Paul Roos schools, his children understood what the issues were and soldiered on. The personal and the political came together for Durand and his family with the coming of the tri-cameral parliament in 1984.'We all knew that this was going to be crunch time, because of blacks being left out of it,' says Durand.

So-called enlightened Afrikaners could not understand his opposition to this new development, which from their perspective seemed a step in the right direction.

'At UWC we were under a lot of pressure. Students were jailed, we had demonstrations and there was tear gas. It was really a bad situation. And then we marched.'

After marching, he says, 'I picked up my son Jaco and we had a game of tennis at a small club just outside Stellenbosch. He was in standard eight at the time. And as we were driving home, I told him about the march at UWC and that it would be in the papers the next day and that he should be prepared for any adverse comment. He asked me, "Het Pa gemarch?" (Did you march Pa?) and I said yes. He then threw his hands in the air and said, "Pa maak my naam toti by die skool!"(Pa, you are rubbishing my name at school!) and then he laughed. So I knew then that he'd crossed his own Rubicon. He was no longer being intimidated.' The sense of pride in his son is tangible.

Durand says that Dick van der Ross, vice-chancellor at UWC, wasn't sure how to handle the student demonstrations and marches. 'I said, "Dick, let's go with them." And then we started to organise it on a university level. We had the lecturers as marshals and we marched right into all the television cameras. It was even in the London *Times*. "Dons on the March" was the headline. When we got to Modderdam Road we saw the Caspirs lined up.'

He tells this story with the glee of a small boy who has got away with naughtiness. But he adds as an afterthought, 'I have been shot at by the police. You can't imagine what it was like. How we kept that university going is still a miracle to me.'

As I sit listening to Professor Durand, I become aware that I am listening to a good man, a truly good man. It is not often one feels this. But in his presence I feel that I am with true goodness allied to courageousness. It is a rare and heady combination. Yet he could not be more gesellig (chatty) and unpretentious. He's quite ebullient, in fact, the earlier formality forgotten. It must be profoundly satisfying to see your position vindicated in the court of history and in the eyes of the world.

I ask him to explain what the situation was when he was shot at. He says it took place in 1984 and the *Cape Times* was on hand to record the incident. A photograph taken at the time received a journalism prize. 'It was just one of those things that happened,' he says. 'The students were demonstrating, and I went to the police and told them I would get it under control. As I turned round to go back to the students I was shot with a rubber bullet. Then they started shooting on campus. I still have the photos from the *Cape Times*. That photographer was in just the right spot at the time,' and he laughs delightedly.

He says he had a wonderful relationship with UWC students. 'They knew I was completely behind them. We had quite a few black students there too and they knew of my experiences in the Transkei and that I could speak Xhosa too. So it made it much easier for me to get the support of the black community.'

I ask him to explain why Afrikaners chose to go quietly when I had expected them to fight to the death rather than live under black rule. 'That is a very, very difficult question to answer,' he says soberly:

> What developed here over three centuries is what I would call civil religion in the Afrikaner community, in which the church played a very significant role in developing the ideology, giving it a kind of Christian or Biblical foundation. Things started to change in the '80s. The church was already moving away from the apartheid position but it was ambivalent. However, it was already clear that there were cracks in the foundation. And then it began to unravel.
>
> The big factor was the business people. There was an acceptance that there was no way that we could keep on like this. You had some hardliners, the Masada types, (preferring group suicide to capture as in the story of the Jews encircled by a Roman army on Mount Masada), but

> gradually they were marginalised for different reasons: pressure from church, big business, and then of course De Klerk, influenced I think to a very large degree by his brother Wimpie. There are so many factors that it is not possible to give one answer to your question. I think that the major factors were economics and materialism, but I would not call those the only factors.

I ask him to explain just what he means by 'civil religion'.

> It means that everybody is in an all-embracing religiosity of life. It means a people's church and that even the public square is religious. It doesn't matter if someone is a committed believer or not. He calls himself a member of the church. The whole of life, even the politics, your private life, the public square. All, all of life, is covered by this concept of a civil religion. Giliomee coined that phrase, the 'civil religion'. It would also be the main force behind political decision-making.

Once again, it is clear just what a powerful hold the Dutch Reformed Church had on the Afrikaners and, as a result, on the country. The dominees had so much more power than any Anglican vicar in South Africa – or England, for that matter. Church and state were one. And the child of this evil marriage between religion and politics was apartheid. It takes a very special sort of person to walk outside of that ring and an even greater one to oppose it, as Jaap Durand did.

I ask about the dramatic growth in the charismatic churches. He says, 'In a transitional period, when some of the certainties of life have been completely undermined, suddenly you find that people move into these charismatic movements. It is a moral and sociological phenomenon.' I suggest that they are seeking skuilplek (a hideout, a place of safety) and he agrees:

> Ja, and they find it in that intense religious and private way where they get that security. They had that in the established Afrikaner churches too, but now they find that they have been wrong all along, so you have this

> charismatic phenomenon as a result.
>
> The Dutch Reformed Church is struggling to find a new agenda, a new identity. When you have a crisis of identity, as the church has just had, you immediately have a spiritual fragmentation. You then find that large numbers of people go to that place where they feel they get a feeling of security again. The Dutch Reformed Church is no longer a guarantor of the people's ideals and aspirations. So the charismatic movements are benefiting.
>
> It was not only the Afrikaners who were kept under control by the Dutch Reformed Church; it was the whole country. Now suddenly all those things that they professed have gone. They controlled the public square, the 'civil religion'. They were remarkably successful in keeping all foreign influence away from South Africa. So it is now belated enlightenment that has come to South Africa.

There is a great appeal, a tremendous lure, to charismatic religion, he says. 'When all the intellectual things of the church are suddenly taken away from you, all the certainties are taken out of it, then you go to the other extreme. So now, for some people, it is nice to escape into the charismatic churches.'

In Stellenbosch, he says, the charismatic church is part of the Apostolic Faith Mission, but it's usually a charismatic person who leads. He describes two very dynamic brothers – one in Stellenbosch, the other in Randburg – who draw large numbers into their churches. 'They are so charismatic in their personalities that they draw people to them,' he says.

People in South Africa today are looking for places where they can escape into communities where they can give expression to their feelings. 'The charismatic churches fulfil this function, as they're less dogmatic. Faith in dogma has been eroded because apartheid has been shown to be a sin, where previously it was considered to be the will of God. But by doing the happy-clappy thing, you live in a spiritual bubble,' he warns.

The way people cope with change is fascinating. Some leave old certainties; others cling to them. He gives as an example the coloured people who remain wedded to the National Party, despite its discrimination against them. Durand says the reason for this strange link is a simple but powerful fear of blacks. 'This goes much deeper with some coloured people than it does with some whites. They are much closer economically to blacks than whites. That is where the tension comes, that is where the crunch comes. You will find the same thing with Afrikaners,' he points out. 'It is among the poor Afrikaners that you find the real hard-liners.'

We move on to the land issue and I ask him if it is going to be a threat in the future. Are we going the Zimbabwe way? 'No,' he says:

> I don't think we will go the Zimbabwe way because the South African setting is quite different, and if you look at the economic and financial policies of the ANC, they have completely committed themselves to capitalism. To my mind, socialism is closer to Christianity, so I have my criticisms, but on the other side of the coin, what they have been doing on the economic and financial fronts in South Africa, they have done remarkably well. And so, given the direction they have taken, they cannot afford to have a land issue problem.

But he is concerned about corruption on the land issue. 'I think there is enough intellectual integrity in the ANC to prevent a Zimbabwe style land grab. But they will have to come away from what has been happening in their own government departments. That is one of the serious things that is happening: we are seeing corruption and incompetence. When you get incompetence, you get corruption.' He says he has seen many examples of land being shared in one way or another. 'We have seen this operating here in the Western Cape, where a farmer says, "OK, this piece of land is yours. We all farm together, but what you get from this piece of land is yours." It is small, but the idea of sharing is there.'

I ask if this is Ubuntu. Yes, he says, Ubuntu means menslikheid (humanity). He gives an example that speaks directly to this issue. A friend of his went to visit a black employee who was in hospital. 'It was this woman's birthday so he took her two small tarts. His idea was that they could both have one to celebrate the occasion. But there were six other people in the ward, so she said, 'Let's share with everybody.' He said, 'No, this is so small, you will get almost nothing if you share it out.' She said, 'It doesn't matter.' Suddenly the whole atmosphere in the ward changed as the tarts were shared. 'You see, it was not the size of the piece they got that mattered, but the idea of sharing. That is Africa!' Jaap Durand smiles.

He says that in the Eastern Cape, where he spent a long time, things are 'chaotic' because they forced affirmative action and as a result the best people left, because they got demotivated. In education, particularly, they have paid a very big price. 'My fear is that the same thing will happen in the Department of Land Affairs.

'I'm quite convinced that you will get a lot of cooperation from Afrikaans farmers, a lot of willingness on the land issue, once they have seen that the government is serious about land reform. Those Afrikaners who have accepted change are willing to go far.'

He adds, 'Keep this one thing in mind. The Afrikaner is basically not a capitalist. Some people forget their history. The Afrikaners linked up with the Communist Party in the 1920s. The Afrikaner at the start of the last century was much more socialist than capitalist. Capitalism within the Afrikaners only started with the Sanlam and Volkskas financial institutions.'

This is a busy man. He makes his apologies; I thank him and he dashes off to his next appointment. I think to myself, 'Wel, slaan my dood met 'n slap snoek en sleep my weg!' (Well strike me dead with a floppy snoek fish and drag me away!) I feel a bit like Alice who has fallen down the rabbit hole. Everything is topsy-turvy. My abiding impression of the Afrikaners was that they were in favour of Christ and capitalism. Now here, it seems, they are socialists and, heaven help me, with communist sympathies! And the ANC that now runs the country, who were once seen as Godless communists, are in fact fully paid-up capitalists. What a strange old world it is.

But Jaap Durand has not changed. He remains where he always was, on the outside looking in, speaking his mind, whatever the cost. If I had a wish, it would be for some of his courage.

A Political Centurion

I am keen to meet 'JG', as I believe he is actively engaged in politics as a member of the Democratic Alliance and the name 'Gagiano' comes up a lot – at least three people have suggested that I speak to him. His wife Annie is a professor in the English department at the University of Stellenbosch.

As I enter the coffee shop, I notice a bull of a man with huge shoulders sitting at a corner banquette. His presence dominates the place, which is fairly intimate. I ask the manager if this might be Jannie Gagiano? She smiles and nods. He is speaking on his cell phone in a hugely loud voice, so I wait at an adjoining table.

He is giving the person he is speaking to a hard time. 'Jy lieg, jy lieg! Jou kop en my kop werk nie dieselfde nie!' ('You lie, you lie. Your head and mine don't work the same way!')

The coffee shop's patrons look round to see who this rude person is who is disturbing their quiet pleasure. He makes a new call before I can get up out of my chair. He explains, 'Daar is 'n kinkel in die kabel.' (There is a kink in the cable). He is rather more civil to this second person, trying, it appears, to unravel some problem to do with an email that has gone astray. Finally, he snaps the phone shut and sits back.

I go over and am 'introduced' by the manager, who says there is someone to see him. He has a large, belligerent boxer's face. He is casually dressed in a polo neck under a jersey and slacks. He tells the manager that I am 'an author from England'. She looks at me dubiously.

Gagiano booms, 'I was expecting a tall, thin 6-foot-3 horse-rider,' he says, alerting me to the fact that he has read this morning's *Cape Times*, which carries a review of my book. The tone of his comment makes out that he is disappointed to find that I am, in fact, a fat dwarf. I shrink a bit inside, as is no doubt intended. And he booms once more, 'Have you got a hole in your soul? Have you come back to South Africa to fill it with a meaningful, healing experience?' Now we definitely have the attention of the whole place and perhaps even a few pedestrians outside.

Suddenly I relax. This is familiar territory. The trick is to give as good as you get. To appear intimidated is fatal.

Finally, we get down to business. He speaks with relish, passion and a love of ideas. He is not easily interrupted. When I do interrupt, to ask for clarification or to make a point, a look of deep pain crosses his face, followed by one of resignation; it is like watching a balloon deflate. And then once more he's off, as seemingly unstoppable as the Nile, but clever, witty, crude, emphatic, irreverent and informed. It is an intoxicating mix. He is strong stuff. If he calls Tony Leon 'Boss' as he does, then Tony Leon must be something extraordinary. Speaking of Tony Leon, he says to me, 'Dis nou 'n fokken hardegat Jood!' (Now that is a fucking hard- assed Jew!).

He says, 'The Afrikaner now has a Jewish situation. There is limited access to roles in society. They have become second-class citizens. They have become de-nationalised. There is a distinct echo here of the Jewish situation throughout the centuries.'

His cell phone rings again and, excusing himself, he takes the call. He tells the caller that he is busy for a few hours, then he has a meeting with ''n klomp Amerikaners en sulke ander goggas.' (a bunch of Americans and other such insects). I can't help but wonder how he will describe me. He explains that his own heritage is Scottish-Corsican. One can see it plainly – the mix of robber baron and shrewd peasant. It is a formidable combination.

Finally, he begins to explain how the surprising political change took place in South Africa. His description is a tour de force. 'There was no miracle. That is just magical thinking, made by people who really don't know anything, because they are stupid and just don't understand what actually happened.

Miracles are bullshit. Fuck miracles, fuck magic!' As he says this, it feels as if the coffee shop's patrons cross themselves instinctively and barely repress an overwhelming desire to flee, to be anywhere but here, just so long as it's away from Gagiano before the lightning strikes. He seems unaware of the effect of his words, or pretends to be.

He explains that the way political élites behave cannot be isolated from the environment around them. The nationalists faced constant pressure from within the country and from without. This pressure was not very successful. If you could not offer the Afrikaners some sort of vision, some form of respectable middle-class life with all the material gains that had been made, assuring them that it could be sustained, you would not have been successful in persuading them to go the route that they took, he says:

> But this route became more available. And it became more available, to my mind, because of, firstly, a major resource to liberation movements suddenly buckled, the collapse of communism.
>
> You must also not underestimate the role of Margaret Thatcher's government at the time. Margaret Thatcher was perhaps 'the right sort of person', in inverted commas. She had the right sort of style, the right sort of face, the right sort of kragdadigheid (vigour) and, shall we say, opposition and hostility to liberation-style politics in her own makeup. She spoke that language and she instilled a little bit of confidence in our politicians by saying it. She also had a very interventionist diplomat here, Robin Renwick, the ambassador. So Britain played an important role.
>
> She could tell FW de Klerk, perhaps not in these words, 'Look, the idea that there is a fatal threat to your type of social values and social order has practically disappeared. The ANC hasn't got international backing to the same extent anymore, so you can now go into a negotiation process which will probably have a good outcome. There could be a beneficial deal for you now.'

Gagiano maintains that transitions occur when international pressure starts producing intra-élite conflict about how to deal with that pressure:

> That is what happened in South Africa. The economic and political élite, and particularly the security forces, which had to bear the brunt of maintaining public order under conditions of diminishing political activity, all started saying, 'Hey, come on, let's look for a way out of this.' So the international situation, the collapse of communism, made it easier to find an exit.
>
> Secondly, there was already a debate going on in South Africa since the '70s of how to exit the situation. Afrikaner intellectuals were alienated. It was quite clear that you could not get back to the style of solution that authoritarian logic offered us. You could not go back to separating people into different states within one country. That style of accommodating people while also emasculating them was no longer on.

Another factor hastening change was the impending bankruptcy of the country. 'The rand was going for a bloody loop. So, as Giliomee says, FW de Klerk looked at the books like a good country lawyer and said, "Oh God! We're not going to be able to fucking take this shit any longer!"' Gagiano laughs at the thought. 'Not with sanctions and isolation and skewed markets and all that crap.'

Once more, a little shudder runs through the coffee shop and a display of rapid-eye movements lasers our way. These bounce and ricochet off Gagiano like peashooters off a Cape buffalo. Blithely unaware, he continues his lecture.

'The hydraulic pressure from the bottom also played a part,' he says. 'The ANC seem to think this was the only factor. That is nonsense, but it cannot be disregarded as a factor. The way in which the ANC could bring havoc to the black townships and get their international allies – the Namibians, Angolans and the Cubans – also to bring pressure to bear should not be disregarded. This was part of a process, though it had stopped by the time of the negotiations. So we had, in effect, a negotiated revolution, all done nicely and cleanly; no night of the long knives.'

Why, I ask, did the Afrikaner masses go along with all this when they had been told for years to distrust blacks – and when most had a visceral antipathy to blacks? Racism hardly covers these feelings. To be racist, I suggest, one has to dislike another group as a race, a human race. Many Afrikaners saw blacks as animals, not fully human. Gagiano explains it thus:

> When masses are held in sway and enchantment by their leaders, that is always imperfect. The masses are not just a bunch of complete idiots. But of course there are beliefs that get established in their minds.
>
> The question of trust is key. When the leadership started committing themselves to some negotiated alternative, what they said to their followers was, 'Trust us. We won't sell you down the river.' The leadership told them, 'It's okay. We know where we're going. It's a new situation.' And despite the indoctrination of Afrikaners and their negative perception of blacks, they went along with this because they trusted their leaders.

But, Gagiano points out, the Afrikaners' trust could not be relied on utterly. Twice it had faltered in recent years, first when the HNP (Herstigte Nasionale Party) broke away because of the Nationalists' retreat from the Verwoerdian model, and then with the introduction of the tri-cameral parliament. So the volk's trust wasn't total.

However, there was still a lot of trust. 'The referendum in 1992 was an endorsement to proceed with negotiations voted for by 69 per cent of the electorate. 'We trust you to proceed,' they said, in effect. They gave a general sort of warrant to proceed. Had every detail been explained, they probably wouldn't have endorsed it. If they'd seen what they see now, they certainly wouldn't have endorsed it.' Gagiano laughs delightedly. 'That's the trick. Smoke and mirrors, smoke and mirrors, smoke and mirrors.' He repeats the phrase three times with glee.

Suddenly there is an interjection from stage left. A man

with the sad face of an old salesman leans towards us from the corner of the coffee shop and says hesitantly, 'Jannie, I agree with your thesis on change and why people voted "yes" in the referendum, but mustn't we consider the role that sport played? We knew that if we voted "no", we wouldn't have been allowed to take part in international cricket.'

Jannie swings his head slowly in the direction of the interloper, rather as a lion might look at an interfering hyena that is harrying him at his kill. He is not amused that this man wants a bite of the conversation. He gives him a direct stare and a curled lip. I can see that he wants to pooh-pooh the interjection, but finally acknowledges that the man's point might have been a small contributing factor, and he says, 'Ag, I don't agree with the weight you attach to it, but it might have been one of the factors, the straw that broke the camel's back.'

The man says it was a factor in the mind of 'Mr Average'. Jannie snorts. 'I don't want to let Mr Average's model confuse mine.' He laughs hugely. The man gets up and goes.

Jannie turns his attention fully back to me, and as he looks at me I know just how a half-dead springbok must feel when a lion bends down to feed. 'So, where are we now?' he says, wanting urgently to get back to eating politics.

He speaks about the Nationalists' attitude going into the negotiations with the ANC. 'The mindset with which De Klerk and the boys went in was 'Ons kan die donners se klomp blackies op hulle gat sit. (We can put this bloody bunch of blackies on their asses). We've got them by the short and curlies.' That was the mentality with which they entered into the initial negotiations:

> I'm saying that De Klerk wanted a deal but I think they entered the negotiations with assumptions that made them believe they could get a pretty credible deal for themselves. That was the mentality. I talked to a couple of government ministers about that – Kraai van Niekerk among them – and they said to me there was the belief that 'We can get these guys!' It was hubris coming out of having had a powerful 40 years in government. An aura of invincibility. You just can't think of yourself as not being regarded seriously, that you're not important. It

> was a case of psychological carelessness from which they proceeded in their negotiations with the ANC.
>
> The ANC had the same problem. They had an exaggerated idea of the extent to which they could control things.

Gagiano then explores the central dynamic of the negotiation:

> Once you have decided you want some sort of negotiated outcome and the way to go into that outcome is through negotiations, then the logic of sustaining the ambience of a negotiated type of intercourse is already a part of your commitment. Jy kan nie nou hardegat raak nie! (You can't suddenly become hard assed). Jy kannie sê, fok jou, jou hoer, laat loop nou! (You can't say, fuck you, you whore, bugger off). So you are playing a number of games. You are saying, 'I can still handle this.' Roelfie [Roelf Meyer] believes when he talks to Cyril Ramaphosa – hand om die blaas met hom, soos ons sê (hand around the bladder as we say) – he's actually getting somewhere in terms of the larger project, not only in terms of 'I'm giving expression to my Boere gemoedelikheid.' (my Boer agreeableness). Though I'm not so sure about that.

So, I suggest, looking for a deal sets the agenda for civility? Jannie nods vigorously and pays me a compliment: 'That's a nice way of putting it. A better way than I put it.' And he adds, 'Civility then becomes a requirement to continue with the negotiations. But there were some episodes when that was challenged. The one between De Klerk and Mandela, for instance, when civility burst asunder, so to speak, and other such incidents that were not so well reported.'

I compliment Jannie on his insight into this diplomatic dance of the seven veils. He brushes aside the compliment, but says with a grin, 'I'm glad you said that because deep down, I'm very shallow.' And he shouts with laughter.

I'm just glad I'm giving him such a good time. One doesn't mess with lions. He reminds me more than a little of the mafia don in the TV series *The Sopranos* who occasionally enjoys doing his own dirty work with a baseball bat.

Suddenly, just as I'm thinking this, he picks me up on my use of the word 'moegoe' and tells me that I use it incorrectly. It is, he says, an old Transvaal word meaning 'skollie'. I tell him that my understanding is that it means a foolish person, a stupid person. The manager, an Afrikaans woman, is called over to adjudicate and declares me correct.

'Well, I've learnt something,' Gagiano says.

Bravely, the manager says to me, 'Daar is nie baie mense wat vir hom iets nuut kon vertel nie. Dit is 'n verassing!' (There are not many people who can tell him anything new. This has been a revelation!) She grins and bustles away before he can reply.

He tells me about a proposed military putsch contemplated during the time of the CODESA discussions. The ubiquitous Hermann Giliomee told him of a discussion between General Meiring and Constand Viljoen. Apparently Viljoen said, 'Ons kan die plek vat. Ons kan dit in een dag vat.' (We can take the country. We can take it in a day) And Meiring then said, 'Ja, en wat doen ons die volgende dag?'(Yes, but what do we do the next day?)

> This [he says] shows the predicament of the security system in the country that built up over the '80s. It ties in with the intellectual responses they developed to exit the problem. The security system always had the capacity to crush [he savours the word, rolling it round his mouth], to crush ANC-style resistance and bottle up hydraulic pressure from the masses. But the more it did that, the more it dug its own grave.
>
> I always use the image of stepping on ants. You step on a few. They attack and then after a while you are overrun by ants and, the more you stamp and the more you kill, the more they come. It was that kind of slippery-slope logic that was part of the predicament of the security forces and the government.

He explains further with this story:

> Johan van der Merwe, the head of police security, said we had a verknorsing [predicament]. The more we started playing a role in the suppression of the opposition, the more we lost our legitimacy as a police force able to uphold the law. When you collapse the moral logic of policing into the immoral logic of political repression, it means that a policeman can't walk down a Sowetan street to help and protect people from gangsters. Instead, he is seen as an evil representative of the regime. Even black policemen had this problem and they had to build protective sites to isolate them from the 'wrath of the people'.

He exaggerates this last phrase for effect.

> This more and more disturbed professional people. You mustn't underestimate the extent to which an Afrikaner policeman wanted to be a good policeman in a good police force. They were not happy with running a state agency in such circumstances. [Jannie points his finger and says with emphasis:] As soon as the public image of the military gets dragged down by the political role they have to play – then it's putsch time, pal! Look at South America.

He says that contrary to popular belief, the police were not happy campers:

> There is an agency-specific kind of code these people have. They said, in effect, 'You're asking me to kill terries now? I'm not here to kill terrorists. I'm not here for that!' All these internal pressures made themselves felt. You could speak about the fragmentation of the functional efficiency of the entire state. You find the setting up of state agencies against one another. A very good example of this was the way in which Pik Botha and the military were at loggerheads. Intra-state conflict was a big reality.
>
> On the day that the Commonwealth Eminent Persons Group, who were brought in here by Pik Botha,

> the day they left, the security forces hit Harare. 'Whaaaaack!' Just to make the point: 'Hey! Pik Botha, you think you're going to make a deal without consulting us? We'll spoil the cake for you!'

Speaking of cake reminds me that I am starving, not having had any breakfast. Jannie and I order coffee and anchovy toast, which arrives in tricksy little wicker baskets, with balls of chilled butter, balls of anchovy paste and warm toast folded into napkins.

He makes short shrift of the belief that the Afrikaner, softened by materialism, came quietly. Had the ANC been set on massive wealth redistribution, that would have threatened the swimming pool and BMW and the rest, and there would have been a spirited resistance, he says. A real threat to a middle-class existence would have seen a very different response from the Afrikaner, he maintains. The ANC's understanding of the Afrikaners' commitment to their current lifestyle and the ANC's preparedness to let it stand was one of the things that turned the key to a political solution.

He laughs off the thought that the Afrikaner is just resting, waiting for 'Der Tag'. There will be no return to power. 'I will tell you where their best minds are. They are resting in the diaspora, or taking retirement down at a nice strandhuisie (little beach house) where they can privatise their Afrikanerdom through ethnic nesting. I don't see them returning to the public fray.'

We speak about Afrikaans and the concerns I have heard expressed about the survival of the language. He is uncharacteristically fuzzy about this, or perhaps it's me. He speaks of the relationship between government and Naspers, the giant Afrikaans publishing company, and that M-Net, its TV company, is one of the government's main 'financial arteries', and the trade-off that occurs. He also explains how with brown Afrikaans journalists – people with different political agendas and commitments – taking up positions in Naspers, the nature of the Afrikaans press will change.

He also seems to say that with the loss of power, Afrikaners cannot expect to hold onto gains they made 'because of their superior access to the state and state funding'. He adds, 'They can't retain all of those things that are still associated to being attached to power.' But then, confusingly, he says, 'But that doesn't, of course, mean that the new government, with whatever theory of nation-building it has, can just start evacuating a very valuable commodity and piece of cultural equipment that is still available to the Afrikaans community.' He makes the point that there is nothing that can be said in English that cannot be said in Afrikaans, that it 'is part of the entire cognitive store of knowledge on this planet'.

I ask Gagiano briefly about his own politics and he tells me the following story. 'I'm a liberal, but that is a liberal with balls, because that is the type of liberalism you have to exercise in the world we are living in here.' He is committed to speaking out and has warned Tony Leon against any signs of 'wetness'. He uses this expletive most beloved of Margaret Thatcher, whom he met when she was in South Africa, trying to persuade the Afrikaans community that a deal was the way to go:

> She asked me, 'What do you do?' I told her that I was a political scientist. She said, 'What does a political scientist do?' 'Well,' I said, 'you know how biologists put bugs in a bottle and then stare at them, observing their behaviour? Well, I do that with politicians like you!' She moved on quickly to the next guy.

His whole body shakes at the memory of that delicious encounter with the Iron Lady.

On this happy note, we close. It has been an informed briefing, perhaps the most joined-up thinking I've come across. But then, Gagiano is a political scientist, after all. The unexpected bonus is that he is both a political centurion and a robust communicator. My heart goes out to Tony Leon, just thinking of the energy it must require to keep abreast of both Gagiano and the ANC.

To the River

The 600m sandstone buttresses of the Hottentots Holland mountains are lit by the setting sun like some enormous theatrical backdrop for a cowboy movie. Such magnificence seems incongruous, dwarfing as it does the squatter camps we drive by.

I have dashed back to Constantia from my morning with Jaap Durand and Jannie Gagiano in Stellenbosch, had lunch, thrown a few things into a bag and am off on the next stage of the journey.I'm off to the Breede River, my old fishing haunt, with my sister and brother-in-law and nephew for the weekend. We will stay at their cottage at Malgas, which will give me a chance to kick back a little and write up my notes. I have been looking forward to it hugely.

Guy is driving us down in his old Kombi which has just had the engine reconditioned. He and I sit up front, Kirsten is on the next row of seats with enough reference material on bird and plant life to sink the *Titanic* all over again, and Jay is at the rear with Monty the Schnauzer. From time to time, he wanders to the front of the car to inspect the oncoming road from the vantage point of my lap. He is not an entirely welcome load, but one that I put up with. My affections for this dog are tempered by his barking and semi-aggressive nature. Ever since he nipped Kirsten for having the temerity to sit on his mother's bed, I have kept a wary eye on Monty. The little bastard is well named; his namesake also had a bark and was not averse to taking a little nip out of underlings.

It is good, though, not to be driving myself, to be free to observe and make notes as we go, north-east out of Cape Town.

There is much to see and muse over. As we pass the interminable kilometres of pondokkies, (shanties), homes to a million squatters, I wonder about my response to these pitiful places - outrage, pity, fear, resignation? I feel all these things and also acknowledge that these feelings don't stack up to a hill of beans.

These homes and these people are a constant if mute reminder of the inequalities of life in South Africa, and so many other countries. Christ said the poor would always be with us. Is that an excuse? Does it mean we should be comfortable with the fact?

Today, if you choose, you can view these squatter camps in a new light. They have been artistically depicted so often they have become an artistic cliché - kitsch. They are now culturally colourful, rather than merely pitiful. There is a book titled *Shack Chic*, which makes this very point. I wonder if the homeowners are happy to see this distinction.

I know for a fact how house-proud they are. Many of these tumbledown homes are immaculate inside. And these residents and their neighbours form a tighter, more meaningful community than Constantia, says Kirsten. I suspect he is right. In Constantia, the neighbourhood where I'm staying, dogs and cats are probably on more intimate terms with each other than their owners. In Constantia, there may well be a closer bond between homeowners and their security people, the 'rapid response units', than with most other families living in the area. This, I suppose, is true of all such wealthy suburbs the world over.

An ironic comment on community now comes up on my left - Hazelden Park. This is one of the new breed of 'secure communities' where South Africans are taking refuge in ever-increasing numbers. The realities of crime, violence and security are such that the estate agents do not have to work hard to sell the benefits of these places. Guy's father lives in one such in Constantia, my parents-in-law live in another, at Hermanus.

Now we begin to climb Sir Lowry's Pass and I look back at the peninsula unfolded, always, always, a view to cherish and be amazed at once more. At the top of the pass we are soon amid the strange rock gardens of Grabouw, leagues of rock that have burst through the earth in a million jagged shapes, the size of one or two-storey houses.

As we pass Houw Hoek, one of the pleasures of this trip manifests itself. The three people I share this vehicle with are hugely well informed about just about every aspect of this place. Guy says that the name 'Houw Hoek' comes from the word 'Ho', shouted at oxen to stop them at this point, where leather brake straps were placed on iron wheels to slow them for the coming descent, turning the wagons into sleds. In some instances, the wagons would be dismantled and carried up or down the pass after being unloaded. Later they would be reassembled and re-loaded. What a business! It used to take three weeks to get to Swellendam, a journey that now takes three hours.

The countryside in this winter-flowering area is awash with fynbos blossom. There is suikerbos (protea) everywhere. In the small farm dams there are carpets of waterblommetjies (water hawthorn flowers), a staple food in these parts in times past, and still considered a delicacy when made into a waterblommetjiebredie (water hawthorn flower stew). A sign of the times now appears at intervals to our right and left.

It is something I have not seen before, the presence in these vast fields of signs announcing to passing motorists what is being grown. We see 'Barley', 'Canola', 'Koring'. It is all part of the burgeoning agricultural tourism. I can't help wondering at the reaction of these farmers the first time they were asked to put these great yellow signs in their fields, announcing the name of the crop. 'Is julle gek?' (Are you mad?) might well have been the response. I assume that there is some kind of payment made to clinch the deal. Even then, it does seem a bit odd.

That distinctive way-marker, Boontjieskraal, flashes by at the bottom of an immense rounded hill – low white walls, Cape Dutch architecture and the incongruity of three palm trees among these wheatlands.

Up ahead in the darkness we see a massive cross, lit up with electric light, shining above Caledon. 'Caledon has been claimed by Jesus,' says Kirsten dryly. But he is wrong. A sign reads 'Caledon – A World of Rewards', a billboard announcing the Caledon Casino.

But Kirsten is not to be out-argued. 'If you have temptation on one hand, you need to have redemption on the other!' The cross, he says, appeared at the same time as the casino.

Soon we are past this distraction – the standoff between God and mammon, Christ and cash – and the dark settles once more on the land.

We pass those rare picnic places under a few lonely gum trees, a concrete table and concrete chairs, painted white or pale green, which jog my memory. I see my father having a pee at the rear of the car as my mother shells hardboiled eggs and unwraps paper twists of salt and pepper. The chicken and sandwiches are in foil. The coffee, in a thermos, is hot, tasting different and delicious, with the mixed smells of big country and plastic mugs.

Stands of distant blue gums in tightly grown copses speak to me of heimwee (homesickness). In the distance, 20-odd kilometres off, on our left, the Riviersonderend mountains march beside us.

We pull into the petrol station at Riviersonderend. Beside us, a grey funeral hearse is having its tank filled. I feel relieved not to see a coffin in the back. On its side there is a painting of proteas and the words Shalom/Alijac Begrafnisdienste (funeral services). Inside there are tasteful but chilling oyster-grey ruched curtains. They would not soothe me on my last ride, I fear. There is something pretty final about that lifeless colour.

But I am soon distracted from these morbid thoughts, and the easing of my bladder also helps. There is a splendid display of proteas and other fynbos flowers stacked in boxes outside the petrol station shop. We are paid a flying visit by the woman who keeps the toilets pristine. She appears to be deeply religious and manages three biblical references in the minute that she chats to my sister through the open sliding door of the Kombi. It is evident she feels we need saving, and tells us, 'God is everywhere.' Jay acknowledges this truth graciously and the petrol-station priestess then departs.

We turn off the N2, onto my old friend, the 70km corrugated gravel road to Cape Infanta at the mouth of the Breede River. We will stop short of the sea at Malgas, where Jay and Guy have their cottage.

We arrive after dark, and the southern night sky is there to meet us in all its magnificence. Away from the flare of city lights, the full spectacular display of starlight is almost artificial in its brightness and complexity of pattern. After the dim northern night skies I have become used to, this sky is almost too much, too rich, too gaudy to seem real. It is almost unseemly. It is a stellar version of a fat American in a Hawaiian shirt. At some level it offends my toned-down sensibilities. It is incredible.

I stand on the lawn in front of the cottage. The river, about 50m off, is silent. Above me, the misty millions of the Milky Way are stretched like gauze, making a silhouette of the old pine that dominates the garden.

Monty is quiet, quartering the grounds, criss-crossing the lawns in olfactory heaven. I wonder what he scents. In the headlights of the VW Kombi (campervan) I noted earlier that the grass is thick with surings, those yellow flowers whose sour juicy stems we liked to chew as children. They are wet with dew and closed for the night. I pick one and crunch, and childhood is back.

The cottage, too, smells of childhood, of fishing trips heavy with the scent of nostalgia; a paraffin lamp on the dining-room table sends out its old exciting aroma. I am in my own kind of olfactory heaven. I sit like 'Lord Oom Piet' (this is a family saying, but comes originally from a 1962 film by Jamie Uys of the same name, about an Afrikaner who laid claim to being a lord), scribbling, while my Cape Town family unpack boxes and, passing me, look indulgently down on my bald patch.

Kirsten tells me that in this region, as recently as 50 years ago, people lived marginal lives, surviving with aloe tapping, collecting prickly pears in season, keeping a few goats and the odd ostrich or two and maybe a pig, helping to make ends meet. The law of verlate erven (abandoned acres) meant that land left by owners became yours by right if you paid the back taxes owed.

Wheat farming in the 1960s brought a new element to the local economy, but the rainfall is unreliable, and canola, grown for its oil used in margarine, is a more common crop now.

The people who live here permanently are an interesting lot. Their lives are precarious – they are either semi-subsistence farmers or people in flight from the cities. To survive, they take on a range of skills to get by – road grading, selling eggs, collecting rubbish, excavating dams, bulldozing plots clear of scrub and mining shale.

The farmers have fought to survive in this sometimes arid place. They have not always been clever. They shot the caracal – a lynx-like cat – virtually to extinction, with the result that there are now thousands of dassies (rock hyraxes). The farmers have also shot the porcupines that eat through plastic water pipes. But farmers have embraced one form of wildlife: the blue crane, the country's national symbol. Their greatest fear is that one day the jackal, unknown in these parts, will break through the mountains from the Klein Karoo and then, as they say, 'As die jakkals kom, dan is dit verby!' (If the jackal comes, it's over!) For the jackal is seen as a committed and enthusiastic sheep-killer. And sheep are one of the few things that keep this place ticking over economically.

We finally all head for bed. I am tired but I do not fall asleep for a while. My mind is too active. I have not been sleeping well; I'm too stimulated with all the new information and new people buzzing round my brain. I think of my wife and children back in England. How are they coping? Is this trip really justified? Finally I fall asleep, lulled by the country silence.

I wake early, refreshed but bursting for a pee. It is Saturday, 28 June. I don't want to wake the place up by using the bathroom, so I creep outside into the morning darkness and have a leak in the grass. I return as quietly as I can and get beneath the covers. For the first time I appreciate the room. It is simple and charming, with starred chiffon curtains, a hanging bunch of lavender, bags of pot pourri, long glass candleholders and two paintings of distant yachts.

The call of the Cape turtledove, that most typically Cape sound, announces dawn. In front of me speckled mousebirds with long tails and feather crests on their heads look like avian rats as they go up and down the bird feeder, making short work of the oranges and apples that have been put out for them. Cape weavers, chunky yellow balls of energy, sit on the aloes, alongside a single spectacular iridescent blue-green malachite sunbird that cheeps between drinks, its elegant scimitar beak penetrating deep into each flower flute as it sips. There are Cape white-eyes too.

Guy appears with a flag – the Union Jack, in my honour – which he runs up the flagpole outside the cottage. What does it symbolise to me? Two decades and a bit abroad, more than a life sentence. But also peace of mind, access to a larger world, personal growth and not a little pain.

In among the syringa trees and a pepper tree before the cottage I can hear the southern boubou, and then I see it with its go-faster white stripe on a black back, making its distinctive call. A fiscal flycatcher in black, white and grey flies in. These are just some of the birds I see in the first ten minutes on the stoep.

There is a lull and I glance right, down the length of the veranda. The morning mist has lifted now and there is the Breede River. This is my first glimpse of it for a decade. This is the river that almost cost me my life some 37 years ago, when the dinghy in which I was fishing with my father and Pascoe Grenfell nearly came to grief on the vicious bar at the river mouth. Now, the river – here it is 24km from the sea – gleams quietly as a pond, wisps of mist ghosting across its surface, still, still, still. The noise and movement are all avian – Egyptian geese, Cape turtledoves and the constant cicada-like sound from the colony of weavers to the left of the cottage.

Beyond the river a rounded hill rises, its side indented like a cupped hand, filled with renosterbos (rhinoceros bush). A speedboat is launched from a ramp next door and thrums downstream and back up, its engine being tested by a neighbour. At this noise the dew is dashed from the syringas as the birds fly off.

I close my eyes, dozing in the gentle sunlight, and when I open them, I think I see an Angolan pitta. I could swear I see it. The red undercarriage and blue-speckled wing and pinkish throat latch, surely? But I am in need of new lenses for my specs, so I accept that I could be wrong and so won't tempt the wrath of my ornithologist nephew, who would doubtless be scathing.

After a while we take a gentle stroll downstream on a path behind the houses that front the river. Kirsten has gone off to meet some birding friends, so it is my sister and brother-in-law and I who meander down the gravel road past gardens bursting with flowers. Surely this can't be winter? But it is, and the sunshine is costing farmers dear.

At the farthest point of our walk we notice a cottage, number 274, for sale, just a kilometre downstream from Jay and Guy's place. Its garden is dominated by two huge fever trees hung with weaver nests, a mad African take on an English Christmas tree hung with gifts and baubles. A sign says 'Te Koop/For Sale' and invites you to ring Anneke or Lynn to discuss terms. The cottage has a green tin roof that I know will amplify the welcome sound of rain amid these dry, sun-scorched, aloe-covered hills. I look at this place, imagining myself on its deck, overlooking the river, and I dream a little, and for just a moment it's mine. But I know that I will never phone Anneke or Lynn, that my life is now a 12-hour plane ride away. But one can dream.

We walk on a few metres and Guy shouts, 'Look!' Across the river, descending the hillside, are fourteen horse-riders, a frieze against the skyline, and my heart beats harder for a moment and for a moment that cottage is sold. And in the nanosecond that these things take, I build a riding, fishing, writing life around this place. And then I turn my face away and trudge up the hill behind my sister and brother-in-law.

Later, I read this passage to my sister as she prepares a salad for lunch and, hearing the catch in my voice, she says, 'You know you have a place down here whenever you want it. Ours!' And now I can't speak at all, and pretend to continue writing.

On our walk along the river, we have passed cottages with marvellous indigenous gardens, ablaze with winter-blooming flowers. We see two Cape francolin, a black-headed heron on a telephone pole, lesser double-collared sunbirds, Cape weavers galore, Egyptian geese on the riverbank, crowned plovers overhead and Klaas's Cuckoo calling 'Meitjie' (little girl) from the aloes. There are three house sparrows on the thatched roof of a pretty Cape Dutch-style cottage. Hadeda ibises fly over. We see a Cape bulbul and a yellow canary. There is a long-billed lark in a wheat field and there's a clapper lark also, near it. There is a laughing dove without its collar and the Cape Robin looks a bit like its English cousin. The place heaves with bird life.

We stop in the deep cool shade of a massive milkwood tree. I look up carefully and Guy, who has an uncanny ability to read my mind, says, 'Look out for boomslangs.' Suddenly the shade is not that welcoming and I walk, as nonchalantly as I can, out into the sunshine again. He grins.

Back at the cottage, the weavers are hard at work, flying long grasses to their nests in a constant repair process that keeps them busy. I walk down to the river past Guy who is braaing (barbecuing) lunch – cheese and tomato sandwiches on the grid. I've never had a smoked sandwich, but there is a first time for everything.

At the river, I put my hands in the water and time stands still, and then falls back thirty years. I dab it on my forehead, re-baptising myself in bliss. I walk back across the little beach and turn once more to stare at the river. I see my footsteps in the sand, marching down to the water and back again to where I now stand on a grassy knoll, and the tears come at last. I wonder how many years it will be before my feet will once again mark that beach. Irritated with myself, I brush my hand over my eyes and go up for lunch.

After lunch, we pile into the Kombi. Kirsten is back from his walk in search of some rare owl that turned out to be fruitless. Two kilometres from the cottage, we strike lucky with no fewer than 35 Stanley's Bustards in a wheat field. There are also 10 blue cranes and six sacred ibises. Kirsten counts in a rhyme I've never heard before, 'One for sorrow, two for mirth, three for a marriage, four for a birth, five for England, six for France, seven for a feast, eight for a dance.' As he finishes, we spot a lone mongoose.

Our aim is to drive down to Infanta for another meeting with the past. My father has put his cottage up for sale. It is a heartbreaking decision, but my brother lives in California and I am in Sussex. The days of our trips to fish the Bankie at Infanta stopped years ago and the cottage is deteriorating. It makes no sense to keep it.

On the horizon, the Langeberg mountains are a distant smudge. We cross the Melkhoutrivier and all about us now are birds - giant birds, free-range ostriches. A female lowers herself regally onto her clutch of eggs. There are windmills for pumping water from below ground for these birds, but their blades don't turn; there is no wind.

In the distance, the sand dunes of Witsand show up and I know we are approaching the river mouth. Just beyond Kontiki, twelve baboons lope across the road into Port Jackson scrub, swing up onto a farm dam and are gone. A rock kestrel flies over.

And now, suddenly, we are at Die Bankie. This is where I once caught a 102-pound kabeljou (Cape Kob) on a moonlit summer night so many years ago when I was thrilled to be taken along on one of my father's fishing expeditions. I was just 17 then, and some of the intensity of that time and that emotion comes back to me as we walk down the dune from the car-parking area. Jay and Kirsten wait for us in the Kombi. Guy and I stride slowly along the beach to the flat rock formation where I once stood - not often enough, not nearly often enough - to fish this magic place, heavy now with meaning, but once just a place to fish.

I stand on the rock and stare out to sea. It is quite still. For once, there is no wind and the tide is at its height. I see the now and I also see the then - sunshine and moonlight.

I think of the 24 years I've lived abroad, of the decision to go and why I took it, and of the fact that I was wrong in my analysis. That in the end, when the hard question was asked, the Afrikaners finally chose sense over nonsense, turning their backs on all they apparently believed and held dear. I had been wrong about them and as a result my life was now in England, my children English. Had I stayed on, I wonder, how different would my life have been? One thing I know, life has taught me: life demands a price; whatever you do, wherever you live, it's not free. As my mother would say, 'Nothing for nothing and very little for a sixpence.'

I look down at my feet and find an oyster lying just at the

edge of the tidemark. Unusually, it is still alive, shut tight. I pick it up and hurl it back into the embrace of the sea, returning it to its element. I wish I could so easily return to mine. What is mine? Thoughts, feelings, emotions, form a kaleidoscope in my mind. Throwing the oyster back pleases me greatly, however. This bivalve, which might have held a pearl, I return as a gift to the place that gave me such a gift, once upon a time.

Reading my mind again, Guy says, 'For old time's sake, hey Jules?' My large, quiet, unemotional brother-in-law, so different from my sister and me, has summed it up once more.

Returning to the Kombi, we are quiet. As we drive off, I tell Jay and Kirsten what has just happened on Die Bankie. Kirsten sniffs at this and mimes vomiting, finger in mouth. It's all too much. It's a bad case of magical thinking, he says, and gives me a crooked grin. I smile inwardly. Just wait, I think. One day you will understand. Or perhaps not. I hope not.

Just then a lanner falcon flaps past with prey in its talons. The mysterious, banal fact of life and death. To our left, black korhaan, small bustards with black and white wings make their mechanical cry.

Now we head for the village of Infanta itself. A tractor tows a black ski-boat with two fishermen inside, heading home, away from the sea. We drive into the village and find our old cottage looking good on its corner plot overlooking the sea. It has been freshly painted and a sign says 'For Sale'. Beside it there is a group of ploegtydblommetjies (ploughing time flowers), little yellow stars with six petals – the sign hereabouts for farmers to start ploughing.

I turn my back on this place with its shuttered windows. I walk onto the rocks in front of it and watch a cormorant diving in the waves 100m out. I find a sun-warmed saddle of rock and sit down. It is part of a stone formation that wind and tide have turned into rolling convoluted shapes that collect rainwater and bums, both, equally well. The sound of the sea fills the bay. There is no one around but us, four members of a family who no longer come to this place. It is filled with ghosts and memories: Dad, Pascoe, Martin, Henry, Ferdie and Piet. Many of them are no more in this world; they, too, are gone from this place. I say a silent prayer for them and their lives that so enriched my own. Guy joins me and we sit in companionable silence.

He tells me there is a large, tarpaulin-covered woodpile behind the cottage that is a complete snake pit. It is infested with all sorts of local reptiles and I pity the person who has to clear it away. It will require agility, Wellington boots, gloves and a panga. Even then, it will be nervous work and I wonder if a mole-moving smoke bomb might not be a useful precursor to such a task.

We take some pictures, get back into the Kombi and drive through the village vir oulaas (for old times' sake), as they say. On a grass verge we spot a small tortoise dozing in the late afternoon sun.

The few kilometres back to the cottage are into the setting sun and Guy drives carefully. Now we have the Potberg on our left, and three bontebok graze its slopes. Approaching cars on this road come at you like an army on the march – a roiling cloud of red dust erupts behind them, a comet trail of grit. At Lemoentuin we turn in. A sign stands at the crossroads announces the house names on the river here – 'Whispering Waters', 'Doo-Little', 'Shambala' and 'Stumble Inn' catch my eye.

And so to bed. It has been a memorable, bittersweet day.

Sunday morning, 29 June, dawns bright and sunny once more and my thoughts go to the farmers watching the skies for cloud. Selfishly, I don't think of them long, for breakfast is being served on the stoep – croissants, butter, marmalade, Cape gooseberry jam, apricot jam, a sheep cheese and coffee. In the trees about us a Burchell's coucal burbles its lovely call. The river glides by and my mother speaks to me through the call of the turtledoves she loved so much.

My eye is distracted by the sun shining on a large, black, ridge-backed lizard, about half a metre long, which lives on a flat rock beside the bottom of the steps into the garden. I have to pass it each time I walk off the stoep onto the lawns. It gave me quite a turn the first time I spotted it, as I have half been expecting to see snakes – puff adders or Cape cobras – which live here too. I now know that the 'lizard' is made of clay, and is a dubious sort of garden ornament. But it is so lifelike, caught as it is in mid-movement, its head tilted right, towards the lowest step, that I can't help but give it a passing glance each time I descend the steps. Each time I half expect it to twitch into life and run across my feet.

Guy suggests a canoe ride. We collect the white and orange canoe from among the clutter of speedboats, a tractor and a wooden-hulled dinghy with four rowlocks that looks familiar. It is the same little boat in which I nearly checked out from this mortal coil nearly four decades ago. I touch the wooden plank in the prow where I sat as we approached the maelstrom of the roiling river mouth sandbar and recall how I was ordered by my father and Pascoe to put on the only lifejacket in the boat. It seems like yesterday.

How can this dinghy still be here, when all these years have passed and the memory of the event has taken on the dimensions of myth in my mind? It is a bit like having Tutankhamun walk through the door and say, 'Hi!' Time has had a kink put in its cable, as Jannie Gagiano might say.

I shake myself and get a grip on the silver handle at the front of the canoe. Guy and I carry it down to the sandy beach below the cottage. We launch it and paddle downstream past 30 cottages or so, then turn and row back. Monty, who has come along for the ride, stands in the prow, a bearded presence, an old river dog. He ignores the three dogs we pass on the bank – a black Doberman on a balcony, a small Cocker Spaniel on a lawn and a handsome brown and white Boxer standing on a floating dock.

On the next dock, there is a sun-bronzed woman waiting for us to pass so that she can cast her line. 'Pull,' she says encouragingly and smiles. Instead, I stop paddling and ask her what she's fishing for and what bait she's using. 'Steenbras and prawn,' she replies and adds, 'A steenbras was taken here yesterday.' We wish her good fishing and paddle on.

Back at the cottage we put the canoe away in its spot on top of that blue and brown dinghy that so nearly carried me across the Styx. Mentally, I bid it farewell. Life goes on.

After lunch, the cottage is packed up with the skill and lack of fuss that comes from long experience. The Kombi is soon loaded, the water turned off, the flag removed, the front door locked.

The sun shines from a cloudless sky. It is a steady 22 degrees. There is quiet, a lazy peaceful Sunday afternoon somnolence, just the lapping of water caused by a speedboat that swept past minutes ago. There is also that Sunday feeling of pleasure run out, of the call of the workaday world, of Monday on the horizon. I also sense about me a greater African reality, the uncommercial, timeless, agrarian way of life that is the true character of this still largely undeveloped continent.

We climb into the Kombi and ease our way uphill, heavily loaded in so many ways. Almost immediately, we spot two blue cranes and a brown and white bustard, looking to me like some giant goose. On the long gravel haul to the N2 we pass wheat fields contoured round the slopes and flats of hills, the steep cliffs and gullies left wild, too steep and rocky to work. Yellow fields of canola and a hundred-odd herd of brown and white cows mark the foreground; behind are vast spaces, lines of hills folded into lines of hills, folded into lines of hills – the space goes on forever.

We pass the turnoff at Ouplaas for Hamerkop, the other place of childhood magic where my father also kept a fishing shack – another place, another time, more memories. There is a jackal buzzard in an agave tree. We stop on a bridge dated 1959 and look for birds. About us the land unfolds. We are held, in place, in time, for a moment and then move on, breaking the spell.

We crest a rise and there, to our right, clustered round a farm dam, are no fewer than a hundred or more blue cranes, just 20m from us. Kirsten says they flock together in winter and pair off in summer to breed. There are also about 50 ostriches, and it seems as if the cranes have been attracted by the combination of water and the food put out for these birds. We spot a male ostrich with the distinctive red legs they get in the breeding season. At this time of the year they can be dangerous to approach. These birds cost around R2,500 each. Sometimes, with a thousand birds in a camp, there is R25 million walking round in feathers, on stilts.

We drive on and to our left, there are two Egyptian geese

flying level with us, one behind the other. We reach the N2 and turn for Cape Town. As we cross the Freek Botharivier before Riviersonderend, the talk turns to white beggars. There are a few in Cape Town. Guy says they often wear a sign saying, 'Unemployed Breadwinner. Please help. God Bless'. He adds that there is one, a woman, who moves round between Cape Town and Somerset West, sometimes begging with her children. Some beggars have been offered jobs, he says, but when they hear what the pay is, they opt to stay with the begging life.

Buzzards top the telephone poles like Roman battle standards. All are collectively known by farmers as hoenderdiewe (chicken thieves), says Kirsten. There are lonely-looking farms atop hills with their stands of gum trees, grown for firewood and shade.

Just before Sir Lowry's Pass, we pull in at the Peregrine Farm stall and buy springbok pies, rose-petal jam (later we have this combination for supper and it proves delicious), green-mango atjar (pickled vegetables), a warm aniseed loaf and some koeksisters. In the Kombi, we tear off chunks of the warm cake-like bread and drive over the pass, munching contentedly.

We talk of my trip into the hinterland, which starts tomorrow, and I say that I might sleep over at Velddrif.

North-West Into the Hinterland

It is Monday, 30 June and I'm finally off round the Western Cape to look at the country and to listen to people, anyone who will talk to me. I'm not sure if this is going to work, but I feel I have heard enough from intellectuals for the moment.

I drive away from Cape Town in the early-morning dark. My plan is to head up the west coast first, then back along a different route to Paarl and on up to Oudtshoorn and back to Cape Town via the east coast. This is the plan; it may change along the way, depending on a number of variables - my mood, the people I find and the things I see. It cuts a sweep across all the places that have a power to lure me back - my old biscuit-selling routes, my time in the army. It is nostalgia-led and -driven, no question about that. But, conveniently, it also takes me into Afrikanerdom, for this is farming country, where Afrikaans is still the lingua franca.

I hope the old Merc is going to behave. So far it has done well and has not let me down once. I head out towards Blouberg, aiming to drive up to Velddrif and from there to Piketberg where I hope to meet up with Mariette Odendaal and her husband Kobus and see their farm library, and from there travel on northwards.

At Table View, there is a huge electronic sign at the Checkers supermarket, which reads 'Do not leave bags unattended'. I think how bizarre this sign would have looked had I been able to see the future, fast-forwarding 40 years, through my 13-year-old eyes, as my pony Don Juan and I sweated our way through what was then virgin scrub, with nothing around but bush and space. That sign would have seemed such an apparition, a visitor from Mars, not the everyday piece of suburban paraphernalia that it is today.

I drive under the power lines of the Koeberg Nuclear Power Station, which takes electricity into the city, and shortly afterwards see a huge sweeping bay on my left. I'm amazed afresh by the sheer scale and openness of the country around me.

As the sky lightens, I realise I'm back to a strange but pleasant bit of South African driving etiquette – pulling over onto the tarred hard shoulder to let the car behind overtake in safety. One does this whether there is oncoming traffic or not. The driver of the overtaking vehicle gives you a flick of hazard lights to say 'thanks'. Now and then they don't, and I'm annoyed.

As I cross the Modderrivier, I think about how difficult it has been to tear myself away from the safe haven of my sister's home. It has been so peaceful to return there each afternoon, or evening, after a day of interviewing, that I have been a bit reluctant to break loose and head off on my own for a week up-country.

To me it seems there are a number of key issues. I think of them in terms of cash, crime, land, language and AIDS, and though this last does not as yet seem to have impacted on the life of whites, or Afrikaners particularly, it is the real hidden hand of devastation. This is, after all, the country with the highest level of HIV infection and AIDS cases in the world. Few, too few, will live to enjoy the new democracy.

On the language issue, it is clear that older Afrikaners feel Afrikaans is under attack. Many middle-aged and elderly Afrikaners feel sold down the river by the deal de Klerk struck with the ANC, which does not protect minority cultural rights.

These and other, lesser, issues are what concern those I have spoken to. Each alone is a major problem; together they form a witch's brew that the government seems ill prepared, or unwilling, to tackle.

The sun comes up out of the east on my right just as I

pass a burnt-out bakkie (pick-up truck), lying by the side of the road. On either side of me an immense Port Jackson scrub country stretches to the horizon.

We thrum along comfortably at 90kph. The car is happy at this speed but will not do much more. The problem with this old Merc is that it's heavy and it doesn't have much oomph. I think the suspension may also be fairly shot. I worry about how it will handle the passes out of the peninsula and the Outeniquas on the approach to Oudtshoorn, if and when I get there. But on these long, flat stretches the old car goes well enough.

This is truly now the start of a walk down memory lane. I recall driving this road in the years between my 20th and 27th birthdays, coming this way to sell biscuits up the west coast.

To either side of me, there is the odd sand track through the scrub, heading down to the sea on my left or away inland, the kind of path I knew so well in my horse-riding days in the Cape as a boy.

Again, I catch a distant sea view. The South Atlantic stretches north and south and west, and it takes my thoughts with it across to South America and those Afrikaners, the Bittereinders, (Bitter-enders) who left after the Boer War, a century ago. I have an Afrikaans friend whose 80-year-old father has recently visited that part of the world. He had gone, I suspect, to check it out, to see if it presented a viable alternative to life in the new South Africa. He came back and does not talk about going. His question has been answered. One does not change one's life that easily at 80. I know. I found it hard enough at 30.

South America seems a long way off, but who knows? If things get truly bad here, that far-off community might get an injection of new blood. One thing is for sure: the movement of people out of this continent has gone on for millennia. A new Afrikaans push westward would just be another pulse of old Africa's heart.

I pass the turnoff for Darling, where Pieter-Dirk Uys has his 'Evita se Perron', a former railway station converted into a museum, restaurant and theatre and dedicated to Uys' alter ego, Evita Bezuidenhout. Here is another who made his protest bravely, in his case by staying and mocking the white regime, and now their black inheritors. His has been a lonely voice of mad sanity in this crazy place. He, too, is a Boerejood. I decide to pass by Darling. It does not fit with my view of the grassroots. Pieter-Dirk is a mega-celebrity. His nay-saying about white politics at first, and now his naai-sayings about AIDS, (nay saying in Afrikaans is a double entendre, meaning sexual intercourse language), have given him a huge popularity, justly deserved.

A sign says 'Velddrif, 67 km'. I'm half thinking of spending the night there or in Langebaan. I'll see how I go. As I drive, I feel that I have my brother for company, as this is a route he knows well, driving up to stay with his in-laws who had a cottage at Velddrif. Today he lives in California. I feel that he is close by me in spirit, but physically he is half a world away. My thoughts are with him, though, and I send him a wish for sterkte (strength).

This is virtually a tree-free area but for the introduced blue gums at the roadside beside picnic spots. The rest is low scrub country. Two pied crows lift lazily off a piece of mashed roadkill. All around me lies vast open country with distant rolling hills. In the west, off to my left, I can spy a bit of sea through hills. The road runs ruler-straight into the distance, then there is a slight angle, and it continues dead straight to the horizon once more.

It is strange to be alone with a week of travelling ahead of me. I haven't been alone now for the best part of 26 years – ever since I met Janice at university we have been together almost constantly. We've been apart at most for a few days, and then I've had the children for company. So I feel my aloneness strongly and I have a slight feeling of vertigo, agoraphobia too, in these huge empty spaces. I feel exposed in some way that is hard to describe.

This slight sense of agoraphobia explains, perhaps, why it is I've managed to sit in a made-over garden shed behind my house in Sussex for 10 years, writing for a living. Or perhaps that is why I now feel so exposed? I don't know.

I feel a little nervous but also lucky, excited. In many ways, I wish I had Janice with me. It would be wonderful to do this with her – but of course then it would be a very different experience.

But this is a lonely thing to be doing, it strikes me. If you are driving from A to B for a reason, that's one thing, or if you have work on the way; but to just go, meandering round like this, observing and noting for something as insubstantial as an idea in your head, which you hope one day to turn into a book, does seem almost surreal.

I remind myself that I am driving into a disaster area. This glorious weather that I am so enjoying is not good news for the farmers. Unless they get rain soon, the harvest this year will be lost and animal stocks decimated.

I pass the first farm I've seen so far, tucked away among blue gums. In the middle of a vast field, which abuts the farmhouse, an old chestnut horse stands basking in the morning sun. An even older windmill sags in a distant corner of the field.

To my right I see a sign for a fossil park, but I don't want to delay for fear of missing the Odendaals. There is a huge industrial complex belching smoke far over on the left.

I pass a farm called Kleinberg and I think that it will have to be a very small mountain hereabouts, as the land is almost uniformly flat. The biggest hill is just 60 to 100 metres high. Cattle and sheep stand in fields.

The Weskus Spens flashes by – a small farmstall advertising honey for sale, attracting travellers with promises of coffee and breakfast. I realise just how hungry I am. I might stop somewhere ahead, after the farm at Piketberg. It strikes me that I have come a roundabout way, taking the coast road rather than the road through Malmesbury and past Moorreesburg, but I have enjoyed the absence of traffic and the reintroduction to a landscape I haven't seen for years.

I pass a duiker (small antelope) on my left, and then the turning for St Helena Bay and Stompneusbaai, (Stumpnosebay), which takes you up a hill, behind which I suspect the sea must lie. Ahead of me the road stretches for at least ten kilometres and I cannot see another vehicle on it. I compare this to the M25 around London and shudder.

Velddrif appears on the other side of the Berg River. I cross what looks more of a lagoon than a river, a marshy area with saltpans to my left. There are fishing boats tied up. Municipal workers are out watering plants at a time of year in which the heavens would normally oblige. Apart from them, there is hardly a soul about. I turn right, east towards Piketberg, and I pass a sign that reads 'Kerrie-vetkoek' and the thought of breakfast comes again, but curry in fried bread doesn't appeal. Not at this time of the morning.

A line of a hundred short, stubby palm trees planted beside the road overlooks a vast marsh with cattle egrets and what looks like an avocet or a black stilt.

The farm I am headed for at Piketberg is called Nieuwedrif. Beside the road, a man and a woman stand by a small fire they have made to keep them warm while they wait for their lift in what must feel to them like winter chill. The surroundings do not look salubrious – there is a sad, unkempt feel to this place with its cacti, Port Jackson, blue gum scrub and small, rundown one-room shacks.

A huge raptor flies off ahead of me. Where's Kirsten? He'd know what it is, instantly. Wonderful grasses grow a metre high by the side of the road. There are at least twenty pages dedicated to grasses alone in the South African botanical guide. This road is not in great condition and I slow down to 70kph for fear of further damaging the car's suspension. A range of mountains begins to emerge ahead. It seems I'm now leaving the coastal plain for higher ground.

There are signs of fire damage, which spread for a considerable distance. An old bathtub stands alone in the middle of nowhere. Two men sit on their haunches by a tiny fire the size of a cup.

I reach the mountain that I first saw from 30km off near Velddrif and work up its flank. Beyond lies Piketberg. Looking down from the side of this mountain the land looks parched – dor, verlate vlaktes (dry, forlorn plains) – red, brown and grey.

In Piketberg, I stop to ask for directions to the farm from a middle-aged Afrikaans woman with the most artificial red hair imaginable. She tells me to drive south for five kilometres and I'll be at Nieuwedrif. There are indeed four homes on this large farm. The half-a-square kilometre of red gravel homestead area is also filled with various metal hangars and barns for farm machinery. I stop and ask a party of blue-overalled workmen chopping wood if Kobus and Mariette Odendaal are here and they point me down to a house. This stands open to the four winds, doors and windows ajar. I knock and ring the bell but no joy. I should have made a firm appointment instead of turning up unannounced.

I decide to turn round and head back into Piketberg, where I will stop for breakfast, and then go on to Citrusdal. Piketberg nestles under its mountain, its main road generously broad, ludicrous really for such a small town, but it is like all other such main roads in dorps (small towns) across the region, designed for another age, to allow an ox wagon team the space to turn round.

I stop at a coffee shop and ask for breakfast. The décor is based on the skin design of a Friesian cow – large black and white patches on the walls and black tablecloths. I am the only customer and after a while the smiling young woman who runs the place and who cooks my breakfast of bacon and eggs, toast and coffee, introduces herself as Anele de Vries. She speaks accentless English. Her father, she says, worked for Anglo American, so she has moved round quite a bit. She is tall, with the blue eyes and the open face of her Dutch heritage. Her light brown hair is cut short. She is charming. She tells me that she grew up in Springbok in the Northern Cape but went to school after a time, to La Rochelle in Paarl, my mother's old school.

British tourists love Piketberg, she says, and that more and more appear here each year. As I eat, a young man who runs the plant nursery next door and also farms with tomatoes and citrus op die berg (up the mountain) comes in. His name is Joop Vorster. We get talking and Joop speaks about farm attacks in the area and he says that they had a spate of these some time back. A person known as 'Skiet Piet' terrorised farmers in the area, murdering a number before he was arrested and sent down for life. Farm security remains an issue, but locals are not too worried, he says.

Jeff, a retired accountant from Cape Town, arrives. He has bought a citrus farm on the mountain and he says it will take him years to make it pay. Meanwhile, he's enjoying the good life, but if I know any Brits who might be interested, they could have the lot at a price, he says, laughing.

Joop says that one of the biggest changes that has come

with the new South Africa is a polarisation of white society. 'Today whites are divided into upper class and lower class. The white middle class is disappearing.' He believes that whites are either doing well and remaining on top or not doing well and heading down to a lower-class existence. The middle-class gap is starting to be filled by successful black and coloured people, as the more successful whites move up and the less successful down.

As I eat, I notice a small poster about Mariette Odendaal's paintings on the door. I tell Anele that I have just missed her on the farm, and she suggests I drive over to Tulbagh, where there has been an art festival the past weekend. Mariette is probably still there, taking down the pictures she exhibited. I adjust my route accordingly.

There are vast valleys, but always, the mountains are there to lift one's eyes to the heavens. The land grows wheat and wine and fruit and sheep and cattle. It is dramatically different from Holland, Belgium, Germany and France, wherever these settlers came from originally. Table Mountain would have announced that fact to them on the first day of their arrival in this land.

Mountains define the place. There is the mountain range that marches down the spine of the Cape Peninsula, and across from it the majestic Hottentots Holland. Moving inland, there are the Hex River mountains, the Langeberge, the Swartberge, the Overberge, the Cedarberg, and then a gap through the Klein Karoo and the heights of the Outeniquas await the traveller. These stony outcrops are like a giant's hands whose fingers grip the soil; and between the fingers, there are valleys of breathtaking beauty and fertility.

Has this landscape moulded the Afrikaners' character? How could it not? Its gorgeousness has wedded them to it while its richness has helped them celebrate ownership with fine wines and a cornucopia of good things. And there have been enemies enough to hold them together: first, the indigenous tribes who resented the incursion into their own land, and then the British, stealing first the land and then all that lay beneath it – gold and diamonds. The Afrikaners have not been free to enjoy this land without threat, without opposition, without bloodshed, heartache and death. Perhaps that is part of what drove the excesses of the apartheid years? The wish, at last, to enjoy a sense of ownership of this place, a belief that they would find a way to own it forever? But it was not to be. Now, once more, the Afrikaners are bywoners (tenants) in the land they made their own.

Nelson Mandela has said that the horror of apartheid 'in no way detracts from our sense of appreciation of the role of Afrikaners in building our common land.' And Madiba has chosen a blonde Afrikaner woman, Zelda la Grange, to be his personal assistant, a woman he refers to as 'Darling'. But Mandela will not live forever.

I head for Porterville and Tulbagh, crossing the Kromrivier, which bisects a vast, rolling plain reminiscent of Spain near Salamanca. The land has been tilled but nothing is coming up yet. Dams are dry. Ahead, more serious-looking mountains stand guard.

Another pass takes me into Tulbagh, a beautiful town that has been rebuilt since an earthquake devastated it in 1969, the year I did my army national service. Today the town boasts more national monuments in one street than any other town this size in the country, and although it is charming, it has for me the slightly unreal air of a museum. Historic Church Street has no fewer than 32 national monuments, a row of fine Cape Dutch homes.

Besides heritage, Tulbagh produces another wrinkled crop – it is the main producer of plums for prunes in the Cape. The place also boasts some very well-known local wines, as well as wheat, apricots, pears and, more recently, olives. In fact, this Mediterranean crop is enjoying something of a local boom. People pickle their own and there is even an annual olive festival in the nearby town of Riebeek Kasteel.

I park the car and stroll down Church Street, looking into one or two of the old houses, some of which are now boutiques selling local craftwork and tourist tat.

It is just before 5 p.m. as I drive over the bridge into Citrusdal. I have had thoughts of pushing on to Clanwilliam, but decide not to risk my luck on the accommodation front. The broad high street of this country town is busy with farm workers as I drive slowly, looking for B&B signs. My route takes me gently uphill and I find myself off the main road at a small curio shop.

The curio shop owner says she has accommodation on her farm but unfortunately it is booked up and she makes a call to the Olifantsrus guesthouse just outside Citrusdal. They have a place and she gives me directions. I ask her where I should eat and she suggests Patrick's in town.

We chat briefly and she tells me that she studied at Stellenbosch but instead of pursuing a career she married her husband, a farmer, and moved here. She says there's not a bookshop for miles and that if she wants books she has to go into Worcester or Cape Town, which are equidistant. The local library isn't particularly well stocked either, she says. A request for Steinbeck's *Grapes of Wrath* was met with the question, 'Is the author alive or dead?' She giggles.

About 5km out of town, I find Olifantsrus in an isolated spot amid deep green gardens backed up against a koppie. My hostess, Ilse, says she has three dogs to protect the place against intruders. The first, a Fox Terrier, alerts everyone; the Rhodesian Ridgeback sorts them out; and I suspect that the young Boerboel, once he is fully grown, will eat them.

I have the feeling that in places like Citrusdal, the skin over the new South Africa is stretched pretty thin, too. Little seems to have changed and I suspect great shocks await people. If tourism dries up and access to work diminishes further, things could get very tough for whites. To be born into poverty is hard, but so is having had a good life and finding it gone. I drive into town to have supper at Patrick's restaurant on the main road through town, which now is as quiet as a graveyard. The sign outside the restaurant reads 'A cut above the rest'. It's a proud boast and I enter to check it out.

I look out the window and realise that there is some human traffic outside after all, one or two brown people out on the pavement walking along tiredly. In here it's all white, staff and the few newcomers who are shown to tables at distances from each other. Across the road, a huge double-trailered truck is parked with its hazard lights blinking while its driver shops at a store bedecked with Coca-Cola signs. This huge 24-wheeler, owned by one DJ Bosman, finally moves off and I see revealed a single-storey house with a veranda featuring a thin tracery of broekielace (wrought iron latticework). The walls of this place are painted in an out-of-character African motif, huge blue and yellow diamonds running horizontally across the front, the kind of thing one might see on a rondavel in the rural areas of the Eastern Cape. A sign outside reads 'Drop Zone Restaurant and Pub'. It is dark and closed. Death by décor?

Allesverloren (All is Lost)

I telephone Danie Malan early on 2 July. I have never met him or spoken to him before, but within a minute, he has invited me over. 'Het jy al ontbyt gehad?' (have you already had breakfast?) he asks. I say thanks, yes, I have already eaten breakfast, and he says don't worry, come and have a coffee and we'll talk. He has a deep, guttural voice. I am not surprised by this instinctive hospitality, it is one of the marks of the Afrikaner, one of the most disarming and heartwarming. When English friends visiting South Africa for the first time ask me: 'How dangerous is it really?' I like to tease them a little by saying: 'It is dangerous. You could die there!' And when a look of alarm crosses their faces, I add: 'It's the hospitality that will kill you!' And it seems this remains true.

I drive out to the farm and within 10 minutes I'm seated at a stunning yellowwood table in the dining room of the farm Allesverloren. The walls are adorned with old photographs and above the fireplace there is a framed baptismal gown. The table, which can seat 20, it soon becomes apparent, is an historic one, like so much else on this farm. The room is like something out of a museum, with riempie (plaited rawhide seat) chairs, stinkwood and yellowwood cupboards and a grandfather clock. It has the feel of a large sailing ship's stateroom, all the joinery, including floors, walls and ceilings, made lovingly by the hands of craftsmen.

I ask about the pictures, particularly one in which the man seems vaguely familiar. It is Dr DF Malan, who became the country's first Nationalist prime minister in 1948, the brother of Danie's grandfather. By luck, I have come to the home of Afrikaans 'royalty'. The table we sit at has had all the country's political leaders, including Dr Verwoerd and most recently Kader Asmal, sitting at it. The former Minister of Education was at the farm recently and he said to Danie, 'Allesverloren is not only about Malan history. It is our history too – it is part of all of us.'

Danie approves. He knows that the farm is 'his' for 30-odd years at most and then a new generation will take it on. As a farmer, one is at best a custodian, not an owner.

But I soon find that the old truism, don't judge a book by its cover, is as true as ever, and that there is more to this man than at first meets the eye. It becomes apparent that he is something of a philosopher, and shrewd to boot.

To farm in Africa is tough, he says. He is the eleventh generation of Malans to farm. He says the political change didn't surprise him, but to a lot of people it was a shock. 'There were people bunkering up, stocking up on food, saying there's one hell of a fight that's going to happen.' Personally, he couldn't see it happening that way.

His experience of national service on the border and in Angola made him grow up fast. 'It also made me very reluctant to think aggressively in 1994, because I know what fighting can do.'

He says the Afrikaner was tired of war, everything from the Boer wars through to the war against communism. They were fed up with fighting. Blacks, too, were tired. The ANC wanted to do a deal just as much as the Afrikaners. 'We were two tired nations sitting round a table saying, "Why fight? We're wasting time."'

Mandela, he says, was 'not a miracle worker, just a very broadminded guy. He's what we needed at that stage, and of course De Klerk was also a help in the process.'

The Afrikaners have changed for the better, he says, and adds that since the change in 1994 the farm is also doing better, both with local sales as well as exports. Happily, he says, 1994 did not turn South Africa upside down. Each side expected either the best or the worst to follow, depending on their politics, but neither happened. Life just continued much the same.

'Change there has been, dramatic change. But if you're living with it every day, as we are, you don't really see it that way.'

His own children never speak of black or brown or white children – they are just children. He points to the parallel after the Boer War. 'We, English and Afrikaners, became the South African nation, klaar! Finished! That was it.' He believes the same process is now under way. Old enemies, intractable issues, all gone into history.

Something that is not yet safely in the preserve of history is the land issue. This does not concern him that much, he says, though he'd like to see President Mbeki make a stand on Zimbabwe and the ongoing dispossession of whites from their farms.

In South Africa, he says, there is enough land available to start reforms. However, he believes that one can't force the land issue too quickly because there wasn't a farming culture among black and brown peoples. 'You can't put somebody on a farm who can't farm!' I ask about the experience of all the thousands of farm labourers.

Africa needs food and the security of knowing that food will be produced, he says. Small farmers grow for themselves, not for the national economy. It will take training and education to bring on a generation of black and brown commercial farmers.

Malan makes a clear distinction between theoretical and practical farming experience. He did his agricultural course at Elsenberg Agricultural College and then went to Stellenbosch University to study agricultural economics. His lecturer there told the class that they now knew more than their fathers and should send them, the older generation, packing. 'I stood up then and said his statement showed why he was lecturing rather than farming!'

Farming is inherited and each generation learns from the last one. So the land issue should proceed gradually, he believes, so that the production of food is not endangered.

We speak about race relations today and he tells how he was carried shoulder-high by the coloured rugby team he coached when they won the coloured Farm Rugby League. It patently touched him. He adds that there was a nice irony in the fact that on that same day PW Botha, the former Prime Minister, was making a political speech at Allesverloren. He adds a story of how, when his relative, Dr Malan was prime minister, he shook hands with farm labourers and what a revelation that was at the time, back in the '40s. 'That was an unthinkable thing to do back then. They asked him why he had done it and he said, "We grew up together. We are friends."'

At Stellenbosch, he says, he was told by young Nationalist supporters – Jaap Marais' granddaughter among them – that Dr Malan would be turning in his grave if he knew what was happening in South Africa today. (Jaap Marais, late leader of the marginalised far right Herstigte Nationale Party.) 'I told her my parents believed that if Dr Malan was alive today and prime minister, he would have done what FW de Klerk did, only much, much sooner.' He speaks of a sermon at the local Dutch Reformed Church in which the dominee said Desmond Tutu was the biggest Christian he had ever met.

He also makes the point about the Afrikaners' closeness to black and coloured people. 'When you are out on the land, working or hunting, your workers sit with you, by the same fire, and you talk and drink coffee together. You talk about the land and about the livestock and about the rooikatte (caracal cats) that kill the sheep. Ons sit langs dieselfde vuur (We sit next to the same fire).'

I'm not too sure about this last idea. But Danie is sincere; he believes it, he's not trying to shoot me a line. The stories he tells are aimed at showing that there has always been a greater complexity between the races than outsiders would believe. But one can only wonder how much value a farm worker would have placed on a prime minister's handshake when his own children did not have schools or much of a future?

However, Danie is frank enough about the nature of the Afrikaner. 'Look at Australia. It started with bandits and criminals chased out of England. I don't think we were that different.' I pass on that one.

He says that the Afrikaner approached farming on a rather socialist system – a form of protected economy. 'It was very nice for farmers. But now it is everyone for himself. I welcome that because I am a total free-market man, but it is a high-risk environment.'

His personal philosophy is inherited from his father, he says. 'My mantra is, "Make a difference!"' He says that the advice his father gave him was, 'As jy stap, los net 'n spoor.' (When you walk, just leave a trail.)

And now he says something that touches me. We talk about who and what the Afrikaner is and he says no one may claim that title – to call himself an Afrikaner. '"Afrikaner" is not a label you can claim for yourself. It is up to others to acclaim you an Afrikaner. If you leave this a better place one day, and they say of you, "Hy was 'n Afrikaner", well, that is another thing. But you cannot, you do not have the right, to acclaim yourself an Afrikaner. It has to be earned.' He adds, 'The Afrikaner is not just another brand. It's a total commitment to your country and your people.'

He likes the image of the Rainbow Nation. 'It is so appropriate. We get a rainbow after all the hardships of a hard, dry summer. The good rain comes and with it the rainbow. For a farmer, this is a potent symbol.'

Speaking of symbols, it seems like a good time to ask him about the meaning of 'Allesverloren' and to ask if he thinks alles is verloren? He is happy to oblige. The name, he says, was given to the farm after it was destroyed by a local tribe in 1704. The owner, a widow named Cloete, had gone to Nagmaal (communion) in Stellenbosch – a two-week journey in those days. On her return she found the farmhouse burnt to the ground and the farm wrecked. Thus it became known as Allesverloren (All is Lost).

But here is the magical thing. By a curious irony, the fate of Allesverloren has since been an unusually happy one. By 1806, Allesverloren's owners had already harvested the estate's first wines, and since the estate passed into the hands of the Malan family in 1872, Allesverloren has gone from strength to strength. The estate has increased to a size of 227 hectares (560 acres) and continues to make wines of renown.

So here was a symbol indeed. Out of catastrophe, a phoenix farm had arisen. Faced with the worst fate could do, short of death, the widow Cloete did not pack for Perth or

Amsterdam or go back to Cape Town. She started all over again and built for the future. Today the farm makes Shiraz, Tinta Barocca and Cabernet Sauvignon wines as well as a stunning port. When all seemed lost, a widow had the strength of character to begin again.

There comes a moment in each journey when a synthesis occurs, when fruition or its opposite is achieved, when the trip becomes a success or a failure. It is not always something that one sees till long after the journey is over. Now and then, one has the privilege of recognising it at the time. This was one such moment.

As I sit speaking to Danie I realise that if the Afrikaners could but hear this story, and take on board its central message, then indeed was alles nie verloren nie – all was indeed not lost. Yes, power was gone, but there was hope of a peaceful, prosperous future, and all there was to fear was fear itself. If a widow could find the fortitude to continue in the face of devastation 200 years ago, then today's comfortably off Afrikaners had no excuse but to travel in hope.

Danie says that if the future were managed properly, the Afrikaner could live without politicians. What was needed was good government. What was needed from the ANC was accountability. 'The government must realise the responsibilities of freedom.'

I listen and smile inwardly. Perhaps the ANC government would take this lesson on board – a lesson, some would argue, the Nationalists had never learned.

It irritates Danie that young Afrikaners, the very ones who had shouted loudest for change, are leaving the country. 'I'll stay, come what may, but I won't force my children to stay,' he says. His children have right of residence in Italy, thanks to their mother Juanita, whose maiden name was Firmani, a family of Italian extraction.

The point Danie makes about those who wanted change leaving touches me personally. I wanted change but I left and am not coming back anytime soon. And this is the strange thing. I can see now, today, that thanks to apartheid, we had stability in this country – stability that came at a terrible price for blacks and coloured people. But what would the alternative have been if liberals like myself had got our way in the '60s with one man, one vote? A civil war sponsored by America and Russia? Quite possibly. Possibly not. I will never know. But the irony is not lost on me. I am old enough to know now about the politics of unintended consequences and that the road to hell can be paved with good intentions.

Danie believes that in another 20 years the country will have a totally integrated multiracial government. He looks to the lessons of the Great Trek and says that it had no one leader. Every community or group had its own leader. 'Today, no group in South Africa has a strong leader – even Mbeki is having trouble sustaining his support and popularity.'

Women are the true leaders, he says, surprising me once more. 'The only way that the English could beat us was by taking away the women and children. Our women are our best leaders.'

The Afrikaner must also continue to depend on himself, not on others. 'Glo in God, glo in volk, glo in jouself!' (Believe in God, believe in the volk, believe in yourself!)

The problem with the Afrikaners was their independence, he says. 'If you get four Greeks together, they build a café; four Jews will build a synagogue; but get four Afrikaners together and by the end of the day they will have formed four different political parties.' Danie laughs.

He says a definition of the Afrikaner is being an optimist against all the odds; to farm in Africa, that view is essential. He tells the story of a Vredendal farmer who had lost two farms. Asked why he was so relaxed, he said, 'I'm not worried. It's the bank that's worried!'

'I'm passionate about life. I'm a totally committed optimist. I eat, drink and laugh too much and work too little! But you only have one life!' He adds, however, that his passion and his hobby are his work. One only has to look over the immaculate farm or see his awards to know the truth of that statement.

Finally, we talk of the need for rain. Yesterday's brief shower has made little impact. The churches are once more filled with farmers praying for rain. This leads to a brief aside on religion. 'Christianity as practised by the NG church offers a sombre life but a good life. But today the younger generation want religion to be fun,' he says, and smiles wryly.

His wife Juanita pops in briefly and tells of a recent trip to Sweden where Danie was described as the 'Naked Winemaker', because 'what you see is what you get'.

It is not an apt description of this man. There is much more to him than one at first supposes. As such, he is a good example of his breed: phlegmatic, flexible, a survivor. Enough Danie Malans and surely sal alles nie verloren wees nie! (and surely not everything will be lost!)

The Afrikaner in me warms to this man and his open-hearted hospitality and warmth; and the Jew in me is equally warmed by the welcome. In my strange bi-focal vision of the world Danie Malan is a symbol of hope and pride. As I depart the farm, I feel somewhat choked with emotion.

North Again

I stop in Paarl to pay my respects at my mother's grave. I have carried a small stone from England with me to place on her tombstone, a nice Jewish tradition that outrages nobody alive or dead among the cypress trees in this Dutch Reformed graveyard. I remove the two dozen dead roses, brought here by my father on his monthly visit to his wife. I place them in a dustbin, except for one, which is still in fairly good shape. I place it beside my Sussex stone.

As I sit by my mother's grave, I am no longer sad. I get no sense of her presence but thoughts of her fill my head as I look at Paarl Rock across the valley. Her sense of humour sustains me, her irreverence. I wonder what she would have made of this trip, this book? I think she would have been much amused, but pleased too.

The step she took in the 1930s, marrying my father, was so huge, so brave, I can only wonder at it and at the power of love. Fortified once more, I climb into the car and drive gently away, this time headed for the Du Toit's Kloof Pass.

For some unfathomable reason I miss the new highway that punches a tunnel through the mountain, and find myself instead on the steeper slopes of the old pass. The car seems fine with this route and I slide back the sunroof to get a better view of the rock faces above me. We take it slowly and stop once or twice to take in that spectacular view back to Table Mountain.

And then we are over, and start the descent to Worcester, which I find is no longer a large dorp (village) but a small city. I work my way through the afternoon traffic and head out on the road to Robertson. This is the road I'd use driving back to the army camp in Oudtshoorn, at the end of weekend passes when I was doing my national service. So for me, this road is dredged with that Sunday afternoon feeling of sadness that is a forerunner of the dread of Monday and all that it means. Today, Route 62 has become a favourite South African excursion, taking in as it does so many wine estates, fantastic scenery and charming towns along the way.

I'm distracted by roadworks in Robertson but eventually find the road I'm looking for, east to McGregor. I've never been to McGregor but have heard many good things about it. In England I have even inspected it via the Internet and, hearing of a new Rudolf Steiner School started there, wondered if this might not be my new Jerusalem, like so many other places briefly looked at and then discarded, for one reason or another. I intend staying the night and seeing what the place is like. I book into the Green Gables Country Inn, a collection of old Victorian cottages turned into a comfortable country hotel. The couple that runs it is busy preparing this evening's dinner when I find them in the kitchen.

McGregor does seem something of an oasis, but an English oasis rather than an Afrikaner one. The place is a small collection of green and white cottages, many with staircases up the side to a solder, or attic, where in the old days everything from dried fruit to coffins would have been kept. Brooding mountains and hills give the place a Tinus de Jongh kind of feeling, a sense of being away in a far country, captured so well by this popular South African artist.

My hosts, 'Tiger' and Jill Meyer, are former Jo'burgers, anglicised Afrikaners who've worked together for all the 35 years of their marriage. Here in McGregor, they have created a gem. The place is packed for supper; without doubt this is the heart of McGregor after dark.

This village recommends itself in many ways beside its physical charms. Its English character here at the edge of the Klein Karoo is unusual. There is a spiritual retreat at the centre of the place. And, perhaps most exceptional, it is an integrated white and brown community.

Tiger tells me the place started as a base for cutting bamboo whip-handles for ox teams. Bundled up, they were exported all over the world. Today, McGregor is growing thanks to tourism and retirement homes. The valley is blessed with good underground water and there are some 32 wine estates in and around McGregor and Robertson.

The British nature of the place owes something to the Scottish ministers who were brought in to serve the Calvinist churches. Tiger is gently amused by the fact that in graveyards hereabouts the whites have black gravestones, and the coloured people, white gravestones.

This latter fact further broadcasts that the realities of inequality are obvious here. There is an unusually intimate mix of wealth and poverty. Tiger says, 'When a man brings you a bag of wood to sell, the money is urgently needed for that night's food. If you see someone dragging a length of Port Jackson wood, you know that's his fuel for tonight's fire. Here we have learnt the value of a rand.'

There is a tree full of weavers' nests and a splashing fountain in the Green Gables garden. I feel content. It has been a good day. My talk with Danie Malan and the beauty of the drive here have left me feeling upbeat and positive.

As I sit writing by the fire, an older woman in a black coat walks over and asks if she might share the fire. She apologises for interrupting my writing. I tell her she is not interrupting at all and we start chatting. In the first five minutes she reveals that she is Jewish and soon it emerges that she is a convert – an Afrikaner who married a Jew. Briefly, I outline my parents' story. She is amazed and tells me more of her own life.

She has children and five grandchildren, is well travelled and still speaks excellent Afrikaans, and yet is committed to the strictest Jewish dietary laws. She speaks of how the Jews look after their own. 'No Jew ever lies in the gutter. There is a Jewish old-age home. My Jewish friends are wonderful, unbelievable. When they do a thing, they do it.' I say that the Afrikaners are also a warm people. She agrees but in the final analysis she opts for the Jews. She is, in this, very different from my mother, yet both opted to throw in their lot with the Jews when very young. It seems an astonishing thing to do, given their cultural conditioning. I can only respect them for it.

She asks me a question that I have often pondered. 'How

much did your father have to pay to have you and your sister and brother accepted as Jews?' I tell her that I don't think money changed hands, but when I get back to Cape Town I intend to ask my father for the answer to this question.

Speaking about the Afrikaners, she says, 'Today people are proud to be Afrikaans,' and adds, 'The previous government messed with our minds!' Today she feels the Afrikaner is learning that other people, other nationalities, other religions, have morals and ethics too. At the end of the day she believes 'all will be well in South Africa.'

We have supper together and I forgo the delicious roast pork out of respect for her convictions and settle for one of the chicken pies I saw being assembled earlier. Once again, I have bumped into a Boerejood, this one by adoption, as it were.

The next morning, I have the pleasure, if that's the word, of Vincent, Jill and Tiger's grey poodle, as a breakfast partner. Tiger, who's very proud of this pooch, coaxes him up onto the chair opposite me and, watched by all in the breakfast room, proceeds to dress Vincent (who, it must be said, seems up for it) in a tartan tam o'shanter, a tartan bowtie, a bib and specs. Once dressed, the dog is served bacon at my table. I feel the smile muscles in my cheeks ache. Monty's revenge, I think!

Life is strange. Last night I shared a table with an Afrikaans Jewess who would not touch pork. This morning it's a French poodle in Scottish rig, eating bacon.

South Again

I drive east, through a landscape filled with the burning candelabra of aloes in full bloom. It is 80 kilometres to Mossel Bay. The old Merc, slow but steady, takes on the Robinson Pass at 860 metres and wins. The mountains are like sharks' teeth, row upon row of serrations. The view from the top, down across 30km to the curved hook of Mossel Bay, lifts the heart. I am in another world, one edged by sea, with all the possibilities that brings. Within an hour and a half, I have left Oudtshoorn behind and am booked into the Post Office Tree Hotel in Mossel Bay with a view of the sea.

I call Cape Town and get my messages, including a telephone number for Max du Preez, one of the country's most distinguished writers, broadcasters and editors. He is the former editor of the brave anti-establishment newspaper, *Vrye Weekblad,* distinguished TV commentator and author.

I phone him, introduce myself, explain my business, and find that I have virtually driven past his new home in Barrydale at lunchtime. He is hoping to start a literary festival there soon he says. He tells me that many leading liberals, including Jannie Gagiano, who used to lecture him at Stellenbosch, are now becoming less liberal. Gagiano and other 'so-called verligte intellectuals' are increasingly worried about Afrikaans and the lack of Afrikaans as a medium of education, he says:

> I would like to destroy the last 35 pages of Hermann Giliomee's book, where he says that FW de Klerk sold the Afrikaners out. I wish Giliomee could have been as cool and dispassionate about the most recent chapter in

> our history as he was about everything else he wrote about. Still, you should read his book at some stage.
> All these Afrikaners, as I've begun to think of them, have gone all ethnic on me, worried about Afrikaans language and culture. We must become part of a bigger whole. Besides, the language has never been richer than it is now.

The debate over the future of the language is creating deep rifts among Afrikaner intellectuals. The taalstryders (Hermann Giliomee et al) have been called 'taalbulle' (language bulls), by Max du Preez, as an insult – the inference being that bulls charge at nothing and bulls in china shops are a damned nuisance. The answer of the taalbulle was to label Max, Willie Esterhuyse and the rest of the non-stryders as 'taalosse', (language oxen), saying they were too meek and mild to fight for Die Taal (The Language of Afrikaans).

I can only think that this broedertwis (fraternal friction) must be highly diverting to many non-Afrikaners, who are surely rubbing their hands with glee.

On another contentious issue, the presence and influence of 'black' and 'brown' blood in the Afrikaner, Max and I find agreement. We believe that we have a common ancestor in Anne of Bengal, and I add that if we go back to the anthropologist Christopher Henshilwood's Blombos cave on the Swellendam coast (in which man's presence at the Cape goes back millions of years) we are all related. He seconds that.

I am intrigued by Max. He has a quality of grounded intelligence that is very attractive. There is none of that self-importance that so often accompanies great intelligence and a national profile. He sounds a very nice human being. He is part of that twinkling blanket of light – an intellectual firmament – that echoes the magnificent African night sky over South Africa.

I am very sorry to have missed him in Barrydale. We share stories about Piet Cillié, a neighbour of my family at Blouberg and Max's first editor at *Die Burger*. He wasn't a fan, he says.

After coffee I brace myself and walk over to a group of locals. They invite me to pull up a chair once they know that all

I want is their opinion on South Africa's current situation and nothing more.

Their concerns are mainly about jobs and the problems of affirmative action. 'If our kids follow us into our business, they will be OK in the future, otherwise I don't know,' says the young woman on my right. She adds that for professionals there doesn't seem to be much future. And she says that drugs and crime are becoming a problem. 'In 10 years' time, it will be as bad as Jo'burg here.' Pragmatically, she says, 'We can't live in paradise forever, I suppose. We live for the day. We worry about crime, but if it happens, we'll deal with it. It may never happen. But if it affects my children, then I'll go.'

Emigration is rising, they say. Among Afrikaans school leavers, the 18-20-year-olds, many are going, as they don't see a future for themselves here.

But, life, the group agrees, is still good. 'We live well. The quality of life in South Africa is still very good. We have all this space – die ruimte. Here a nine-year-old boy can walk three kilometres to his friend's house, or ride his bike there. That's how we grew up also.'

Racial tensions remain, but it's disguised, they say. 'Mossel Bay is too conservative for the races to be integrated. It's not cosmopolitan at all. There is no open racism, but when you're with your own trusted friends, then it's a different matter. Everyone puts on a nice face, hey, but really it's not like that. In private it's another matter.'

They say that racial mixing is easier in cities, but in small communities like Mossel Bay, it is not much different to how things were. 'The races do not mix socially.'

The young redheaded woman at the other end of the table says suddenly, 'Speak to me. I'm the intelligent one!' She looks as if she has had slightly too much to drink. She says that she and the girl to her right are lesbians. Her friend does not look happy to be 'outed' in this way in front of a stranger, and glowers. Undaunted, her friend continues that they want to have kids and would I be prepared to help? I reply that as this is a common male fantasy, they have only to ask to find a queue of men forming round the block. She takes this as a no, and returns to her own conversation. I thank them all for speaking to me and take my leave.

I have a disturbed night. At 2 a.m., someone is busy outside my window hosing and brushing down the pavement. I lie awake thinking of the trip, the people I have met and the places I have seen. My mind is buzzing.

Breakfast in the hotel restaurant offers place mats that shout 'Good Morning!' and 'Live life slowly in Mossel Bay'. The restaurant is called the Oyster Bar. There are African-print tablecloths and on a wall there is a backlit seahorse.

After checking out of the hotel and loading the car, I stroll round the corner to have a look at the Post Office Tree, an 800-year-old milkwood of enormous size. Letters were left here, hanging in a shoe, suspended from one of its branches. The tree stands 100m up the slope from the beach, next to the freshwater spring where the early Portuguese mariners stopped to fill their casks. They drew water here from 1488 onwards. In May 1501, Pero d'Ataide, captain of a homeward-bound ship of Pero Cabral's fleet, left a message here, which was found on 7th July 1501 by the outward-bound ships of João da Nova. I'm standing here 502 years later, to the day!

I touch the tree softly on its trunk and branches. This is living history. Doubtless it will be here long after me. A sign near the trunk reads 'No Loiterers' in a harsh, local-authority orange and black script. Below me, the sea is calm and the air temperature a comfortable 20 degrees. There is no wind and just a light cloud. The beach abuts a rocky headland on which my hotel stands. Looking down, I can so easily imagine the small ship in the bay, the rowing boat lowered from its deck and the men straining at the oars. The landfall just below me, and the easy climb up the slope to this tree. What is 502 years?

I stroll over to the museum across the lawn to see a replica of the caravel that brought Bartholomeu Diaz here in a six-month journey from Portugal. The new caravel on display did the same journey in three months. It is beautiful, a small, stoutly made boat with fat bulging sides, around 15m long by 6m broad. Amidships there are two masts and from them hang long curved beams from which the sails are suspended. Bold red crosses mark the sails. What brave, brave men! What would have possessed them to undertake such a journey into the unknown? Was it a desire for fame, action, money, status? Perhaps it was, as Danie Malan said, a wish to leave a spoor, a trail in the sands of life? A trail that said, 'I did something. I made a difference.' Probably it was a mix of all these various things.

I get into the car and head south. I take a wrong turning, which brings me to a luxurious estate overlooking the sea from the cliff top. It is reminiscent of Hamerkop, where my father kept a fishing shack. I like Mossel Bay. I like the sea, the bay, the views, though I don't like the stories about the great whites out in the bay. I do like the town, the hill that it's on, the history. In fact, I think I could live in Mossel Bay. It's a town that would make no demands on you. And you'd have fishing, swimming, boating, horse riding in the hills beyond, up at Eight Bells, where friends have a holiday home tucked into a mountain fold. It is not a town with pretensions of its own, nor, I imagine, would it expect much of you. There is a peace in that. People might be surprised to hear you were living in Mossel Bay. I like that. I find the route out of town eventually and head for Riversdale, Swellendam, Caledon and Hermanus. The latter half of the road is the one I travelled with Guy, Jay and Kirsten only last weekend. In a way I have come full circle.

On the horizon is a gas flame, I assume from the offshore gas field, the Mosgas Project. There is an enormous plume of pollution across the sky.

I recall Danie Malan's story of the Afrikaners, the Greeks and the Jews, and think to myself that the Greeks and Jews, in my experience, are infinitely more disputatious than the Afrikaners. Four Jews would probably form five political parties and sell the extra one off at a profit! I'm reminded of the old joke about the presidents of the United States and Israel meeting. The American boasts that he is president of 250 million people. The Israeli president compliments him and says in response, 'Mr President, that is a lot of people. But you must remember this. In Israel, I am the president of five million presidents!' Israelis are lekker moerig (pretty aggressive) and that pleases me greatly.

The country is gently rolling, with sheep and cattle in the

fields. The old car touches 100kph, stretching its legs. To my right there is a line of mountains, running north to south, that stride across country for some 80 kilometres, before disappearing into the far distance.

I pass chunks of tyre retreads cast off by the side of the road. To my left, there is a sign for Ystervarkfontein, (porcupine fountain) and later, an aloe-extraction factory to my right. A car with CAW plates flashes past – a big white BMW – and I recall that CAW used to stand for 'cold and wet'. It is the registration for George, a small town up the coast whose airport runway my brother helped to build during his national service in the air force. On the roof are two slim canoes and on the back hang two bicycles. This is a sports-mad country. Bugger politics, just let's play!

There is a grey-green feel to this countryside, the stands of trees and whitewashed bungalows and cottages remind me of Ireland. A farm stall sign reads 'Kom Rus 'n Bietjie' (Come rest awhile). The road is wide, flat and empty once more, but watched by a thousand eyes – ostriches. Another farmstall advertises biltong, honey and dried fruit.

A boat with flags and the words 'Love Boat' on its side marks the road to Stilbaai. Is this a honeymoon destination or an invitation to a dirty weekend?

I get the whiff of khakibos (khaki-bush) and try to unpack it. There is a menthol quality, also camphor, and a bitter taste in the back of the throat. It is a very distinctive smell that conjures up my time in the army.

Cars towing speedboats or carrying racks of surfboards barrel north. People, still mainly whites, are having fun in this country – those who can afford it.

Riversdale lies under a blanket of mist between hills. A rusty 12m hull lies at the southern entrance to the town, announcing breakfast – what an indignity! The place has a magnificent setting. It's easy to see why one of my great-grandfathers (my father's mother's father, Solomon Rosenthal) settled here.

I cross the Jan Pienaars Rivier into the breadbasket of the Cape with wheatfields as far as the eye can see. Windmills stand still; I have not seen one moving on this trip. I'm tuned into

KFM 94.5 whose selection of music is dismal beyond belief. Country and Western and old ballads. Depressing stuff.

At Swellendam, I fill up the car with diesel. The light plays on the mountains and across the rolling hills dotted with farms. It does not surprise me that in 1795 the locals declared their own republic here, independent of the British-controlled Cape Colony. The temptation to feel a sense of ownership of this place must have been overwhelming.

At Riviersonderend, (River without end), I stop to buy gifts of proteas and wine for my parents-in-law. As I drive on, I think back again to my conversation with Danie Malan and his comment of how others must define you as an Afrikaner. Having thought about it, I must take issue with this. In my experience, the pillars of personal identity are not conferred by others, but adopted by oneself, out of conviction. This both limits your options and defines you. That is why I feel that I am a Jewish Afrikaner. If I had to ask myself the question my father put to himself recently, 'Where should I be buried? Among the Christians or among the Jews?' I would say, 'Put my body next to my mother, among the Christians, but bury my heart among the Jews.' Or should that be the other way round? That is the central conundrum of my life.

This countryside is like a land sea, swell after swell after swell. There are huge, plunging hills down which you swoop, levelling out briefly before you climb and climb. You top out for a bit, seeing far across the hills, then once more you begin to descend into the next trough. It is a bit like being at sea in a small boat.

But, confusingly, it also feels like flying. As you top these hills, you look down on such enormous stretches of country that it's reminiscent of the view from a plane. One hardly has to think of driving, because the road is arrow-straight but for the rising and falling of the hills.

I pass Boontjieskraal and the Cape wind finally finds me. It stirs something in my mind about my love of this country. It is, after all, the country of my heart. I think about that for a moment and have to admit that this is no longer the whole story, for I now also love England. It has become a part of me. And a nice conceit comes to mind. The heart, after all, has two chambers – there is space enough for both countries in my heart. I have a double-barrelled nationality now. I'm a soutie, I suppose. 'Soutpiel' (salt penis) was the word Afrikaners used for their English-speaking neighbours, who, they said, had one foot in South Africa and one foot stretched far for England, leaving their penises hanging in the sea.

I pull into Hermanus at 1 p.m., exactly four hours after leaving Mossel Bay. I greet my parents-in-law, George and Lynne Warman, and am taken off to have lunch at a restaurant overlooking a small lagoon and the sea at Onrus. Then, after an afternoon nap, we go to a fund-raising dinner. Lynne has recently joined the Church of Scotland, having abandoned the Church of England after a lifetime, for reasons that elude me.

An Expensive Little Operation

Returning from my trip round the Western Cape, I slip up to Bishopscourt to see my father, to check in, to report my findings, and to ask the question that I'm dying to ask: 'How much did you have to pay to have me, my sister and brother accepted as Jews?'

He is 90 years old, not that you'd know it. He is as sharp as a tack and misses nothing.

He has lived alone since my mother's death six years ago. But 'alone' is a misnomer, for he has a wonderful staff taking care of him. 'I have lived like a king and I intend to die like a king,' he has said on many occasions. So he lives in the home he built us when I was 15, all of 38 years ago. And there, in bed wearing just a pyjama top, he grows older.

His success and his 90 years count for little with him. 'My advice to you, my boy, is don't get old.' This is his mantra. In the meantime, he has a routine that includes a steady stream of visitors, acupuncture, massages and regular medical check-ups for his back pain. But other than a pill to balance his blood-sugar levels, he is healthy and in better shape than most other 90-year-olds, by a long shot.

His staff are remarkable. They include the newest recruit, Matilda Strydom and the longest serving, Pieter Brill – who drives and cooks and generally manages the place as he has been doing for five decades. He is himself now almost 80 years old, but does not talk of retiring. He is an amazing, patient man. Suzie Meyer has been the cook for 30 years, and Doreen

Strydom, Matilda's mother, has been there for years. Ben Winslow, the gardener, has been there as long. Together, this team comprises more than a century of service to our family.

My father is generous, and helps many people in many ways. He gives advice to all who seek it – and many do – for he is shrewd. He is an unpaid executor in many estates and has watched families tear themselves to pieces for money – sons against fathers, mothers against daughters, children against each other. 'People will kill for money' is another of his truisms.

After I have told him of my trip, I ask the question I have been waiting to ask. 'How much did you have to pay the rabbis to have us accepted as Jews?' He looks surprised. 'Pay the rabbis? I never had to pay anyone anything to have you, your sister or your brother accepted into the Jewish faith.' He thinks a moment longer and then something comes to mind. 'The only time I had to pay anything more than expected was for your bris, your circumcision. When the mole [the Jewish specialist who performs the operation] heard that your mother was Christian, he didn't want to do the operation. So I had to pay him twice the going rate.'

The fact that my Jewish credentials, such as they are, came at a price, fills me with a strange satisfaction – and a sense of the ridiculous.

Julian Roup

A Place in my Divided Heart

I pay a visit to the South African Jewish Museum which is situated in the downtown neighbourhood of Gardens in Cape Town. It is located in the grounds of the Gardens Synagogue, and is in the same complex as the Gardens Jewish Community Centre and the Holocaust Centre. It is also close to the Iziko South African National Gallery and Houses of Parliament.

The Holocaust Centre is new to me and I am moved and greatly impressed. It makes a powerful statement in an intelligent and informative way. The first fact that hits me there is that of the six million Jews who died in German gas chambers, 1.5 million were children. There are drawings done by kids in concentration camps, which depict former lives and express a longing to return home. Few survived to see that wish fulfilled. How blessed I am that I can still return to the haunts of my youth and childhood.

A picture of Dr JFJ Hans van Rensburg, the Ossewabrandwag (Ox-wagon Sentinel, the Afrikaner nationalist organisation) fascist leader, flanked by torch-bearing members at a rally in Stellenbosch 1941, catches my eye. Next to it is a cartoon titled 'Coming of the Scum', a perfect forerunner of the kind of image the Nazis used so successfully to pump up race hatred. It shows a hook-nosed caricature of a Jew, loaded down with cases, stepping off a ship. This one is from a South African publication called *The Owl*, published in 1904 that gave rise to the Quota Act (1930), which aimed to control the influx of

European Jews to South Africa.

There is a story from the 1930s in the *Cape Times*, which tells how 1,000 men and women marched to the docks at 11 p.m. at night intending to halt the docking of the SS *Stuttgart* carrying 538 German Jewish immigrants. Happily, they failed.

The 1930s and 1940s witnessed a surge of anti-Semitism in South Africa, ensuring a prominent position for the 'Jewish question' to be placed on the public agenda. Anti-semitism formed an important component of the Afrikaner nationalist worldview, as was evident in such movements as the pro-Nazi Greyshirts, the Ossewabrandwag and the New Order. This was the time, the point in my own story that my crazy, stupid, brave, loving mother chose to marry a Jew. What could she have been thinking? The power of love astonishes me.

In the Gitlin Library, just below the Holocaust Museum, there is a useful collection of books and informed authoritative opinion. I'm told that in the past 25 years around 50,000 Jews have emigrated from South Africa. Today the local community of Jews, a mainly ageing population, stands at around 80,000 people, a small part of the 13 million Jewish community worldwide. Jews clearly, then, do not form two-thirds of the 250 million population of the United States – as one highly educated Afrikaner informant told me, using this 'fact' to explain the attack on Iraq.

In the Gitlin Library, I find something that fascinates me. Few Afrikaners will know that a Jew made a significant contribution to the literature of early Afrikaans. The South African author Charles Press, in his authoritative book *The Light of Israel – The Story of the Paarl Jewish Community*, writes, 'Jan Lion Cachet, a renegade Jew from the Netherlands, played an important role in the early history of the Afrikaans language. He was a regular contributor to *Die Afrikaanse Patriot*, the first Afrikaans newspaper, published in Paarl. It was said of him that he was proud to be a Jew, a Dutchman and an Afrikaner.'

Press continues, 'His poem *Die Vierkleur* was crowned victor in a competition in *Die Afrikaanse Patriot* and was later set to music by Jan S. de Villiers. He also published a history of the Huguenots and perhaps his most famous book, *Die Sewe*

Duiwels en Wat Hulle Gedoen Het (The Seven Devils and What They Did), became a classic of early Afrikaans literature. His allegorical poem *Die Afrikaanse Taal (The Afrikaans Language)* displays such prophetic vision that it is considered to be one of the jewels of the first Afrikaans Language Movement.'

It fascinates me, this mingling of Jewish and Afrikaner intellects – a sometimes troubled, sometimes happy relationship between the two races.

I think of an old Cape Town friend, Larry Schwartz. In his book *Wild Almond Line*, Larry (who now writes for *The Age* in Melbourne, Australia) has this to say about the South Africa-Israeli link. He writes, quoting from Gavin Cawthra's book *Brutal Force: The Apartheid War Machine*:

> While casting around in the 1960s for allies outside NATO, South Africa established economic, military and political ties with Israel. South Africa had been among the first countries to recognise Israeli independence in 1948. It had renewed its support in the 1967 Six Day War. There had been a series of subsequent military and political exchanges, culminating in a 1976 visit by the then South African PM, John Vorster, a sour and slow-speaking man who had been interned during WWII for pro- German sympathies.
>
> The South African Defence Force (SADF) had acquired a wide range of weapons and armaments and Israeli fast-attack boats had been assembled in SA. A number of Israeli military specialists had visited in unofficial capacities. Military links had been established with the Ciskei 'homeland'. Twenty-three Ciskei air-force pilots were trained in Israel in 1983. Israeli mercenaries were hired as bodyguards to cabinet ministers and advisers to the Ciskei Defence Force.
>
> On 22nd September 1979, a US Air Force surveillance satellite registered a double flash of light in the South Atlantic-Indian Ocean area that some attribute to a nuclear explosion....

There has been much speculation over the years about nuclear links between South Africa and Israel. Strange indeed, the links between my two peoples.

So what about anti-Semitism and other forms of religious intolerance in the new South Africa? Personally, I try to wear the six million chips on my shoulder as lightly as possible and avoid seeing monsters in every dark corner or shining face, but I know it is there. One has eyes and ears. Anti-Semitism comes seeking you; you don't have to go looking for it.

Religious intolerance stalks some of our best universities. This issue has surfaced in the past year at Stellenbosch. Yvonne Malan was devastatingly clear about it:

> On Christians and Stellenbosch: it's a problem that's far deeper than the race issue. When I was a member of the Student Representative Council a faction among the Christian students demanded that I quit because I wasn't a member of their church. Only one member of the university management, Kobus Visagie, was willing to stand up and say that it was wrong. It was an unpleasant experience, but also causes me not to be surprised by statements like that from the university official who declared last year, after a request that there be more religious diversity at official university functions, that 'allowing non-Christians on stage is the slippery slope to satanism'. This was said, of course, in Afrikaans, with eyes cast to the heavens.

Yes, there is a long way to go yet.

Against this, one must never forget the best of the Afrikaners. I think of people like Jaap Durand and another remarkable Afrikaner, Bram Fischer. Bram Fischer was born in 1908 into a prominent Afrikaner family. He was the grandson and namesake of the last president of the Republic of the Orange Free State and his father was a respected lawyer, judge of the Free State Supreme Court and Judge President of the Orange Free State.

Bram was a brilliant student who went to Oxford as a Rhodes scholar before returning to South Africa to practise law. He was committed to social justice, joined the Communist Party and defended many black activists, including the future president, Nelson Mandela. For his convictions, he was hounded and finally imprisoned.

I leave the Holocaust Museum and the Gitlin Library and head back to Constantia. As I've driven round the southern suburbs I've seen signs for a book sale at the South African College School (SACS), my old school. Finally I give in to the impetus to go and take a look at this former place of personal torture.

I walk into the Jan Hendrik Hofmeyer Hall, where I used to stand in assembly, and there are just six people, wandering round in a disconsolate way looking at the book displays. I stand next to the stage where Robin Whiteford, my former headmaster, who wielded sarcasm like a rapier, once held court. I look at the books he would have seen had he stood here now – cookery books, romance, spiritual guidance, children's books, South African history. What would he have made of it, I wonder.

On the wood-panelled walls are the gold-leaf reminders of former pupils who did the school proud. My name is not among them. I look at the first-class Matrics for 1968 and 1969, recalling the faces as if it were yesterday.

I leave this hall, so filled with bad memories, and make my way into the school up a brass-handled staircase. There are the same facebrick walls and the same smell. It affects me strongly. I walk down the corridor to my old headmaster's study and find among the many photographs on the walls a picture of my uncle, Nathan Roup, taken in 1918. He is part of the Under-17A rugby side that won the Inter-Schools' Shield. He is 16 years old in the picture and so has just 10 years to live before he will die of Black Water Fever and so break his parents' hearts. He is good looking, with large, dark, expressive eyes, a handsome forehead and dark, straight, shiny hair, neatly parted on the left. He is tall, with broad shoulders – 'n beeld van 'n klong (a handsome boy).

I turn and look through a window up to Bishopscourt, where I can make out my father's home. He has outlived his eldest brother by 64 years but takes little pleasure in that.

As I stand, leaning my forehead against the window, my

mind is filled with thoughts and images of Jews and Afrikaners, my own personal history and the larger canvas of South Africa. Nothing is resolved. My forebears bear down on me, their successful and unsuccessful lives neatly complete, the stuff of books or family myth and legend. I straighten up, look one last time at the door of my headmaster's old study, where more than once I stood waiting to be caned for some trifling misdeed, and I wish him a hot day in hell, and walk out of the school to the car.

At the traffic lights at the end of Newlands Avenue there is a young boy carrying a large plastic sack. He has a note that says he will take the rubbish from your car for a small sum. The gap between rich and poor is as wide as ever, possibly wider. There are mansions now going up in Bishopscourt that must be the homes of human 'rhinosceri' – people with skins so thick and hearts so cold they feel no pain. I can't help but wonder at this opulence – Tuscan villas, French chateaus and Spanish haciendas. Men and women pass me in their open-top BMWs, Mercs, Alfas, Porsches and God help me, a Ferrari! The party for the few, still in full swing?

These issues continue to intrigue me. I am no closer to finding any deep understanding of myself or my society, here or in England. There is, though, a place in my divided heart for both South Africa and England, for the Afrikaner and the Jew, for Christianity and Judaism. It has all coalesced into something new and different which I but dimly understand.

I do not regret my decision to leave South Africa, based as it was on a fear that has not come to pass. I could not have lived with the insecurity and the horror of what might have happened here and what I might have been a party to if called up to serve in the army. Europe, though, has not been an easy ride either. There, too, there have been costs. I am, perhaps, stateless in a way, but also a citizen of a greater world than just one country. My mixed heritage has given me strong roots, a sense of self, and these have helped me to forge a new identity.

In England I am not a Boerejood; they don't even begin to understand what it means. I'm just another damned colonial with a funny accent. Jy weet? (You know?) And there is a price – and a peace – in that.

TOTSIENS (TILL WE MEET AGAIN)

This journey in search of answers has certainly given me a better understanding of how the South African 'miracle' occurred, how Afrikaners feel now and what they think about the future.

Why the Afrikaner went quietly, with a whimper rather than with a bang, seems to be for a whole raft of reasons; there is no simple answer. But I believe the answer lies among the following factors.

First, there is a moral element. Leading Afrikaners - writers, intellectuals, some theologians, some politicians - increasingly felt a genuine discomfort and unhappiness about the path apartheid had led them down, which required brutal force to keep blacks in their place. Van Wyk Louw's words come to mind once more, 'Ons moet liewer sterwe as 'n volk as om in ongeregtigheid te lewe.' (We should rather die as a volk than live with injustice).

The internal debate among Afrikaners about the injustice of apartheid was given new impetus by young Afrikaners burdened with an army commitment that seemed endless. In the army, they saw first-hand in the townships, on the border and in Angola just what they were up against and how unsavoury were the tools needed to stay in command. This brutality led to a growing moral repugnance and self-doubt.

The sheer simplicity of the maths was also compelling: five million against 30 million could not go on forever. As more than one person said to me, it was like the elephant fighting the ants. Constand Viljoen and the army had the foresight to see this and they became a force for reason over madness.

The economic reality was also concentrating minds. The country was facing bankruptcy. Big business wanted a solution found, and fast. Sanctions were biting. The Afrikaners' newfound wealth seemed in imminent danger of being lost. The desire to hang onto material possessions was great.

International condemnation and disgust were no small thing either. The wish to be liked and respected and once again to be a part of the 'Community of Nations' called to the Afrikaners. Another Afrikaner, Jan Smuts, had once shown them they could be a significant member of the world community. They were tired of being the world's skunk. Some were simply tired, tired of it all. After all, they had been fighting for a century, the Anglo-Boer wars, the Depression, the black masses oppressed by apartheid. They wanted an end to fighting.

Then, fortuitously, came the timely fall of communism, and the moral justification for holding back the perceived black communist hordes suddenly dissipated. Now there was only one game in town, and it was American-led capitalism. Rooigevaar (the Red threat) was gone.

And then, crucially, there was Nelson Mandela. Cometh the hour, cometh the man. Here was someone who seemed to offer a way out of the impasse, a black Moses, a man of reason, of integrity, of great dignity and Christian ethics. A smart man. A man the Afrikaners finally felt they could and must do business with.

And, finally, perhaps dimly perceived, hardly referred to by any of my informants, is the issue of gold and diamonds and precious minerals. One cannot consider South Africa's past, its present or its future, without reference to its mineral wealth and those foreign companies and countries that play a role in extracting it. These forces have one powerful drive: to preserve an ordered society in South Africa, which will facilitate such work with a minimum of interruption.

The distinguished historian and author Rob Shell said to me that South Africa had never truly had an independent government – first it was influenced by the Dutch East India Company, then the British East India Company and later the mining interests inside and outside the country. South Africa has always been a company town, so to speak, with one in seven of the population employed directly or indirectly by the mining conglomerates, some of which were part of companies so huge they eclipsed many nation states in their size and power.

Floating like a klipvis (rock fish) over the reefs and banks of information about South Africa available on the Internet, I found here and there a seam of gold, or just a nugget, just like the Jo'burg miners working thousands of metres below ground on the real thing. Among the gleams that caught my eye – and you will have to be the judge of whether it was 'fool's gold' or the real thing – was a report in the publication *International Journal of Intelligence and Counterintelligence* (Summer 1995) by Richard Cumming, titled 'A Diamond is Forever: Mandela triumphs, Buthelezi and De Klerk survive, and the ANC on the US payroll'.

The article describes the role America played in persuading the Nationalist government not to hang Mandela and his associates, but to give them life sentences. America did not wish to hand the communists a public relations triumph.

Later in the same article, the role of Sir Robin Renwick, the British ambassador to South Africa at the time of the power change, is applauded for his 'highly skilful work' in helping to obtain Nelson Mandela's release from prison, thanks to the leverage his government could exert, having never imposed sanctions.

The article also notes the 'continued role played by the great companies and families that have controlled the South African economy since the Boer War'. And it concludes, 'Politicians may come and go, but as the De Beers advertisement claims on television – 'A Diamond is Forever'.'

Could anything be plainer? Here, obliquely referred to, is a great truth about South Africa. The article, as I see it, represents a flick upwards, just for a second, of the sheet of secrecy and misinformation that covers the face of the truth about realpolitik in South Africa.

These factors, as I see it, were the ingredients for 'the miracle'. Like Rubik's cube, all these elements suddenly locked into place and a solution was on hand, a solution that promised hope of peace, of a future for Afrikaners in Africa. Sense prevailed. And so, as FW de Klerk reportedly said to Van Zyl Slabbert, the Afrikaners decided: 'Let's take a chance.'

Inevitably, this journey, this personal odyssey of mine, has raised fresh questions in my mind.

At present, South Africa appears on the surface rather like post-war Germany – not a Nazi to be found, only 'good Germans'. The talk I found was of how immoral and unsustainable apartheid was. But scratch the surface just a little and the older reality is still there. A joke doing the rounds is revealing. 'What is the difference between a white racist and a white tourist from abroad?' The answer: 'Fourteen days in South Africa!' The wife of a wealthy farmer, who had some mighty impressive connections to the old regime, told me this. Things have not changed that much, it seems.

The old uneasy relationship between Jew and Afrikaner is also there. I did not have to go looking for that. It arrived on my plate, gratis.

What has changed are the ugly scenes and the ugly signs. One sees white Afrikaans youths serving black and coloured families in restaurants, with a smile; one sees interracial couples walking hand in hand; one sees mixed beaches, mixed facilities. Make no mistake, things have changed.

If you have been generous enough to read this far, may I be permitted one single piece of advice to Afrikaners? Wees geduldig. Be patient. Here in Britain and over the pond in America they are still making movies about the Second World War over half a century after hostilities ended. It must be damned hard if you're German, but there it is.

My advice to you is to be patient and gracious in the face of black anger over the past. Do recall that many Afrikaners are still fighting the Boer War, and that's a century back now! You feel your hurt strongly, and you hate the injustice that was done to you. Do, then, accept that others might feel the same. So refrain from calling on blacks to forget the past. You have not, why should they? Be patient, and gracious. A great hurt was done them, and it will take a long time to forget. And do remember how generous they have been in victory.

The Afrikaners have become what Van Zyl Slabbert

once predicted, a nation of non-discriminating racists. The old feelings are there, but now it is illegal to do anything about them; there are powerful sanctions in place, and the law is on the side of the black majority. And there are those BMWs and swimming pools Afrikaners do not want to put at risk. Holding onto what one has is still the name of the game, but it requires a new set of manners, new rules.

An image comes to me from the past. It is of the baboon, that cleverest and most adaptable of Africa's animals. I think of how a baboon will raid a farmer's fields. I think of how a farmer will place pumpkins for it to find. With ingenuity, the baboon manages to burrow a paw inside and grasp the cool seeds and the wet pith within, making a fist, greed overcoming fear as the farmer approaches with the shotgun. The baboon's fist is now too wide to get back out through the hole; the animal is encumbered with loot, which is now its trap. And the bloody death. Greed can be a trap. Just in time, the Afrikaner unclenched his fist, released the country and now lives to tell the tale.

The country faces massive problems. Poverty is endemic and sits alongside great wealth. The impact of crime is both subtle and brutal. It takes up mental and physical space, requires a constant vigilance, wariness, houses like fortresses and armed rapid-response guards on patrol night and day. The danger is not only an urban phenomenon, but affects the most rural farm. Rural crime and farm killings are a daily reality. Police are stressed out, and can only take so much.

Affirmative action is a swear word, a curse, for many white South Africans who previously enjoyed all the protection of a white state; merit then was not the issue, colour was all. So what has changed? But now there is a very long way to fall, and so doctors emigrate, young people go abroad. There is a haemorrhage of white talent.

There is a real fear for the future of the Afrikaans language by the people who make their living in it and for those to whom it means more than a language, a culture. Afrikaners seek cultural spaces like Oudtshoorn where they can celebrate a sense of togetherness and a blossoming of culture, though some question the quality it provides. There seems to be a definite generation gap among Afrikaners. As always, the older people are less optimistic and there is fear of crime, of loss of identity, of impoverishment. The young are less concerned, have greater options, and have time on their side.

There is the enormous effect of AIDS on the country, the loss of talent, the growth of an orphan underclass, breeding more crime and impoverishment. There is concern about corruption.

People find different ways of coping and, as one put it, 'die tronke is vol, die kerke leeg.' (The jails are full, the churches empty). The NG church is in the process of integrating brown and white congregations. Meanwhile, many find solace with the charismatic Christians' feel-good faith. Young Jews have immigrated in their thousands to Europe, America, Australia, some to Israel.

The Afrikaners' dream of racial purity is long gone and now they simply hope to hang onto their material possessions, and as much of their culture as they can salvage from the churning machine of change. Their options, as outlined by Professor Grundlingh, are to buy into nation-building; make money, emigrate, or find a safe, nostalgic past to live in. Violent white opposition is not an option. Afrikaners are living day by day, taking each one as it comes, hoping for the best, but expecting that many of their young people will leave. Finally, I load my suitcase into the car and head for the airport. There, I sit with my brother-in-law, Guy Louw, killing time till my 7.30 p.m. flight for London. We look out at the welcome rain, which has finally come on my last day, but which ends all too soon, leaving a rainbow out across the runways. It rises directly behind the tailfin of Kaapstad, (Cape Town) the aircraft that will shortly be taking me home. I think of my nephew Kirsten's generous wish for me, hoping that there will be a moment of synthesis, an epiphany if you like, that will somehow wrap up the journey symbolically, and here it is – the second one of this journey. Here in this moment I feel it taking place. It arises out of the plane with its flag-draped tailfin, behind it the rainbow and, perhaps most importantly, Guy, sitting beside me. Here is an Afrikaner, an anglicised Afrikaner, working happily in this new

South Africa.

His pragmatism makes this all possible. He has survived seven lean years, a personal drought, with ingenuity and quiet dignity. He turned himself into a tourist guide while continuing to do as much contract-engineering work as he could find during a severe downturn in the industry, to help make ends meet. As a result he has made friends all over the world. Surely here, right beside me, is the best message of hope for the Afrikaner? The qualities that have helped them survive and thrive in Africa are still at work in him. Their genes live on in his and my sister's children, an ornithologist and an actress. They have no wish or intention to leave the beloved country. And Guy will be helping to construct key new facilities that will help Cape Town to grow and thrive.

Guy seldom speaks Afrikaans; he thinks of himself simply as a South African. He loves rugby and cricket, braaivleis (barbecue), kortbroeke (shorts) and kaalvoet stap (walking barefoot), and goes regularly from the city to refresh himself in the platteland by the Breede River. He is of Africa and would never leave willingly.

Perhaps, here, in my quiet brother-in-law, is the new, best hope for the Afrikaner, an ongoing commitment to Africa, pragmatism and a continued contribution to building the future. He will continue in service to South Africa, helping it to realise its potential. His work began in what was once a cursed country on a continent awash with catastrophes; now, there is hope. He stays and lives with optimism. The Afrikaners still have work to do, it seems to me as I sit there, and here is one Afrikaner just getting on with it.

Later, as the plane rises into the African night and I feel my throat close and my eyes prick as usual, I look down for one last glimpse of the winking lights of Cape Town and the distant lights of those many country towns I have visited. As we climb out of sight, my thoughts turn to the amazing cast of characters I have seen, none of them saints (perhaps with one exception), all with faults, but all staying on, making a difference, not flying away like me.

I think of the arrogance of the Afrikaners, their racial and spiritual short-sightedness, the hurt they have done their country, its people and themselves. I think of the Afrikaners' wish to hold back all that was foreign, be it Jews, Catholics or blacks. I think of the hurt they have done the coloured people, the brown Afrikaners they themselves bred. I think that there is much to ask forgiveness for and much to forgive.

But then I think of Ampie Coetzee at UWC, teaching reduced numbers, but teaching, and fighting to save his language for himself, his son and his coloured students.

I think of Anton Meyer, that huge mass of energy, still in search of meaning, a man who has been in the forefront of change in his school, leading it across the desert of white education to a mixed and fairer educational future.

I think of Professor Albert Grundlingh at Stellenbosch, teaching history to students from all over Africa, not just Afrikaners, looking at the past forensically.

I think of Yvonne Malan and my heart goes out to her and wishes her well, knowing that she will be an ornament to whatever task she undertakes.

I think of Karin Cronjé, at times no longer feeling an Afrikaner exile in her own country, but writing her way to a personal freedom and not a little fame, I suspect.

I think of Henry Viljoen, using his biting intelligence, working for free through a mountain of paperwork to help right a wrong, a feather in the country's judicial cap.

I think of Mariette Odendaal on her farm near Piketberg, painting and spreading literacy among farm workers, opening the door to a greater world.

I think of Fiona Archer, somewhere on her way to Botswana, driving alone on a journey to seek wisdom and shining a light on the African cultures she finds along the way.

I think of Louise Viljoen, loved by many, bringing Afrikaans literature to a wider audience and doing more than her bit for the language.

I think of the sad-happy figure of David Kramer, who brings people of all types together in laughter and in tears, an artist who has made a difference.

I think of Gerrit and Elna Boonstra, family of mine, who have raised fine children, and who have helped to educate and inform their countrymen of all colours. I wish Gerrit well with his book on metaphysics, a new look at how the spirit and politics coalesce, which seems a book that South Africa is much in need of just now.

I think of Pieter Hugo and his Arab horses, showing overseas guests the cradle of the country's wine industry and showing, too, why we all love the place so much; its beauty winning new friends for South Africa. I think of the integrity, the courage and the steadfastness of Jaap Durand and how wisely God chose when He called on this man to take a stand that would one day reflect well on his people.

I think of that human volcano, Jannie Gagiano, and his questioning mind, his devil's advocacy, his bringing an academic rigour to politics and a preparedness to say 'Jy lieg!' (You lie), to anyone he feels deserves it.

I think of the young Anele de Vries, running a coffee shop in Piketberg, dreaming dreams of new horizons and new challenges. Kind, open and undaunted by life.

I think of the artist Rochelle Beresford and her husband Pierre du Plessis, with their art gallery in Tulbagh that displays the work of black, coloured and white artists.

I think of Sabina Swartz, the ANC chairwoman of Lamberts Bay, her courage, her long personal journey and the land she now waited for; land which will be used to grow things to feed people, mentally, spiritually and physically.

I think of Danie Malan, on his farm Allesverloren, which now and forever will be for me a symbol of Afrikaner fortitude and the belief that aanhou wen (fortitude wins). Here is a man with a distinguished inheritance, making fine wines that bring fame to South Africa. He is fulfilling his ambition to make a difference, to leave a spoor.

I think of Jaco Kirsten, of his energy, his intelligence, his commitment to South Africa – part of a chain of 13 generations. His raised voice declaring, 'I'm an African, I'm here to stay and woe betide anyone who tells me different!'

I think of Professor Hein Willemse, a brown man, teaching Afrikaans in a white University, writing his own books, an intellectual at the cutting face of change, and living with an open and forgiving heart. Truly a worthy son of Nelson Mandela.

And, finally, I think of all those hundreds of kilometres of country I have seen of this, my other beloved land. Having travelled those distances and spoken to some of its inhabitants, my feeling is that there is work to do, much work to do, but things are far from being allesverloren. The Afrikaners still have a place in Africa. The continent would be the poorer without them.

The aircraft climbs steadily and the land beneath us becomes indistinct. My Jewish-Afrikaans heart wonders if the Afrikaners have now entered their own time in Egypt, in internal bondage? Is this the start of a 5,000-year-old story, or is it the end of a brief cultural flowering that has lasted but a century, the briefest of life as a distinct people. Do they have the uithouvermoë, the endurance for the long haul? Will they bounce back from international dispersal, from internal tensions and strife?

These are big questions that only the harshest and kindest of taskmasters – time – will finally be able to judge. My head tells me it is doubtful, but my heart, my heart wills them to survive.

Laat dit goed gaan met julle, my moeder se mense. Laat dit goed gaan.

'May things go well with you, my mother's people. May things go well.

Other titles by BLKDOG Publishing for your consideration:

Britannia: The Wall
By Richard Denham & M. J. Trow

THE END OF ROMAN BRITAIN BEGINS.

The story opens in 367 AD. Four soldiers - Justinus, Paternus, Leocadius and Vitalis - are out hunting for food supplies at an outpost of Hadrian's Wall, when the Wall comes under attack.

The four find their fort destroyed, their comrades killed, and Paternus is unable to find his wife and son. As they run south to Eboracum, they realize that this is no ordinary border raid. Ranged against the Romans at the edge of the world are four different peoples, and they have banded together under a mysterious leader who wears a silver mask and uses the name Valentinus - man of Valentia, the turbulent area north of the Wall.

Faced with questions they are hard-pressed to answer, Leocadius blurts out a story that makes the men Heroes of the Wall. Their lives change not only when Valentinus begins his lethal sweep across Britannia but as soon as Leo's lie is out in the world, growing and changing as it goes.

Goblin Market
By Maryanne Coleman

Have you ever wondered what happened to the faeries you used to believe in? They lived at the bottom of the garden and left rings in the grass and sparkling glamour in the air to remind you where they were. But that was then – now you might find them in places you might not think to look. They might be stacking shelves, delivering milk or weighing babies at the clinic. Open your eyes and keep your wits about you and you might see them.

But no one is looking any more and that is hard for a Faerie Queen to bear and Titania has had enough. When Titania stamps her foot, everyone in Faerieland jumps; publicity is what they need. Television, magazines. But that sort of thing is much more the remit of the bad boys of the Unseelie Court, the ones who weave a new kind of magic; the World Wide Web. Here is Puck re-learning how to fly; Leanne the agent who really is a vampire; Oberon's Boys playing cards behind the wainscoting; Black Annis, the bag-lady from Hainault, all gathered in a Restoration comedy that is strictly twenty-first century.

Fade
By Bethan White

There is nothing extraordinary about Chris Rowan. Each day he wakes to the same faces, has the same breakfast, the same commute, the same sort of homes he tries to rent out to unsuspecting tenants.

There is nothing extraordinary about Chris Rowan. That is apart from the black dog that haunts his nightmares and an unexpected encounter with a long forgotten demon from his past. A nudge that will send Chris on his own downward spiral, from which there may be no escape.

There is nothing extraordinary about Chris Rowan...

EST. 2019
BLKDOG
www.blkdogpublishing.com

Printed in Great Britain
by Amazon

49781105R00169